ANDY RUSSELL'S
CAMPFIRE STORIES

ANDY RUSSELL'S CAMPFIRE STORIES

with illustrations by

Don Brestler

M&S

Canadian Cataloguing in Publication Data

Russell, Andy, 1915–
  Andy Russell's campfire stories

ISBN 0–7710–7882–X

1. Canada, Western – Anecdotes.   2. Russell, Andy, 1915–   – Anecdotes.
I. Title.   II. Title: Campfire stories.

FC3206.R87 1998   971.2   C98–931912–1
F1060.R87 1998

We acknowledge the financial support of the Government of Canada through
the Book Publishing Industry Development Program for our publishing
activities. We further acknowledge the support given by the Canada Council
for the Arts and by the Ontario Arts Council for our publishing program.

Typesetting by M&S, Toronto

Printed and bound in Canada

McClelland & Stewart Inc.
The Canadian Publishers
481 University Ave.
Toronto, Ontario
M5G 2E9

1 2 3 4 5   02 01 00 99 98

Page 318 constitutes a continuation of the copyright page.

CONTENTS

Preface / ix

1 The King Elk / 1

2 Being a Kid / 30

3 René and Clarice / 34

4 The Party Line / 38

5 The Man with the Iron Belly / 41

6 The Colonel's Stud Horse / 48

7 A Lesson in Mountain Climbing / 53

8 Kleo / 62

9 The Friendly Owl / 85

10 So This Is Africa / 100

11 The Land of the Sky / 105

12 Sam Lee Captures a Wolverine / 116

13 Dangerous Game / 119

14 "Chalk One Up for Us" / 123

15 Being Your Own Packhorse / 126

16 Camera Hunting / 135

17 First Steps / 142

18 A Joke on Cap / 148

19 Nothing Like a Mule / 154

20 Wild Visitors / 160

21 Green Englishman / 168

22 Meeting the Judge / 174

23 Butts Lake / 182

24 Wapiti Land / 187

25 Wilderness Adventure / 195

26 Mountain Streams / 201

27 Wings over the Mountains / 209

28 Relative to Riches / 218

29 A Frontier Woman's Solution / 227

30 Adventures with Susie / 230

31 There My Stick Floats / 234

32 The Speedster and the Slowpoke / 238

33 Autumn Gold / 245

34 The Way Things Were / 250

35 Horse and Buffalo / 270

36 The Stoneys / 290

37 Cowboy Days / 300

38 People Along the River / 307

Acknowledgements / 318

PREFACE

Growing up on a ranch at the foot of the Rockies in southwest Alberta in the early part of the century was sheer adventure for youngsters. We had our horses, dogs, and lots of rugged country to explore. We had no telephone, automobiles were few and far between, radios were scarce, and television had not been invented. When we went anywhere, we either rode a horse or drove a team. For entertainment we either joined in song, listened to musicians, or told stories. Nearly everyone would tell a story, but some of us were very talented. I have known men who could not write their names take their turn around the evening fire and keep their audience helpless with laughter or spellbound as they told a story.

I was not very old when I realized that if I was going to take part in entertaining people, I must learn to tell a story. I used to practise by telling stories to myself. When I got the chance, I told them to my parents, and when they were genuinely amused, I was encouraged to continue.

Being a professional guide for many years, who entertained guests around the evening campfires in mountain camps, gave me the opportunity to improve my technique. Writing stories for publication in outdoor magazines was a natural step, and writing books came next. Storytelling is to me about as natural as breathing.

This book is a collection of my favourite campfire stories, some of which have appeared in print before, and some of which are published here for the first time. All of them are the kind that have the smell of woodsmoke about them, and all are intended to inform as well as entertain.

1

THE KING ELK

Elk are very gregarious animals. Except in spring, when the cows scatter far and wide to have their calves, the herds sometimes number in the hundreds. They gather into bunches in summer, and when the first deep snows of winter come, these consolidate into even bigger herds.

They feed in a definite pattern according to the season. From the higher country in summer, after the calves are big enough to travel, they go down to the ridges at the edge of the mountains for the winter. When the grass begins greening on the lower slopes and flats in spring, they move down for the fresh feed and then work their way slowly back into high country to avoid summer's heat and flies.

So, in late March, Old Buck led her herd up over the pass out of Horseshoe Basin. She halted the herd at the summit, and for a while they stood outlined in a long rank against the snowy flanks of the mountain called the Horn. She had a choice of two trails descending the ridge – one a summer elk trail pitched at a steep angle across a shale slide, and the other, man-made, on an easier grade. Old Buck took neither of them, but cut across the north shoulder of the Horn where the winds had whipped the snow off, and down into the head of a big draw. From there she picked a trail along the south face to a bunch grass bench, and then on down to the park boundary near the head of Cottonwood Creek. At first starshine the herd came out in a long line onto a flat flanking a swamp by a big natural salt lick.

They were salt-hungry, and many of them began avidly licking the mud where alkali had leached out onto the surface while the rest fed on the new green grass. The moon came out from behind a bank of clouds to light up a pastoral scene of primeval wildness. The whole flat was alive with the moving shapes of the great deer, and the night musical with their conversational squeals. As usual at this time of year, there were no mature bulls with the bunch, only a few two-year-olds, slab-sided and gaunt after the long winter, and still carrying their antlers.

Upon her arrival at the lick, Old Buck walked around the rest of the bunch, stopping here and there to listen and test the wind. It told of peace – a night belonging to the elk, full of stars with the soft, warm smell of spring everywhere. The balmy breeze played with the long hair of her mane, and her ears flickered as a coyote yapped, having discovered the herd. But she was not concerned about the little grey wolf. A great horned owl flew by on silent wings in quest of a snowshoe hare or a mouse. Satisfied, she ambled back through the herd to lick at the salty mud, fulfilling a craving for the minerals winter and the twin calves in her womb had drained from her body.

As spring progressed, the herd began to split up in search of fresh pastures, spending their days in indolent napping among the aspen groves and coming out to feed when they were hungry. The young bulls went off by themselves and the yearlings, no longer encouraged by the cows to follow them, formed their own bunches. By late May the cows were scattered far and wide, each seeking her own private calving place. Well hidden in willow thickets and aspen groves, they began to drop their calves.

Old Buck sought out a willow patch along Cottonwood Creek, where early one morning her calves were born – reddish, light-spotted, gangling little creatures, that seemed all eyes, ears, and spindly legs.

She licked them dry, thus quickening their struggle to get to their feet, and encouraged them to wobble their way to her flanks, where they poked their noses around, fumbling for her teats. When they fastened onto them, they sucked her udder dry, then folded up again to sleep. She left them there, slumbering in the sun-dappled shade, while she wandered out across a meadow nearby to feed hungrily.

This was her routine during those first days of the calves' lives, a vulnerable and dangerous time for them, as it would be two weeks before their legs strengthened enough to allow them to keep up to her. Old Buck was never very far away and continually on the lookout, but in spite of her constant vigilance, two coyotes surprised her one evening.

She would have missed them entirely had she not caught a fleeting glimpse of one ghosting past fifty yards away and heading straight for where the calves were hidden. She ran, and finding a coyote within two jumps of her young, she charged, striking with her front feet. It dodged and streaked away as one of her flying hoofs grazed its tail. She pursued it and, perhaps because she was so close to it, she followed it too far. The coyote's mate streaked in behind her and grabbed one of the calves, quickly tearing its throat before dragging it away.

Old Buck came storming back, a living picture of rage, her hair standing up on her neck, her mouth open, and her ears hanging loosely down on each side of her jaws as she reared to strike. The coyote dropped the calf to streak through a heavy clump of willows where she could not follow, and she quickly turned back to her young. The male was lying still in his bed, his big liquid eyes full of fear, but his sister was feebly retching for breath as her blood ran out of a torn jugular.

For a while the old cow licked her as though trying to bring life back into the limp little body, all the while nervously moving around and stamping her feet as she stood with head thrown up watching for the coyotes. The smell of them was in her nose, along with that of fresh blood, urging her to move. She roused her remaining calf to his feet and led him away. As soon as she was gone, the coyotes came back to quickly tear their kill to pieces. Eating some and burying the rest, they each took a piece back to their pups at the den.

Three days later, Old Buck came whisker-close to losing her remaining calf. He was cached in a small aspen grove by some beaver dams while she fed a hundred yards directly downwind. When her belly was full, she lay down in a patch of cow parsnip to chew her cud, half dozing in the warm morning sun. Suddenly she was lifted to her feet by a nose-ful of the sour-sweet smell of bear. At the same moment, she caught a glimpse of the animal heading through a stringer of low willow growth towards her calf. Letting out a ringing alarm bark, she charged.

The black bear was only a few steps from the calf when she arrived. Without a moment's hesitation she reared, coming down hard with her front feet in a lightning-fast one-two that sledgehammered squarely in the middle of the bear's back. The spine of a lesser animal would have been broken but bears are incredibly tough, and this one rolled out from under her to swivel on his feet, chopping at her brisket with his teeth. A swinging paw lifted a wad of hair off her neck, and she gave a wild, whistling snort and slammed him over the bridge of the nose with a clubbing hoof, quick as a striking snake. Knocked down again, the bear bawled, got up, and swung on his heels to get away.

Another cow had heard Old Buck's alarm bark and the ensuing ruckus, and she came charging in to help. The bear, finding himself overwhelmed by two raging demons bent on pounding him into the ground, fled in panic. Both cows came charging after him, striking at his rump every time they got close enough. The bear came to a beaver dam and hit the edge of it at a dead run while looking back past his shoulder, whereupon the muck and water tripped him up in a great splash. He somersaulted, skidded on his back, and then went completely under in deep water. When he surfaced, he struck out, swimming for the opposite side, came out of the water at a gallop, and was swallowed by the forest.

The cows did not try to pursue him, but turned to go pacing back towards their calves with noses elevated and heads held high.

In a few weeks King was transformed into a little saddle-brown replica of a full-grown elk, still juvenile in his outline, but now fleet-footed and fully able to keep up to his mother in their world of timber and meadows among the folds of ridges and hills at the foot of the mountains. Old Buck joined a herd of about thirty cows, part of the larger one she wintered with, and they wandered from one choice spot to another in the good feed of this lower ground. Their old winter hair was now replaced by short summer coats of rich brown, sleek and shiny over new fat. Most of their feeding was in the cool of the evening, at night and in early morning, for the fly season was at its height. To avoid the insects, the elk spent the hot hours bedded down in the shade of heavy timber.

Now the danger from predators was lessened by the number of elk and the mobility of the young ones; any one of them could outrun a bear. No coyote, however hungry, was likely to risk trying for a calf when faced with thirty sets of keen eyes, ears, and nostrils backed up by a formidable willingness to fight when threatened. The calves were rarely vulnerable, for they were not inclined to wander far from their mothers.

One evening while the herd was feeding on a grassy flat, a grizzly wandered out of the timber on the upwind side. Instantly every cow was paying close attention. The big silvertip did not have elk in mind, but was just following his nose. The cows bunched, with their calves crowding close to their flanks. When the rank smell of grizzly filled her nostrils, Old Buck blew her nose with a sudden sharp snort and broke into a run to lead the bunch away from the flat and up a long slope to higher ground.

When they came to a fence, she took it in one long, easy bound and the rest of the cows did the same. The calves slithered under the wires. One bull calf belonging to a young cow with twins misjudged his stride and caught the second wire full in the mouth. It slammed him back, knocking him off his feet. He was instantly up and jumped again. This time his front feet went between the second and third wires, and he somersaulted with the wires twisted around his legs, suspending him upside down. Squealing and thrashing, the calf struggled to get free, but the wire clung to him, a barb caught in the soft skin of a foreleg.

The calf's mother missed him when the herd stopped in a low saddle flanked by aspens a quarter-mile beyond. But her remaining calf began to suckle, lulling her first impulse to go back, and by the time it was finished, the herd was on the move again. She was nervous, but out of long habit she went with it, leaving the trapped one.

By daylight, the calf was nearly dead. Shortly, a coyote found him, quickly cut the remaining threads of life, and howled a message to its mate – news of a juicy windfall.

King, fed by his mother's rich milk and now without competition in the suckling, grew fast. Like the other calves, he quickly learned to eat the variety of herbage in abundance everywhere. From the beginning, he showed a strong tendency to dominate the other calves as they played.

Regularly every evening and early morning, while the herd was grazing, the calves would explode in play. Much of the time it was a disorganized racing in all directions, but it sometimes followed a pattern. One evening, by accident or design, the calves lined up in a circle that took them single file around the bunched cows in a flat-out gallop.

Seeming to be caught in the excitement, most of the cows lifted their heads to watch. Two of them towered straight up on their hind feet, their noses elevated to the maximum and their briskets touching as they pawed at each other. They shouldered into each other as they came down, then made a full turn and sashayed off to the side to break the ring of running calves, first one cow running ahead of her partner to check her with a shouldering motion, and then the other repeating the manoeuvre. Other cows paired off in similar frolic until the whole flat was a mix-up of playing animals. Then, suddenly, they all stopped and stood still for a while before resuming their feeding.

Another day, early in the morning, they came down to a pond among some low hills to drink. The little lake was shallow and, like a circular mirror, reflected a long line of drinking elk cows standing shoulder to shoulder, their images in a detailed duplicate on the surface. King suddenly shied in mock fright at his own reflection, jumped into the water, leapt back on shore and then in again. A moment later, half a dozen calves had joined him, shattering their reflections as they threw water in all directions. A cow and a young bull with first-year spikes in velvet raced out into the pond, bucking and plunging, pawing and whirling in a wild pas de deux that threw sparkling sheets of water high in the air. The rest of the bunch stood like spectators on the edge of an arena.

Ever vigilant, Old Buck was standing up the slope behind the herd when she spotted the rider on his horse in a dip between two knolls on the other side of the lake. Her alarm bark stopped the play instantly, every elk frozen where it stood. King came running to his mother, and as if that was the signal, the whole herd went streaming away out of sight.

The wavelets of the little lake subsided; the sharp reflections of the mountains took shape again in the mirror stillness. I was left alone with my horse in the wings of a natural amphitheatre, the recent scene of wild action and great beauty.

Outside the breeding season, most of the bulls range in small bunches by themselves, and during the summer months, their growing velvet-covered antlers are tender and vulnerable to flies. So the bulls spend a large part of their time feeding and loafing along the open slopes above and around the timberline. By August, their new antlers are fully grown, the velvet beginning to dry, and an uncomfortable itching sets in around their bases. The bulls rub them on saplings and clumps of brush, stripping off the remaining velvet in long, bloody rags. For a few days the newly uncovered antlers are ugly with splotches of dried blood on their bone-white surfaces, but this is soon changed by much vigorous rubbing against trees. The colour of the antlers depends on the kind of vegetation used by the bulls for the polishing. Aspen or cottonwood stains the antler beams and points a rich tan shade, and willows make them a bit darker. The bulls that polished their headgear on alders had rich mahogany brown weapons. The points, in contrast, gleamed like polished ivory from being repeatedly thrust into the ground.

In mid-August, the proportion of light to dark hours changes as the earth turns towards the winter months, and this brings about a very subtle and delicate hormonal change in the bulls' body chemistry. Their testes enlarge and their summer passivity begins to be replaced by a desire for competition. A certain hierarchy is established between individuals, a prelude to the coming rut. This change prompts no extra movement or effort on the part of the cows; their procreative organs are primed for the coming estrus of the breeding season.

By September Old Buck's bunch had worked its way gradually up among the mountains and the rut was in full swing. She was still the trail boss when the group was on the move, but the females were now in the harem of a mighty bull with a heavy rack of antlers – seven points to a side. The beams curved out from his head and then swept gracefully back towards his rump – mighty weapons, polished, hard and sharp. Because Old Buck was inclined to head out for new ground under the pressure of his herding, she was sometimes roughly prodded back into the herd. King was nervous when this great grunting and whistling male came close, but he was only a spectator in this first mating moon.

The mountain slopes rang with the bugling of the bulls as they challenged each other for dominance over the harems of cows. Each herdmaster's rivals were continually trying to cut out females for themselves. Most of the competing was done by manoeuvring, displaying great antlers and bugling, all of which maintained the social pecking order among the bulls. At times, however, when a lesser one pressed too close, there would be a quick charge by the ruling bull and almost invariably the usurper would give way, fleeing to avoid a clash.

Individual character among the males ranged from the awkward and unsure advances of the novices to the paramount arrogance displayed by the dominant herdmasters. Some of the bulls, regardless of age, were naturally timid, and while they might make a great deal of noise, a few would go for years without knowing the surging passion of covering a cow.

Because of the size of the harem he ruled, the herdmaster of Old Buck's bunch was almost continually harried by questing bulls bent on cutting cows out of his herd. His resting and feeding periods were fleeting. When he was not driving away a rival, he was herding, following individual cows and continually testing the ripening of their estrus periods until they stood still to be mounted. His outline grew gaunt, his eyes took on an almost insane gleam of passion, and he reeked of urine and musk. He was an animal driven, a pawn of the game being played under the mating moon.

By the time the mating season had waned, he was slab-sided, thin and almost tottering with exhaustion, and he went off alone to seek some rest and feed to build up his body for the long, hard months of the winter ahead.

Although she was fat and vigorous, Old Buck was not in calf. Age was beginning to tell on her and so she joined the ranks of the dry cows. But this did not diminish her quali-ties of leadership; she was still the accepted trail boss and once more in full charge of her bunch. It had been joined by others and now included about a hundred cows, fifty calves, and a scattering of adolescent bulls.

Compared to their weight of a few founds at birth, the calves had grown apace, averaging about a two-pounds-a-day weight gain throughout the first months of their lives. Still their mothers suckled and guarded them; they were less vulnerable to predators, but the risk was not entirely gone.

In late Indian summer, when the days were sparkling clear, the nights frosty, and the air had a tang of autumn, King was lying asleep a few yards upslope from his dozing mother on the edge of the herd, when a big lynx crawled onto a boulder slightly above and downwind of him. Its fur matched the grey of the rock, so that the cat was almost invisible as it crouched, looking through keen, cold, yellow eyes down across the mountain meadow, where the herd was bedded down.

Directly in front of the hungry cat, the flickering of an ear gave away King's position, just a bound or two beyond a patch of low, shintangle pines. The lynx sagged back, step-ping down off the rock and slinking like a shadow into the tangled mat of the scrub. Not a twig snapped as it stalked.

The cat came to the edge of the cover, gathering itself for its final leap onto the sleeping calf, when a squirrel feeding on the fat cones on top of a nearby pine spotted him and cut loose in a sudden tirade of chattering.

Things happened fast. Old Buck jerked her head up at the instant the lynx launched itself. The sudden noise had thrown its timing off just the width of a hair, and as King came up on his feet, claws as sharp as razors dug into his back and neck near the forward slope of his shoulder.

The calf bawled in surprise and pain as he and the lynx rolled over in a tangle of squirming limbs. The next instant Old Buck boiled into the mix-up with a sharp snort of rage. A driving front foot came down on the lynx's back and skidded off to pin down a hind leg. The cat squalled and released its intended victim, who rolled out between his mother's spraddled hind legs. Ears dropping and eyes bulging with anger and intent to kill, the cow reared again to trample the lynx, but it dodged her stabbing hoofs to roll sideways and come up at a scrambling run for cover. Old Buck pursued closely, but again the lynx dodged, jumping for a scraggly aspen growing out of some rocks. A broken hind leg threw it off balance and it fell back to the ground. Before it could gather itself up, the cow was all over it, tramping it savagely until it was only a sodden, bloody rag of fur.

When she turned back to her calf, she found him bleeding profusely. A flap of skin was torn loose from his neck and hung down, raw side out, under an exposed piece of flesh. It was a sore wound but not deep, although it was bleeding profusely. King nuzzled his mother and trembled while she licked him, as they stood surrounded by excited cows sniffing the blood and the dead lynx.

The wound soon stopped bleeding, but for several days it was raw and sore. When it began to heal, it contracted and the hanging flap of skin shrunk into a slightly pendulous wattle. Meanwhile ravens eyed the calf with anticipation and magpies hovered close, ready to share the windfall of misfortune. Coyotes smelled blood and hung around the outskirts of the herd. But Old Buck was vigilant day and night and kept King close to her.

When the wound finally closed, it made a distinctive mark that King would wear the rest of his life. At first the wattle was topped by a patch of bare skin, but gradually whitish hair grew over it, making the brand even more distinctive.

At three years old, King was a big elk, wearing new antlers that were exceptionally heavy, with four well-developed tines on each side. He summered high in the mountains with a small bunch of bulls, sharing feed that was nothing less than exotic in its lushness and brilliance of bloom. As the first stirrings of the rut stimulated the bulls, he joined in the preliminary sparring and shoving with such arrogance and gusto that older bulls were sometimes pressed close to an outright fight.

By the time the rutting season arrived, his neck muscles were thick and heavy, his whole body tuned to toughness, and his strength honed to a fine edge by the exercise. It was the third rut of his life and the first in which he would take active part, although young bulls rarely have the opportunity to breed.

That fall I was guiding a professional photographer out to make a film featuring wildlife in the mountains. We were camped in the park among the elk there, taking advantage of every hour of good light to record the rut as part of his motion picture. Drama and excitement unfolded in almost every direction at all hours of the day and night, for the breeding season of the elk was in full swing, and the mountains rang with the bugling of the bulls. We enjoyed those golden moments when everything was right; there was action aplenty, and my friend was beside himself with excitement as he exposed film of the elk playing their roles out among golden aspens and evergreens against the backdrop of peaks. And sometimes we were keenly disappointed by being out of range when something dramatic happened, or the light being bad.

One afternoon we sat on the edge of a meadow in a stringer of low brush listening to the bulls tune up after a lull in the middle of an unusually hot day. Most of the elk were in the timber, the males sounding off with their various bugles ranging all the way from thin high-pitched squeals to deep pipe-organ notes – the music of the bulls on the quest for cows, throwing back and forth their challenges full of wild and primitive lust.

Out of sight in the timber below us, two bulls were working their way down opposite slopes. Although they were completely hidden, we could locate them by their bugles. One appeared on the far edge of the open grassy bottom; a moment later the other walked into view directly across from him. Both were lesser, unattached bulls, the kind that continually harry the herdmasters. There were no cows to fight over – the bulls were coming together for no other reason than excitement and anger at the other's presence.

As they closed the gap between them, stalking along with heads held low, my friend began shooting film. He should have waited, for he was rewinding his camera when they collided. The collision wasn't violent, they just walked into each other like two animated mechanical things converging on the same track. After the first clash, they stood braced, testing each other, their antlers banging and rattling as they manoeuvred for position.

Again the camera began to whir, but suddenly it stopped and as he struggled to clear the jammed film, the photographer muttered words he never learned in church. While he worked frantically, the bulls put on a show that couldn't have been better if they had been directed. Their movements put them in a wash of bare earth along a watercourse where their footwork churned up the dust, all backlit dramatically in the lowering sun. Just as the camera began running again, they suddenly stopped and looked at each other as though mutually surprised at this profligate waste of energy. Then one went back into the timber and the other went up the wash to a place where all but his back and antlers were hidden. There he began horning a steep cutbank, stirring up a cloud of dust. The photographer sat looking on in absolute disgust, punctuating his feelings by spitting into the grass at his boot toes in silent frustration.

Above us a big bull with a small harem of cows appeared on a bare, steep hogback ridge running down into the valley. Behind him we could hear another bull. When this one appeared, I recognized him by the silvery scar in the hollow of his shoulder. He circled onto the ridge above the herdmaster, challenging him bugle for bugle, while the older bull stood facing him. Suddenly the young bull charged like a streak of light. Horns rattled sharply as they tangled. The attack must have taken the older animal by surprise, for before he could set himself, he was being propelled backwards down the steep slope through a tangle of low, weather-twisted aspens. By the time he got his feet set and recovered his balance, they had gone over fifty yards. But age and experience showed as the herdmaster sidestepped, then parried the other's weapons and raked his flank with a fast slash that lifted hair off his hide. As suddenly as it had started, the fight broke off, the brash youngster retreating and disappearing into thick green timber.

We had watched another dramatic encounter, this time out of camera range, and I was beginning to feel sorry for my friend.

As we mounted our horses to head for camp, a shower blew in from the west, soaking everything, but by the time we reached the top of the ridge it was clearing. Vagrant, fluffy wafers of mist hung here and there on the mountain flanks, and the setting sun lit up the sky overhead.

My friend had just set up his camera to record this scene, when a huge old bull with his cows appeared out of the timber directly below us. Leaving our horses, we sneaked down through some scrub to a spot within a hundred yards of the bunch, and suddenly four more bulls appeared out of nowhere, almost walking over us. They passed us in single file, circling the bunch in front.

Putting my call to my mouth, I almost lifted my friend bodily off the ground as I let out a bugle beside his ear, hoping to stir up some action. Instantly, the passing bulls stopped to answer, and their ringing challenges echoed off the mountain slopes. The big herd boss stalked towards us, his nose thrust out and his magnificent antlers laid back along his flanks as he blew a long column of vapour from his open mouth, the prelude to a bell-like sound that resembled water being poured from a huge glass jug. This musical call was followed by a deep-toned bugle that had power, savagery, and an almost frightening quality of utter wildness in it.

The photographer beside me muttered with a fervour that was monumental, "Damn! There isn't enough light!"

There was a movement among some spruces on the far side of the herd as a young bull came into view, and I was astonished to recognize King. Without uttering a sound, he sneaked through a patch of small trees, going straight towards a cow as though drawn by a string fastened to his nose. And to my further astonishment, she stood perfectly still as he reared and mounted her. He fumbled a bit in his steaming excitement, but then penetrated her, thrusting hard in a straining plunge just as the old bull spotted him and charged. Before the outraged harem boss could reach him, King had disengaged and whirled away. He was an enterprising and energetic bull, this one, an individual of character marked by more than his identifying scar.

The photographer, repeatedly pounding the ground with his fist, sat beside me watching him go. Stalking elk with a camera that day had been heavily laced with both excitement and disappointment, long on action and short on success, the vagaries of the game sometimes taxing a man's patience to the breaking point.

The following winter was a hard one with deep snow. Old Buck's herd had a new leader, for the old cow had taken a hunter's bullet through the fleshy part of a ham the previous fall, and though the wound had healed, she was lame. Her face was grey with age, and the prolonged cold weather had worn her down till her bones showed through her faded buckskin coat. But somehow she stuck to the herd, though hard pressed at times to keep up, as they trailed through the deep snow from one feeding area to another.

The season was cruel with heavy drifts and a sharp crust on the snow. As usual, the mule deer suffered most, the coyotes taking them almost at will, for they were weak and vulnerable. The sheep were cut down in numbers too, though not as much. The coyotes left the elk pretty much alone, although any animal that was weakened by age or infirmity was usually quickly found and literally eaten alive. Most of the casualties among the elk were older bulls caught by the early storms before they had had time to recover from the rut. By spring there were very few of these left.

King was ranging with his mother's herd on the wind-whipped slopes stretching from the mouth of Pine Creek to the long open mountainside above Indian Springs, a piece of country stretching over several miles. Like most of his age group, he was gaunt but strong when I saw him pawing for feed over the winter months. He was the biggest bull accompanying the herd that winter, easily identifiable among the cows and a scattering of other young bulls.

The hard weather broke in mid-March and a warm chinook wind melted the snow until only the biggest drifts showed, greyish white in contrast to the new green grass on the hills and flats of lower ground. As usual, Old Buck's bunch left the park about this time, climbing over the pass out of Horseshoe Basin in a long, slow-travelling, straggling line. Far in the rear, Old Buck hobbled slowly along, favouring her stiffened leg, and by the time she crested the ridge, the rest of the herd was out of sight among the folds of timber below.

She stood on the skyline, resting, every line of her frame spelling fatigue, before she began picking her way down the track. At the rim of a steep-sided draw, where the herd had slid down on thawing ground, she half fell on the poor footing and further hurt her injured leg. Again she stood still for a while on a hard-packed drift that bridged a small stream, smelling the track where it climbed through some willows on the opposite side. Under her feet, she heard the muted rattling of the little creek as it poured along a tunnel cut through the snow. Ahead of her was the sharp pitch, while below her the hard-packed crust offered an inviting alternative towards lower ground. Accepting the invitation, she began picking her way down the easier route, till she came to a narrow cleft where the draw's sides pinched in between steep banks, offering no choice of passage. She had no means of knowing that the creek had thinned the crust here, until suddenly she broke through and found her feet in rushing water and snow almost level with her back. She was trapped, and she seemed to accept her fate without a struggle. That night she died. Under a canopy of stars, with the smell of green meadows on the warm breeze – meadows she would never see again – life left her in one long sigh.

At sunrise, a great grizzly, following his nose upwind, hungry for feed after an early exit from his winter den, appeared over the edge of the draw above the dead elk. He went straight for the carcass, grabbed it by the neck with his teeth, and heaved it out of the hole as effortlessly as a terrier would handle a rabbit. Backing up the steep slope, he dragged Old Buck's body into a thicket where pussy willows hung soft and silvery, and tore it open.

When the big bear left the vicinity a few days later, there was nothing left of the elk but a mat of loose hair, the skull, and a few of the larger bones. The grizzly's mounds of dung, thick with the hair he had eaten with the meat, were all deposited in a shallow hollow nearby, where the waxy-green pointed leaves of glacier lilies broke through the leaf mould, reaching for the sun. Like every other living thing in the mountains, the old cow had sprung from the soil, grown to full maturity, raised calves that now propagated her kind themselves, and had returned to the earth. The cycle was complete.

Following that winter, King disappeared. Every time I saw elk I looked for him, but he had completely vanished. It was as though he, too, had been swallowed by the earth, and I decided that a cougar or a hunter had got him. But I kept looking for a bull with a wattle topped by a silvery scar on the base of his neck.

One day I was riding the skyline along the crest of the Continental Divide. On the far side of a big basin near the headwaters of a wilderness creek that ran southwest towards the Flathead River and the Pacific Ocean, I spotted four bull elk. They were lying partially concealed in some timberline scrub, and when I focused the binoculars on them, it was obvious that the biggest one had spotted me.

Half a mile away, he stood up and walked out onto a little promontory where he stood broadside with his eyes fixed in my direction.

Even at that range, his antlers evoked a gasp of admiration – eight fully developed points to a side, heavy in the beams, wide in spread with beautiful double-curved symmetry.

For a while he stood as motionless as a bronze statue, looking my way, then he swung his head a little and I thought I caught a silvery flash at the base of his neck on the left side. Could it be King? My excitement suddenly towered, and I longed for the powerful spotting scope forgotten back in camp. His three companions stood up to join him, aware of his interest, and one by one they fastened their eyes on my horse and me where we stood silhouetted against the blue sky. Finally, they began moving away in single file up a saddle to drop from sight over the skyline. I pursued them through the timber in the bottom of the basin and up the other side. Before reaching the top, I tied my horse in a clump of trees and climbed on foot to a point overlooking the country beyond.

From there I was looking down into a tangle of logs, with second growth and the bone-white, bleached-out spikes of old fire-killed trees still standing. There was no sign of the bulls at first, but then my glasses picked up a spot of colour that might have been the tan hide of an elk among some alders far down in the steep bottom of a draw. For a long while there was no movement, and then, a little beyond, the glasses caught a glint of something, and I made out the gleaming antler tines of a bull.

Slipping back over the skyline, I circled under the crest of a spur to get the wind in my favour and then climbed down towards the elk, making use of every contour and cover. At last, I came out over the ravine on a knoll directly above where I had last seen the bulls, and sat down behind a log.

Not a whisker of them was in sight; they had again vanished completely and my disappointment was keen. The powerful lenses of the binoculars minutely combed every detail of the surrounding slopes without revealing a sign of them.

Picking up a dead branch lying beside me, I rattled it sharply against a dead tree. Like magic, antlers began to rise up from the brush, as the bulls got out of their beds. Three of them were mighty animals, two with six points to a side and one with seven, all grand bulls but the fourth one was magnificent.

His brow tines swung down and curved up almost even with the end of his nose. The bez and trez tines were heavy and long. His top royals were massive, fully two feet in length, their tips gleaming like two upright ivory spears. Back of these along the main beams were four more fully developed points, with the last two forking deeply. When he first stood up his rump was towards me, but when he turned, there on his neck was the familiar mark. I had found King again and he was truly an imperial bull.

A week later I saw him on the crest of the Divide standing in the sunshine over valleys filled with fog. He had changed his territory, crossing two ranges of mountains, and was now located in some of the most remote wilderness in the British Columbia Rockies. He was in the heart of my packtrain outfitting country, so when I headed out with a string of twenty horses and a photographer friend from New York a couple of weeks later, it was with the express purpose of finding and filming King.

My guest was Sheridan St. John, one of the earliest television producers to specialize in nature films, and an internationally famous outdoor sports writer. Like all his kind, he combined business with pleasure, so this expedition with his cameras was also a holiday. To make it even more pleasurable, we were good friends.

There is something special about the companionship enjoyed by two people far removed in their choices of environment, yet close in their common interests and outlook on life. My companion was an old hand at this game – although he spent most of his time in the concrete and steel canyons of the big city, he was passionately fond of getting out into wild country and had been on expeditions into remote parts of the world. Around many campfires over several years, we had traded stories of our experiences. He could tell of stalking oryx, guided by a Bushman tracker in the searing heat of the African desert, or of the high adventure of filming Inuit as they hunted polar bears on the limitless sea of ice of the Arctic.

From the snug camp we set up on this trip, we spent our days wandering on horseback along rugged horizons, dipping into timberline basins set like green jewels among the high jagged peaks. As always this enterprise was more demanding and much more difficult than ordinary hunting, for the photographer depends upon good light to record the drama and magic on the emulsion of colour film. It has its advantages too, for the trophies are brought back on film with no bag limits or closed seasons, and one need never worry about the boundaries of areas closed to hunting with guns. This was early September and all the big bulls had their harems collected: the cliffs rang with their bugling.

Early one morning, after we had been out for several days, we were riding through an old burn in rough country along a divide between two minor watersheds, a place heavily cut by deep ravines full of second-growth timber and mountain meadows. It was slow going and after several miles, we had not seen an elk although their sign was everywhere. At noon we rode out on a rim overlooking a deep box canyon that opened out below us into a heavily timbered valley.

Tying our horses out of sight, we walked out to a point to eat lunch and use our glasses. At first we could see nothing, a situation not necessarily indicating an absence of elk, for there was enough cover in this broken-up place to hide a sizeable herd. When my binoculars were trained on the slope directly opposite, a light-coloured spot showed up at the foot of a big old spruce in an island of mature timber the fire had missed. A look through the twenty-power spotting scope revealed a sleek cow lying half asleep and chewing her cud in the shade beneath an overhanging alder.

At a range close to half a mile, it was like unravelling the design of a picture puzzle wherein hidden figures lie; one after another, six more cows took form with only parts of them visible.

Then up near the top of a strip of thick alder brush, a spike bull stood up in plain view and gave an adolescent squeal. A hundred yards below him, directly above the cows, a huge bull came to his feet, only his head and neck in sight, and bugled back, then twisted his antlers into the brush, savaging the alder bark and making the leaves fly. There was no mistaking those massive antlers. It was King.

Sheridan whistled softly through his teeth at the sight of him. Here was a leading character in an elk movie – the biggest bull either of us had ever seen.

To try to get within camera range in that jungle was impossible even without the capricious mountain air currents to give away our location, so we just waited to see where the elk would go when they got up to feed.

Following the flurry of bugling and momentary excitement, both bulls lay down again, and for a long while nothing happened. Then, as the sun began to dip towards the skyline, the first cow I had spotted got to her feet and began nibbling at a low bush. More cows got up and began to move around, and the spike bull squealed. Instantly the whole valley came alive with the music of rutting bulls; the place was alive with them. When the cows began to move up valley, it was time for us to start our stalk.

We headed down the slope of the canyon through a heavy stand of second-growth lodgepole pine, slipping between their trunks and around and over a clutter of dead logs. We came out on top of a low cliff and climbed down onto the bench below. As we found a way through more timber, it was hot and still and the sweat was running off us. We came out on the rim of another cliff a hundred yards above the creek, directly across from two open strips of grass, uprooted trees, and scattered boulders separated by a stringer of green timber – avalanche tracks. They would give the camera good play – the kind of set-up a photographer looks for. Down the valley at least a half dozen bulls were sounding off.

Sheridan set up his loaded camera on its tripod and we waited. It is one thing to sit still in the quiet mountain, and quite another to do so while listening to a wild symphony coming closer and closer – a concert as primitive as the sight of midnight stars reflected on the mirror surface of a rock-bound lake.

I slipped around a clump of brush for a better view down valley, and then a twisting thermal of wind went by, blowing the wrong way. I held my breath, for which way the elk would go would depend on how that puff of air current delivered our scent. The sharp alarm bark of a cow suddenly silenced the concert.

The timber cracked directly below and there was the tan flash of a cow jumping a log as she headed up the valley. She was followed by several more cows, and then King went by at a gallop, his nose outthrust and his great antlers laid back as he cleared the log at a long bound.

Stepping back, I murmured, "Look sharp! Here they come!"

Timber was snapping and cracking all over the slope as elk burst into view on the grass strips – bulls, cows, and calves all going at a dead run like a cavalcade of steeple-chasers. King was running behind a string of cows low down the slope, a magnificent sight as he galloped over the rough ground.

They milled around for a minute or two at the base of the cliff before doubling back and coming down the canyon directly opposite us. There were fifty-three cows and calves, four big bulls, and three smaller bulls. King stopped on the skyline, outlined against a white cloud, every detail dramatically lit up by the lowering sun. Then he was gone.

"Holy smoke!" Sheridan muttered, letting out a long breath. "What a bull! That's the best shot I ever got of elk on the move." Then he added, "Can we find that bull again? I want some more footage of him."

"It won't be easy," I told him. "It's a big country, but maybe we'll be lucky."

We were lucky. We found King and his harem again in the middle of a grove of big western larches. The giant timber, some of the reddish-brown trunks four feet in diameter, soared aloft for eighty to a hundred feet before spreading out in a broken canopy of foliage, golden with autumn. It was remarkably like a well-tended park, with very little undergrowth and few downed logs, so we could see for two or three hundred yards in places. The golden rays of sunlight filtering through the foliage lit up the forest floor like something out of an artist's dream.

Quietly moving against the wind as close as we dared to the herd, we could see the elk scattered among the trees, some lying down and some feeding. Standing out among them was King.

Spreading the legs of the camera tripod on top of a low knoll behind a screening salmon berry bush, Sheridan began recording a wild and utterly beautiful mountain scene. It was early afternoon, and a lull in the rutting activity gave a relatively placid air to the herd. King was the only bull in sight, though there had to be others close by.

After Sheridan had rolled considerable film of the scene before us, he murmured, "If that big character would stir himself to do something spectacular, it would be perfect."

I knew there was a good chance of blowing the whole herd out of sight by calling in a second bull, but thinking it was worth the risk, I took out my call. Pulling in a chestful of mountain air, I cut loose with a challenge.

Instantly King swung around to face us, and pointing his nose directly at us, he let out a short bugle that sounded deceptively like an immature bull. Then he stalked deliberately towards us, his nose outthrust and his massive horns swinging in cadence with his stride. I kept quiet; nothing is worse than overdoing the calling. Closer and closer he came, an awesome sight moving in and out of patches of shade over the yellowing grass, an aura of power and majesty about him. Thirty steps from us he stopped, his front feet planted on a little mound where a tree had been uprooted long ago. His nose lifted as he opened his mouth to bugle right in our faces.

His head suddenly swung around, and looking in the direction he pointed, I saw another big bull coming towards us. This one had us in plain view. We froze, hoping he wouldn't spot us, but it was too late. For a long moment, the second bull stood with his head high and his eyes pinned on us, then he swung on his heels to leave at a tearing run.

For a few seconds flashes of elk showed between trees as the herd stampeded away, then we were all alone.

Sheridan straightened, exclaiming, "That was something to see! But sure as hell this would be a poor place for a man with a weak heart!"

The weather held good, and for the next week we rambled far and wide trying to pick up King and his harem again. They seemed to have evaporated into the mountain air.

One night it clouded up and began to snow. In the morning our tents sagged under the weight, and more was coming down. It was time to leave, for our grub was running low and Sheridan was due at a meeting in New York in a few days, so we packed up our gear and headed out. Breaking trail over a high pass that afternoon, the horses strung out behind me plodding through a driving blizzard, the trees beside the trail burdened under heavy loads of snow, it was hard to believe that only the day before we had ridden for hours in the warm sun dressed only in blue jeans and shirts.

This was the prelude to one of the toughest winters the country had ever seen. In late October, King and eleven other mature bulls settled on a south-facing slope on a ridge running west from the Continental Divide. The place was open to the sun with a heavy growth of cured bunch grass to give them good feed through the deep snows of winter.

By December the snow was as deep as it usually ever gets. At Christmas, the temperature dropped to forty below and it stayed cold without a break. No crust impeded the bulls pawing for food, but the snow continued to build up. By late January they were wallowing halfway up to their ribs in snow and finding it hard to get enough to eat. They were within sight of a cabin in the valley bottom, and the trapper who lived there often watched them.

One frosty morning in February, he was fastening his snowshoe harness as he got ready to leave for a day on his trapline. He was surprised to see the bulls coming along the trail past his cabin ploughing their way down the valley. They passed not more than fifty yards away, their antlers swinging, steam shooting from their noses with the exertion, and their coats rimed silvery with frost. Their ribs showed, and short rations had dulled their usual caution to the point of paying him little attention, but they were still going strong.

A half mile below his cabin, where the trail comes close to the creek, there is a long stretch of open water where big springs keep the ice from forming. Here the bulls took to the easier going of water travel, and proceeded to fill up on the browse overhanging the stream. Then they bedded down in the deep snow along the top of the low bank.

It was a welcome break for them but also a trap. The snow got deeper and deeper until it was over six feet on the level, so by the time the willow browse that was within reach began to thin out, the bulls' movements were restricted to the half-mile stretch of open water. The cold continued and as the bulls foraged, the splashes their feet threw up froze on the hair of their bellies and sides. The cold armour that only warm weather could remove quickly grew thicker and heavier. The fast-diminishing feed coupled with this extra weight cruelly drained their remaining strength.

One day in the following spring, I met the trapper in town, and he told me about it. "They must have been carrying over a hundred pounds of ice apiece," he said. "And they ate everything off till there wasn't a twig along the creek any smaller than your thumb. They got so weak, they couldn't take it any more. They would crawl up in the snow to lie down for the night and in the morning they just couldn't get up. One by one they died. I've never seen anything like it. It was sure one hell of a winter for the animals!"

In early summer I had a fishing party out in that valley, and I took some time to look for King's remains. Searching through the brush alongside the creek, I found what was left of eleven bulls – just scraps of hair, antlers, and bones scattered by bears. But in spite of searching back and forth for hours, I could find no sign of King.

Had he somehow managed to save enough strength to move to better feed and survive? I stood in a little meadow within a few yards of the cheerfully chattering stream and wondered if somewhere high on the slopes he knew so well, he lay in the warm sun basking among brilliant flowers. It was highly unlikely, for nobody ever saw the great bull with the silvery blaze on his neck again, but it was heart-warming to think that among the survivors of that terrible winter, there were undoubtedly some of his sons and daughters.

While he and Buck have long gone, somewhere among the valleys walk other bulls and cows, maintaining that bloodline and ensuring that each fall, when the first frost touches the mountain slopes, there will be wild music and action in the land of the elk.

2

BEING A KID

DON BRESTLER

Being a kid growing up on a wilderness ranch eighty years ago provided experiences nobody will ever know again. The ranch was located at the foot of the Rocky Mountains. We had three cold, clear mountain creeks on the ranch and they teemed with trout. The hills and valleys were well populated with grouse and ducks and other kinds of small game. There were deer and bears in the bush, with wild sheep up on the mountain slopes.

We had work to do with cattle and horses. If we went some place across the country, we either rode horseback or travelled in a buggy or wagon pulled by horses. We had no radios, T.V., telephones, or automobiles. Some of us could play musical instruments, while others like the trappers or cowboys could tell stories. They were very good at it.

Every kid in the country had a horse – sometimes two. We all grew up riding horses and working with cattle. Sometimes we got some skin knocked off when we got care-less or overly reckless, but rarely did anyone get seriously hurt. When kids and animals are mixed, there are bound to be times when the unexpected happens.

I remember a day when my brother John and I were out fishing with a couple of boys from a neighbouring ranch. It was a hot day, and when the time came for us to be heading home for supper, we got on our horses and lined out down the trail. Carl was in the lead, followed by his brother Ritchie. John was next and I was bringing up the rear. Ritchie was riding an old white horse that was as lazy as horses get, and we were advising him to quit holding up the parade when a fly bit the horse on the nose. He stopped while he put his nose down to rub the fly off his front leg. John's horse kept going, and the tip of his rod, which he hadn't taken down, went under old Scrub's tail and the fish hook, which was caught in the tip guide, got caught on the edge of his exhaust pipe. Scrub was instantly transformed into a three-star rodeo bronc. He broke wind like a string of firecrackers going off, bogged his head and threw Ritchie up into the top of a snow-bent aspen. His fish flew out of the cotton sack he was carrying them in and joined Ritchie as they dribbled down to the ground.

Scrub lit out for the horizon. Brother John's fishing reel screamed as the line went out. John reared back like he was fighting a big fish. The line came to an end and broke off. We caught up to Scrub at the next gate dancing around, snorting and blowing, wider awake than he had been for years. I undertook to catch him but stepped on the line that was still dragging from the hook and set off another riot.

I got back on my horse, took down my lariat, and caught him. Then I tied his hind foot up to his shoulder and examined the damage. A bit of surgery with my jackknife fixed up the problem and we proceeded on our way with no more excitement.

This is the way a culture is built on the frontier.

3

RENÉ AND CLARICE

R ené was a trapper who had his trapline in the valley of a small river running into the Peace in northern Alberta. The Peace is a mighty river that runs through a big piece of land and back in 1895 it was wilderness inhabited by a few Indians, and here and there across the country there were trading posts.

René and Clarice spent their winters on the trapline and their summers at the fort down river. Their trapline was up a tributary above the river. Three years after they were married, they had a son. A bit after a year later, they had a baby girl. When it came time for René to leave for his trapline, a relative who had no children offered to look after their little boy so that Clarice could go with René.

It was a long winter with heavy snow. One day shortly after the ice went, some Indians coming down the river to trade at the fort found a small raft floating in the current with a baby aboard. The little girl was warmly wrapped in fur and although she was starving, she was still healthy. One of the Indian women was nursing a child, so she undertook to feed the foundling.

The woman who was looking after the boy recognized the fur that the baby was wrapped in as part of a coat that Clarice wore. It was obvious something really bad had happened.

Four trappers who were friends of René and Clarice set out by canoe up the river. When they reached René's cabin, they found the bodies of the unfortunate couple. There was no food left in the place, and it seemed that René and Clarice had died of starvation or some sickness. But how did they manage to build the raft that brought the baby down the river? How did they feed the baby?

It was a mystery that has never been solved, for neither René nor Clarice could read or write and there was no message.

The boy's name was Robert, and they called the baby girl Clarice, after her mother. Robert was raised by a man and a woman who worked at a Roman Catholic mission farther down the Peace River. Clarice grew up at the trading post where the Indians who found her had been headed.

The story might be over except that fate decreed that these two young people never met each other as brother and sister. Robert went with his foster father and mother on a long journey back to the original location of their home in Trois-Rivières in Quebec. He was a bright, intelligent child and in due course went to school, where he studied to be a clerk. In those days the requirements of being a clerk involved handwriting and bookkeeping. When he was sixteen, he got a job working for a fur trader, who took him to Europe, where he worked for about a year. When they returned to Quebec, his employer sent him west with an older man, who would be visiting various trading posts dealing in trade goods and gathering fur.

In the course of this work, Robert met many people and one day met Clarice, who was a strikingly lovely young woman. It was a case of love at first sight and it rapidly progressed to a proposal of marriage. But when they went to an old priest, he remembered their origin and of course refused to marry them and told them why.

It was a shock. Instead of a wife, Robert had found his sister. It is one of the strangest stories to ever come out of the Peace River country.

4

THE PARTY LINE

DCB 98

When I was a boy growing up on a ranch south of Pincher Creek at the foot of the Rockies, communications were primitive. When one of the homesteaders or ranchers wanted to send a message to somebody, it usually started with saddling up a horse. The post office was fourteen miles from our door and the telegraph office was two miles beyond that. Telephones were few and far between in the country, and some of the first used the barbed wire of the fences for connecting lines, a not very efficient practice, particularly in wet weather. Wire tied to insulators fastened to the top of a post ten to fourteen feet above the ground worked a lot better, though vulnerable to weather. Our Alberta chinooks that sometimes come roaring out of the mountains at more than a hundred miles an hour had a way of finding weak spots that kept the service man busy. The people who lived in town enjoyed private lines but rural subscribers got along with party lines with anywhere from four to a dozen numbers on each line. When a phone rang in a house, it rang in all the houses on the line and anybody so inclined could pick up his phone and listen. Privacy was on the honour basis, and sometimes the real meaning of the word was overlooked, which could cause friction among neighbourhood housewives. When overheated teenagers came home from school and proceeded to take over the line conversing in deep sighs and heavy breathing, it could tax the patience of a saint, particularly if the saint wished to use the phone. We told ourselves that phones were a highly respected and serious part of our lives, but sometimes this profound reflection went up in a cloud of smoke.

One winter I was boarding on a farm a few miles south of Lethbridge taking my second year of high school at the local place of learning. The place was on a party line and the phone was on the wall in the kitchen, as they generally were on farms then. We were just finishing breakfast one morning when the boss suddenly remembered that he had to make a call. He went over to the phone, picked up the receiver, and put it to his ear to find out if the line was busy – the usual procedure in making a call. It was clear the line was busy but he sort of froze with a rapt expression on his face and, in due course, his expression ran from keen interest through amazement into paroxysms of silent mirth. After he finally managed to hang up, he ended up sitting on the floor hugging himself and roaring with laughter. He finally managed to get himself under control, wipe the tears off his face, and tell us the story.

It involved two characters: One was Mrs. Peck, a notorious woman with a long and colourful career behind her, who owned a dairy farm a few miles away, and the other was Bob Patterson, a tough old rancher who had a purebred herd of fine Hereford cattle. Mrs. Peck decided she needed a Hereford bull to cross with the part of her Holstein milk cow herd she didn't need to keep purebred. So she went to the Patterson ranch and bought a fine young bull. One of the reasons he looked so fine was because he had been on a nurse cow for a big part of his life; in short, he had never been weaned and Bob Patterson never mentioned it.

So it is understandable that when she turned her new bull out with some of her cows he proceeded to get acquainted by sucking his belly full of nice warm milk. When Mrs. Peck became aware of this outrageous behaviour, she rang up Bob Patterson and the overheard conversation went like this:

"Mr. Patterson, your bull is sucking my cows!"

"Mrs. Peck, I thought that's what you bought him for."

"Mr. Patterson, *I said sucking!*"

So much for party lines.

5

THE MAN WITH THE IRON BELLY

When I think about trappers, the name of Harry Simpson comes to mind, which might seem strange for he wasn't a trapper. He was a fur buyer, and he owned a half interest in a store. SIMPSON & LEE the sign said over the door, and likely there isn't an old-timer in Alberta who doesn't remember the place. The partners weren't very much alike. Harry Simpson was an outdoor man. He looked like one, and his dress went right along with it. Lee was a typical city storekeeper. Their store was unique, for it specialized in the kind of gear used by trappers and hunters: snowshoes, traps, guns, knives, axes, and about anything else you might care to name. The business was based on buying fur and was well known to nearly anyone with a skin to sell, from farm boys to grizzled old professional trappers. The fur trade was dominated by the Hudson's Bay Company over most of Canada in those days, but some trappers preferred to deal with independent buyers. Simpson and Lee had a reputation for fair dealing so they enjoyed a good business.

The first time I met Harry Simpson I had a couple of nice beaver skins rolled up under my arm when I walked into the store. They were prime top-grade pelts, a fact that was obvious to his practised eye.

He was smiling when he asked, "Where are the rest of them?"

I kept these back," I told him. "They were still too green to go in the shipment."

"Can I ask where you shipped them?"

"I guess the same place you ship yours," I said. "The Winnipeg Fur Auction."

That surprised him a bit, for most trappers did not know about this market, but it also served to break the ice between us. He gave me a fair price for my skins, and we went on with some interesting conversation. He was obviously a man who loved to hunt and fish and explore remote places. He knew about my work with grizzlies and during the course of our conversation, he undid the buttons on the front of his shirt and opened it to reveal an ugly scar fairly high on his abdomen. It was laced with stitch marks that were not much of an advertisement for the skill of whoever sewed him up. Harry buttoned up his shirt and told me a story.

One day, three years before, a trapper had shown up with a big pack of exceptionally fine skins from the Yukon. Their conversation led to an invitation to dinner. Like many of his kind, the man, whose name was Joe, was enjoying the chance to talk after a long winter alone on his trapline, and Harry discovered that the trapper not only had a licence to trap in his area on the Pelly River, but was also a licensed guide. He proceeded to book a two-week bear hunt the following spring.

In due course, Harry took the plane for Whitehorse, and from there he got a bush pilot with a plane on floats to take him to Joe's cabin on the Pelly. It was wild and beautiful country, the cabin proved to be well built and comfortable, and his host assured him that they should collect a sizeable grizzly with ease for he had seen several along the river. He had a good boat with a powerful outboard motor and with this they would travel the river in search of a bear. Harry set up a target and fired three shots to check his rifle, always a good idea after travelling on a commercial airline, and he was happy to see it was unchanged. His guide noted the three bullet holes in a tight group in the centre of the bull's-eye with satisfaction as well, for it is always a comfort to know that a new man knows how to shoot.

Next morning the sun was turning the high spots along the north side of the river to pink and gold when they launched the boat and headed upstream. The Pelly is a big river running at a good clip through a deep valley, but for the most part there are not many heavy rapids though the current is fairly swift. The slope facing the sun was green with new growth, and this was where the bears were feeding. They had only been on the river about an hour when Joe suddenly swung the boat and landed it on the edge of a gravel bar.

"There's a grizzly up just under the rim below that rock outcrop," he told Harry. "Looks like a good one. We'll have a look with the glasses."

When Harry located the bear with his binoculars, he felt the thrill of excitement, for it was a big golden brown animal with a heavy coat.

"That's a half-hour climb – maybe more," Joe said. "That bear is on the move. The only way to get to him is up that draw to the right. He will be out of sight part of the time from there. If you can handle it, go ahead and I'll watch from here where I can see and I can signal you if he moves."

Harry picked a small pack and his rifle and headed up the steep slope following the draw. He was in good shape, so he made fast time, and for the most part he was out of sight of the bear. It was grazing on the new grass, wandering aimlessly, but was gradually moving higher towards the skyline. When Harry came to the mouth of a small draw branching off the one he was following, he stopped to check on the bear and saw it was barely out of range, but as he watched, it climbed up among some boulders close to the rim. Because it topped out in what looked like a better place to see, a bit farther from the bear, Harry climbed up the smaller draw.

Down below, Joe was watching and when he saw Harry move up the draw coming up on the right, he was relieved, for it put him in a better position to see when he got to the skyline. The bear had moved behind a rock out of sight and did not reappear.

Harry reached the rim among the broken rock, moving carefully and stopping often, as he used his binoculars in search of the bear. He stepped up onto a flat slab of rock and looked ahead. Joe had his glasses up looking back at him and didn't move. Harry suddenly had the strong premonition that he was in a very dangerous place. He froze and carefully looked at every inch of the mess of rock ahead of him. The only place he couldn't see was a partially hidden hollow beyond the edge of the slab he was standing on. He took another cautious step, making no sound. Before he had time to lift his rifle, there was a whistling snort, a flashing picture of teeth and claws, and then something hit him and the light went out.

Joe saw the bear jump and hit Harry and saw the hunter go down. In the same motion, the bear whirled and ran in long bounds to disappear over the skyline. Joe was shocked to the marrow of his bones, but he did not lose his head. He hauled the boat farther up on the gravel bar and tied it to a partially buried piece of driftwood, then he slung a light pack over his shoulders and headed up the slope. When he reached Harry, he stood for a while to get his breath back, then looked him over. Harry didn't look very good.

The front of his shirt and undershirt was torn to rags and he was covered with blood. Joe knelt and ran his hands over him carefully, but aside from a lump on his head where he had bumped it on the rock, the wound on his belly seemed to be his only injury. There were three ugly claw marks, the middle one being deepest. From his pack, Joe took some clean rags to make a pad to cover the wound. Securing it with tape, he took Harry's light rain jacket out of his pack, reversed it, and tied it tightly around him. Harry was regaining consciousness.

"Where's my gun?" he asked.

"Right here," Joe told him.

"Where's the bear?"

"Last I saw he was on a dead run for Alaska! You sure scared hell out of him!" Joe said.

Harry tried to get up and sagged back with a gasp.

"Take it easy," Joe said. "I'll get the pack together. Then we'll see if you can walk."

Getting Harry on his feet was not easy, but when he took hold of the top of Joe's pack with one hand, he could walk. Joe got him down to the boat after a slow painful climb and it wasn't long before they were back at the cabin, where Harry stretched out on his bed and promptly fell asleep.

Joe lit a fire and prepared a pot of soup. He let Harry sleep for a while and then woke him up. Briefly he told Harry that the first thing they had to do was clean the wound. Then they had two choices: they could wait for the plane to come or they could take the boat down to the Yukon River and then up to Whitehorse – a trip that would take days. For a while Harry just sipped soup and thought about it. The soup tasted good and it didn't hurt to swallow it, which encouraged him to believe that the bear's claws had missed his vitals. He remembered seeing some sewing on the skins he had bought from Joe – very neat stitching. It was a sure thing that his belly wasn't going to heal properly if it wasn't sewed up.

"You got needles and thread, Joe. How about sewing me up?"

"Can do, if you can take it," Joe assured him.

Born with good hands and steady nerves, besides having the rudimentary knowledge of how to do a clean job, Joe stitched the wound. Apart from clenching his teeth and sweating, Harry endured the pain, which was considerable because the wound was torn rather than cut, making drawing it together more difficult and slower. When he needed a rest, he asked for it and Joe was glad to give it to him. Finally Joe clipped off the thread and stepped back.

"It ain't very fancy, but I think it will do till you get to a doctor," he said.

By the time Harry's plane came to pick him up, he was feeling good. Back home, he went to see his doctor, who was at first horrified, then amazed, and, when he looked at the pattern of the stitches, puzzled. He called the nurse and asked her if she had ever seen stitches like that, and she assured him that she had; she sometimes used that kind of stitch to mend the kids' jeans. The doctor opined that they should have been taken out long ago and it was going to be a hell of a job to get them out now. The nurse agreed, and Harry assured them both that he wished they would get at it sometime before next week. So they went to work, and Harry's jaw muscles got some more high-pressure exercise and he did some more sweating.

When it was over, Harry was tingling so much he was afraid to move for a while, and when the doctor said that he wanted to book a bear hunt with Joe, he said, "You're welcome."

6

THE COLONEL'S STUD HORSE

DON BRESTLER '88

The Colonel was a client of mine – a fascinating man, whose stories of his life around the world sometimes defied belief, but he could never be called boring or his stories flatly labelled lies, for some careful research would generally reveal that in fact they sometimes lost colour in the telling. He loved to hunt in wild country, not particularly because he got a lot of satisfaction out of hanging a good trophy on the wall, but more due to memories of time spent with the kind of people he admired. He was the kind of man to whom things happened – the born adventurer.

When he came with me on a three weeks' hunt by pack train in the Rockies, it was very enjoyable hunting with him, but the real spice of the trip was the time spent swapping stories around the evening campfires. He had hunted big game from Alaska to Africa and was a counter-espionage agent during World War I, and he was a master storyteller who could hold his listeners in breathless fascination.

Here was a man with enormous experience and a tremendous ability to adapt to just about anything the world could throw at him and land on his feet. Yet he was vulnerable. One evening when he was telling me about his ranch, I sensed that he had a blind spot as most of us have.

He was telling of his tough luck getting colts from his stallion, which was a famous horse once owned by the Duke of Windsor. It was an Arab with an illustrious bloodline. He had owned the stud for three years, yet had not one colt to show for his service. He told me the fate of all the colts seemed doomed, for something always happened to them.

As one who was raised on a horse and cow ranch and had worked with horses from the time I was old enough to do so, this was hard for me to understand. The Colonel told me of all the things that had happened to his colts. "Wolves have been the worst," he said. "I have close to a hundred head of horses on my ranch, but they always pick the colts and seem to have a special taste for the Arabs."

His ranch was on the upper reaches of the Red Deer River west of Sundre, Alberta. It was close to the mountains and was real wilderness country with its due population of wolves. But wolves do not just specialize in killing horses, nor do they stay in one place very long in country where there are good numbers of various big game – elk, moose, deer, and mountain sheep.

Some careful questioning on my part regarding his crew and neighbours revealed the Colonel's unbending loyalty to the people around him. He depended on his crew to look after his ranch, for he was away from it a good deal of the time. His neighbours were few and far between. The signs pointed to a two-legged predator that was raiding his Arab colts, but I said nothing to him about this.

However, the thoughts would not go away and during the winter I occasionally remembered what he had told me. When he wrote me a letter the following spring inviting me to come for a visit, I decided to go.

It was June, with the usual rain, and the road up to his ranch was close to impassable but I managed to get there in spite of numerous mud holes. The Colonel's place was amazing. He lived in the original log ranch house, which was spacious and comfortable, but he had built a big new guest lodge and a private museum that contained the finest collection of old guns and western art I have ever seen.

There were over six hundred pieces in his gun collection, many of them of enormous value, like the matched pair of cap and ball Colt revolvers that Samuel Colt had made and presented to Wells of the famous Wells Fargo company, the early American freight and stagecoach developer that covered most of the western States. This was an elegant pair of pistols engraved and mounted with gold.

They were in a beautiful velvet-lined case made of highly polished walnut. There were also several large oil paintings by C.M. Russell and Frederick Remington and several bronzes by the same artists.

The Colonel and his wife were excellent hosts, and I met some of their friends who were visiting from New York, as well as the crew on the ranch. I got up early the next morning and spent some time before breakfast wandering around the place. At the barn, I found the Arab stud in a box stall. It was a magnificent animal that showed some surprising signs of neglect. I also overheard some conversation between the ranch foreman and one of the hands; they were laughing at some joke they had on the Colonel. I managed to get away without being seen but not without wondering about the loyalty of the crew and also about the fate of the Arab stud's colts that had disappeared.

That afternoon, we went for a ride with the ranch foreman; the guests from New York and one or two of the ranch help made up the party. It was wild and beautiful country and we were strung out on a trail along a steep slope above a creek valley. The foreman, who was in the lead, pointed out a pile of bones on a meadow below us and said, "There's all that's left of one of the Colonel's colts that the wolves killed."

I reined my horse off the trail and rode down for a closer look. One look at those bones told me that they had never belonged to any colt. The horse that once owned them had lived to a ripe old age, a fact that the teeth told me, for they were long and worn smooth on the nipping cups.

We saw another pile of bones that day, and again the Colonel's head man proclaimed them to be one of the Arab colts that the wolves had killed. And again a close look revealed that they were from an old horse.

The Colonel never asked so I kept my mouth shut, but I would have bet money that his foreman was stealing his horses. When I headed back for home, I had the chance to talk to a close friend of the Colonel's and told him what I suspected.

He gave me a long look and told me that he and the Colonel's business manager had told him that his foreman was a thief, but that he refused to believe it.

However, I heard later that the Colonel had caught his man stealing a pistol from his collection. He gave him twenty-four hours to get out of the country and that was the last anyone heard of him for a long while.

The Colonel sold his ranch and moved to Arizona. I was in Calgary on business one day and stepped into the hotel elevator to go to my room. The elevator operator abruptly turned his back to me but I recognized him before he saw me. He was the Colonel's ex-foreman.

7

A LESSON IN MOUNTAIN CLIMBING

DON BRESTLER '98

I was much younger then and I firmly believed that a man who knew how to free-climb could follow goats anywhere they chose to go. Having grown up and lived the greater part of my life among the high crags of the Alberta and British Columbia Rockies, scrambling over mountain terrain was a way of life for me, and I enjoyed the exhilaration and challenges that go with climbing.

Why do people climb mountains? A very famous climber once answered this question by saying "Because they are there." But for me, the presence of the peaks is only part of it; the many kinds of life found on the rugged faces of the mountains make them even more irresistibly fascinating and breathtakingly beautiful.

The highlights of exploration and adventure balance the costs of sinew-stretching exertion, pounding heart, and labouring lungs. The danger is tempered by physical fitness and the knowledge that one may be treading where no man has ever trod before. There are, to be sure, some moments when muscles fairly groan, and when concentration is an exhausting thing, but there are also experiences so utterly beautiful that they are imprinted on the mind forever.

Once, for example, I was crossing the foot of a sheer lava intrusion and I came to a tiny waterfall sparkling and splashing like a fountain into a perfect bowl carved out of the solid black lava. To one side of it there was a small grotto, where a bubble in the molten rock had broken. This was partially screened by the frothy, light green lace of maidenhair ferns. Behind them I saw the glint of reflections from the falling water and when I moved closer to look, there was the sudden flash of wings as a bird flew out. I knelt to part the ferns and found the inside of the hole lined with quartz crystals glittering like jewels. Artfully built in this little cave was the nest of a Townsend's solitaire with four greenish-blue eggs. My camera was primitive and colour film was still in the future, so photographing it was impossible, but the image still lives with me as one of the most exquisitely beautiful I have ever seen, a shrine in lovely homage to a mountain.

Then there was the time I sat on a broad ledge with my back to a rock wall just as morning was opening its sleepy eyes. I was overlooking a secret pass with ranks of massive peaks, miles and miles of them, all purple and rose and gold in the sunrise.

I had spent every daylight hour on that ledge for seven long days hoping to film a big grizzly who lived in the area. My grub was running low back at camp, time was beginning to press, the rock was very hard under my hip pockets, and my jacket was too light to keep out the chilly breeze playing capriciously among the mountain battlements around me. Patience is a virtue acquired by those who film wild things, especially grizzlies, but mine was wearing mighty thin.

Suddenly, out of some shintangle scrub below, the great bear appeared and all the discomfort and waiting was forgotten. Closer and closer he came, walking up the pass into the sunlight, his silvery coat glistening and rolling in cadence with his muscles, and his long front claws glowing dully like old ivory. There was a power and grace about him that is synonymous with grizzlies. He turned directly towards me to come up a steep snowdrift to a point right under my boot toes. For a moment, he stood still, a king of the mountains looking out over his wild realm, and then he sat down to slide in merry abandon to the bottom.

The motion picture camera whirred as it recorded the scene on film, catching him as he came back up to repeat the performance – royalty setting aside its dignity to enjoy a frolic. After such a long wait, it was tremendously exciting to catch this action in the lens of my camera. I did not know it then, but the light was being reflected from the snow as I was shooting into the sun, and my electronic meter was lying to me. The resulting pictures were an unusual record but useless for anything else. Just the same, the scene so indelibly printed in my mind is almost a tangible thing, something of great value to stay with me as long as I live.

That is why I climb mountains, enduring the storms and enjoying the sun. These and a thousand other experiences keep me climbing and make me always wonder what will unfold over the next ridge or beyond the next bend of some wild canyon.

This day I had goats in mind. The solid footing of rock on the cliff face was welcome after the drudgery of climbing the loose rock of the talus fan where my mountain boots slid back a step for every two taken upward. My muscles were loose and I was feeling good as I worked out a route up to the goats' level, although their exact location was now hidden from me by a bulge of the mountain.

I did not hurry. Every handhold and foothold was carefully tested, and following an old rule of free-climbing, one hand and one foot were always well anchored for every move. There is a certain rhythm to this, a fluidity of motion. The climber makes the best use of every feature of the rock and distributes his weight as evenly as possible to enhance his balance. All moves are deliberate and are made with confidence and purpose.

As each step of my route was worked out, I paused to carefully appraise the next. This served a double purpose, giving me a chance to rest and time to plan, for one does not backtrack if it can be avoided. To do so is like taking money out of a savings account; it takes time and more effort to replace it.

Finally I reached a wider ledge on the same level as the goats, about two-thirds of the way up the cliff, but they were still out of sight somewhere to the north of me.

Travelling along the ledge, I climbed to the top of a jutting
buttress just in time to see the shaggy rear of a billy disappear around a corner two hundred feet ahead. I followed,
and this time was rewarded by a good view of the goats, as
they stood in line at a spot where the ledge narrowed and
pitched down at a slant around another corner. Two of
them were watching me, obviously aware of my company
up here in the airy hallways of their mountain fortress.

Ahead of them there was a sheer wall, impossible for
anything but a fly, and I wondered what route they would
choose to get past it. If they cut back above me, they would
be forced to pass close, for there was another impassable
cliff, overhung in places, above me. Their most likely route
was a cutback below, so I stepped ahead into full view and
approached them. They immediately moved ahead, climbing down along the ledge around the curve at a walk.

Upon reaching the point where they had disappeared, I
was astonished to see them all lined up on the tiny ledge
where it faded out to nothing on the sheer wall. In paying
more attention to what is behind than what is ahead, they
had trapped themselves.

Now I cut off their retreat, and they had their heads
turned, looking back at me somewhat quizzically as though
wondering what to do next, their hoofs splayed as they
gripped the ledge, and their high, narrow bodies balanced
perfectly, though mighty precariously, on the bare edge of
nothing. I did not have long to wonder what they would do.
Almost in unison, they reared and pivoted outward on their
hind feet to land facing me, and then they came marching
purposefully back, as though saying that they were getting
out of there, and it would be just too bad for me if I was in
the way. Behind and above me there was a narrow, almost
perpendicular, chimney that could be reached quickly if it
became necessary, so I stayed to see what they would do.

On they came till the leader was only about ten short steps away. There he halted, and I detected definite anger. His ragged, half-shed mane stood up as he bowed his neck, displaying his short, black, curved horns, sharp as needles, and pawing the rock with a front foot. Then he began chewing – grinding his teeth ominously in what appeared to be a towering rage. Ready to retreat quickly into the chimney, I spoke to him softly and took a step in his direction. This obviously surprised all three billies, and again they swapped ends to head back down the ledge. Upon reaching the dead end, they gave the cliff another hard look and once more made that spectacular turn to come back.

This time it was obvious that they meant business, and I quickly scrambled out of the way into the chimney, where I turned my back to the cliff face, braced my boots on each side of it and picked up a fist-sized stone to discourage an invasion. The goats passed me at a fast walk barely fifteen feet below, not one so much as glancing my way, and disappeared around the corner. Although there was a camera hanging on a strap around my neck, I could not use it, being too busy with more important things, like hanging on to the mountain.

When I climbed back down onto the ledge and made my way to the point, I found that the billies had taken a route that slanted down the mountain. As I watched, they switched to their original direction below me, pausing to give me a long stare before disappearing under an overhang. I followed and saw them reappear from under the overhang and pick their way casually along a ledge that led to a long vertical crack, or chimney, in the rock, several feet wide and directly under the face that had so effectively stopped them on their first try. Here centuries of spring run-offs had scoured the rock as smooth as the side of a bowl. The ledge they were following was cut off where it came out from under the overhang, and slanted upward on the other side of the chimney. The gap was about six feet wide. The billies had no trouble passing the overhang, for it was high enough to miss their backs. When they came to the gap in the ledge, they blithely jumped across and proceeded on up the other side. The awesome eagle thoroughfare below they ignored completely.

But I could not help being aware of it – not unduly afraid – just respectful. In climbing one becomes accustomed to heights and develops confidence through exposure. However, this place made me acutely aware of my limitations. It was time to pause and contemplate geography as well as the power of gravity.

The overhang posed a problem; while it had allowed the goats to pass, a six-foot man with a rucksack on his back would be cramped. The ledge was a foot wide in most places, flat and without any breaks till it reached the chimney – a mark for the positive, though no cause for a celebration. It sloped slightly downward, leaving no room for mistakes.

It was not impossible, so I eased out step by step under the overhang. In places I could make headway by stooping low and planting my boots on the extreme outside edge of the ledge, but for the most part I was forced to face in to the rock and inch my way along using every available handhold. Friction was the only alternative to the pull of gravity. It was a kind of crab-wise routine in gymnastics where every handhold was tested, for the sedimentary rock was rotten and sometimes pieces of it came loose before I found a solid hold. The fragments fell in silence for a long way before clattering on projecting rocks below – not something to lull one into any kind of carelessness. It was a great relief to stand comfortably when I finally reached the chimney.

I wondered how any sensible person could ever get himself into a spot like this. The ledge ended here and the six-foot chasm had to be crossed, for backtracking held even less attraction. Not only was it a reversal of original intent, but I was far from sure that it could be done, because my route had taken me around a projecting rock that offered little to hang onto in getting back. I had barred the door on myself – something that can be done in one step in such terrain – so across the gap it had to be, even though the prospect was hair-raising.

On a ledge ten feet above a green meadow such a manoeuvre would mean nothing, but here, with this abyss yawning at me, the prize offered for a slip was final.

As I stood studying the place, one of the billies came back to gaze down at me as though curious to find out what I would do now. The problem in a spot like this is mostly psychological; the difficulty is exaggerated by the surroundings. The trick is to convince oneself of this fact. It's a matter of will and positive thinking, accompanied by the utter certainty that no mistake can be permitted. A hundred times that morning I had been in similar situations where a slip would have been just as deadly, though far less spectacular.

The goats had crossed. What they had done, I could do, I told myself; but they had four legs instead of two, four flexible, spongy hoofs to grip the rock and hold when they landed. If I could make the jump and come down in perfect balance, then crouch and grasp two handholds on the ledge ahead, I would be anchored. It was a contest between me and the mountain.

Stepping back far enough to let me take two quick steps, I took a big breath, and with every nerve concentrating on my landing, I leapt. My boots came down on solid rock. I leaned forward, flexing my knees to take the shock, and my fingers found their holds and dug in. For a long moment I did not move a fraction of an inch. Then came the sound of a little rock, dislodged from the ledge, clattering far below.

When I let out my breath and slowly stood up, my knees were trembling a bit and sweat was pouring off me, even though the jump had been incredibly easy. I had moved on to the top of a buttress before I became aware of sharp tingling pain on my right knee and elbow. A quick look revealed patches of skin scraped off, blood oozing from the raw spots where I had scraped against the rock wall over the ledge upon landing. The scrapes were sore, but it was a cheap enough exchange.

Ahead of me the goats were parading away in single file along a wide ledge leading to an easier portion of the cliff. They paused to stare back, then moved away again, but I did not follow. Sitting with my back comfortably propped against a sloping rock, I ate my lunch and watched them go, content to let good enough alone. It occurred to me that they were probably the most dangerous animals in the mountains – not because of any threat from their sharp horns, but due to the kind of country they led their pursuers into among the peaks.

The lesson learned that morning stuck with me. Mountain goats can go where a lone climber has no business following, no matter how skilled that climber may be.

Now when I see a big old billy posing like a statue atop a cliff against the blue sky and sailing clouds, I am inclined to tip my hat and say, "Happy days, old boy! It's your mountain and you're welcome to it!"

8

KLEO

DON BRESTLER '98

From high up, looking down along its spine, the north ridge of the Horn was warm with the coppery red reflection of a fiery sunset on its western flank, and to the east it was deep in shadow, facing the purple tints of twilight touching the rim of the prairie eighty miles or so away. The top of the ridge was serrated unevenly, like the back of some ancient prehistoric monster lying asleep against the side of the peak; the humps were capped by weathered turrets, rough-hewn by countless years of weather, like castle ruins so old they only hinted at shapes once known. It was cool and very still, the quiet a poignant thing as the mountains and everything in them paused in contemplation of the blazing sky.

Out of nowhere, skylined on the highest point, there came a big red-gold tom cougar. He stalked along with a peculiar grace known only to the cat kingdom, and upon reaching the crest, he stopped. He slowly swept his gaze across the slope towards the forked canyons of Pine Creek, his eyes glowing a blazing yellow, hot orbs betraying his bad temper, a frame of mind accented by the twitching end of his long tail.

For Kleo was a very angry cat. As he walked across the mountains, waving his tail wildly in reminiscence of romance lost, he tingled and burned from a score of wounds inflicted on his tough hide by the claws and teeth of a successful rival.

Two nights before, as he had come down a slope through a tangled mess of wind-tortured timber, he had run head-on into the galvanizing scent of a female coming into heat. Immediately he had followed his nose on down into a canyon, where he found her busy pawing flotsam over what was left of a mountain goat that she had killed, near the foot of a waterfall, a high silvery ribbon of water swaying in the breeze.

The moon was up, several days off the full, a bit flat on one side as though it had run into something in a careless moment, but shedding a pale, ghostly light as Kleo had oozed down across the broken rocks to within twenty steps of the lioness. He had announced himself with a short call, sounding somewhat like a musical burp, and she had whirled around to face him like a coiled spring ready to unwind, answering him with a very unlovely snarl. It was not encouraging. Even though he was a full-grown cat, all of eight feet from tip to tip, she was bigger. He was young, and she looked formidable to him but she smelled very good; the air was full of promise, prompting Kleo to be patient even though he trembled with desire.

He had crouched absolutely motionless, like a dramatic carving of a mountain lion, watching her as she relaxed and continued with the burial of her kill. When she had arranged it to her satisfaction, she stepped back to take a drink from the pool at the bottom of the falls, then climbed up past her claim to dig a hole in the loose shale and urinate. After covering everything with fastidious care, in the way of all cats, she had leapt on top of a boulder, giving him another snarl, composed herself, and began to lick her paws and scrub her face.

Upon finishing her toilet, she had climbed straight up the mountain, pausing at the foot of the broken cliffs to look back, as though daring him to even glance towards her cache. Kleo couldn't have possibly cared less about food. His mind was on one track and that ran directly to her. So when she had moved up, with infinite elegance climbing the massive staircase of broken ledges at one side of the falls, he had followed at a discreet distance as though a string fastened his nose to the slightly curling end of her long tail.

So it had gone for the rest of the night and most of the next day, their trail following a crazy pattern that went nowhere in particular – all over the side of the mountain, in and out, around and over a succession of obstacles, so steep in places that it would have given a goat some pause for thought before he moved a foot. As a matter of fact, several goats had observed this impending romance with such extreme misgivings that they had hoisted their ridiculous excuses for tails straight up and quit the mountain.

During the course of this round of exercise, the female had eventually led the way back down to her kill where she had fed again, after threatening Kleo with murder if he dared step into the invisible circle she had drawn around it.

Upon finishing her feed and reburying her cache, she had led the way, by a circuitous route, along the flank of the canyon into a grove of twisted pines, where she had finally stopped and lain down in a shady grotto, cool under the late afternoon sun. Very carefully and with great patience, Kleo had worked in closer and closer, his whiskers occasionally vibrating to the accompaniment of faint chirps. Her ugly snarls had gradually lost their menace, and she had finally allowed him to gently lick her face. Very gradually, exercising enormous diplomacy, he had finally manoeuvred himself into a position where his front paws were about even with the root of her tail, his body parallel with hers and facing the same way. The long-promised moment was about to be reached; Kleo was on the verge of taking one more step to put him astride her back.

But – as though appearing out of the bowels of the earth – a huge tom cougar had stepped onto a log a few yards up the slope. For a long moment everything had frozen, the atmosphere saturated with a promise of riot. Kleo had lit the fuse with a squall that sounded something like a high-speed saw biting into a hard knot and an explosion of a charge that had taken him to the intruder in three huge bounds. They had tangled in a frightful mix-up of teeth and claws. Rolling over and over in a fast-moving ball of fur and muscles, down the slope they had gone, banging into trees, breaking off snags and tearing up the forest floor, in a battle smoking with rage and the desire to kill.

What Kleo lacked in experience he had made up for in the youthful enthusiasm to wipe out this brigand who dared intrude into his territory at such a moment. But his adversary was an old hand, scarred by many battles; although momentarily taken aback by the savagery and swiftness of the attack, he had rallied. Every move he had made had been backed with purpose and deadly intent. It had been a no-holds-barred fight where second prize could have been severe injury or even death.

Kleo had found himself up against a devil, a giant who not only outweighed him, but who had muscles as hard as steel, and teeth and claws that cut and tore his hide every time they connected. No cat is long-winded enough to carry on a fight of such speed and storm for very long, and too soon Kleo's lungs had run out of oxygen. To his distress, self-preservation won out over procreation, and, with a screech of rage and frustration, he had suddenly torn free to dash away down the mountain. The bigger male had followed him for a way, but he had soon left, for his wind was also running short. He had stood watching Kleo go, his tail waving angrily back and forth and his face a mask of sheer ferocity, blood dripping from a cut across his nose.

Kleo had been beaten and he knew it, but that didn't cool his anger any. A drink at the creek in the canyon bottom, followed by a session of licking his wounds, had not damped it either. So when he appeared on the crest of the broken castle at sunset, he was still seething and boiling, a very angry cougar – so furious, in fact, that he was talking to himself. He continued the soliloquy as he moved down the opposite side of the ridge, his waving tail signalling his rage.

To add to the discomfort of his smarting wounds, he was suddenly ravenously hungry, for he hadn't eaten anything for most of two days. In this frame of mind, his judgement wasn't very good when he ran into a porcupine chewing on the bark of a white scrub pine among a clutter of branches near the ground. It was a situation calling for skill and discretion, but Kleo wasn't charged with such virtues at the moment, so with more bravery than brains, he reached out a paw and hauled out the porky.

This was a grave mistake, for although the porcupine died almost instantly, his memory was to linger on for some time. Kleo's right front paw and the inside of his foreleg were liberally stabbed by over a hundred quills, their stiff barbed points deeply embedded. At first he paid them little heed, as he chewed away at the unprotected, soft underbelly of his victim, muttering and growling to himself in cougar profanity. When he tried to use the wounded paw to clean his face upon finishing his feed, however, he found it paining excruciatingly. He nipped and licked, working on the quills, but the more he tried to get them out, the farther they penetrated, and he only succeeded in breaking some off.

When he started to travel again, he was one very sorry cat, miserable and crippled. There is nothing that throws a feline off balance like any kind of severe injury, and Kleo was one step from being immobilized.

Among all the big cats, for that matter among all the bigger predators of the world, the cougar is one of nature's most efficient killers, matched only by a distant cousin, the African cheetah. A big cougar can kill a full-grown elk or moose. They take ordinary deer with all the ease employed by a common house cat killing a mouse. Cougars are magnificently conditioned animals with every nerve and muscle tuned perfectly for quick killing. To such an animal, a paw full of porcupine quills is a disaster.

Travelling on three legs, Kleo was next to harmless, and the farther he went the worse it got; his paw swelled to twice its normal size, throbbing with excruciating pain even when he rested. Soon he was starving, for in the next two days he managed to capture only a few mice and a half-grown rabbit. At one point he crept out on a big dead aspen log overhanging a beaver pond in an attempt to catch a duck that was feeding in some tall slough grass, but the log broke under his weight and all he got was wet.

That night he hobbled a couple of miles down a creek to suddenly find himself in a ranch yard. He stood, screened by tall grass near the outside corner of a rail fence, observing this alien scene, too miserable to even sniff or growl at its strangeness, when something moving caught his attention. It was another cat – a black and white mother barn cat coming back from a hunt. She was carrying a young rabbit half as big as herself for her brood of kittens cached under a manger in the barn.

She had been lucky in her foraging but now her good fortune ran out as her way brought her within six feet of Kleo's nose. Acting on reflex, without enquiring about identity or protocol, he simply jumped on her, cut off her squall of terror abruptly with a powerful crunch of his jaws, and proceeded to eat her – skin, bones, rabbit and all – without even pausing to lick his chops. He felt some better.

Silent as a shadow in spite of his gimpy leg, Kleo circled the buildings looking for a suitable place to hide, for he was tired. His way took him across the creek, where he took a drink, then through a narrow band of thick willows and up a bank under some big cottonwoods.

There, under the spreading branches of a big tree, he came upon an old truck, a derelict sinking on its rims in the tall grass of a meadow back of the corrals. It had been there a long time; spots of rust showed through its paint, and the window of the cab door on the side next to the creek was broken, offering an inviting hole. After circling around it a couple of times, examining its strangeness, Kleo reared up and peered through the gap left by the absence of the window, and finding it attractive, he jumped in. It was something like a cave, though its furnishings were most unusual. What was left of the seat cushions was soft, so he curled up and went to sleep.

Strange noises roused him early in the morning, as the sun flooded the meadow and buildings with light. Kleo sat in the middle of the seat looking out through the windshield at surroundings the like of which he had never seen before – people and animals moving around, accompanied by sounds alien to his ears. But with typical cat-like deference to his injuries, and an awareness of a good hide if he kept absolutely still, he used his instincts and stayed put, without a thought of taking to his heels. Something told him that this place – close to water and providing shelter – was just what a crippled cougar needed, so he composed himself, even napping occasionally throughout the day.

Intermittently, he licked his festered, swollen paw and leg. No quills now showed, for porcupine quills always work their barbed points deeper and deeper into the flesh. Once, when thirst moved him, he took advantage of the shadows and deep grass to slip out to the creek for a drink, but immediately returned to his hideout.

When day's dusk came and the sounds around the buildings had subsided for the night, he emerged, hungry again, to wander down along the creek. A quarter of a mile away, where trees fringed the edge of a big alfalfa field, he spotted a herd of deer grazing and immediately tensed in anticipation of a stealthy stalk, forgetting all about his sore paw. But at his first step he was quickly reminded of it and stood angrily watching them, the tip of his tail switching. As far as he was concerned, the deer might as well have been grazing on the near slope of the moon.

For a while he poked around looking for something smaller, but he had no luck in that direction either, and for a very good reason. This ranch had a most unusual population of cats, the rancher and his wife being inordinately fond of them. Drowning batches of kittens was something that they just couldn't bring themselves to do, consequently there was a plethora of cats – dozens of them – inbred and half-starved, every colour of the rainbow, and with the exception of four or five pets allowed to stay in the house, all of them almost continually hungry. Thus there were no mice or any other kind of small game within a considerable distance of the ranch buildings. Even the songbirds that managed to survive in the trees did so by exercise of extreme caution whenever they came to the ground. It was a place completely dominated by cats. Now Kleo's presence added a subtle disharmony to the general picture. He returned to the fence corner where he had murdered his distant cousin the previous night. Moonlight bathed the yard in its pale glow as he stood camouflaged in the long grass in hope of a repeat opportunity. The place was strategically sound, for it wasn't long before an orange tomcat, an old battle-scarred sexpot, the father of countless kittens (which he sometimes killed and ate when their mothers weren't looking), came sneaking along the rail fence heading for some distant hunting ground. All unaware of his impending doom, he came right up to Kleo's nose and was dispatched with lightning swiftness. Kleo carried his catch into a willow thicket by the creek and ate it with gusto, even though it was extraordinarily tough. The repast whetted his appetite for more, so he went back to his stand, and by the time the first pale streaks of dawn gently fingered the eastern sky and the tops of the mountains, he had killed and eaten two more, orphaning another batch of kittens in the process. He then took another big drink and retired to his hide in the truck.

While the hunting was good, even though highly unorthodox, Kleo did not exactly bask on the fat of the land. His inroads on the ranch cats were sufficient to keep him alive, but he was gaunt and his fur had lost its sheen. However, his wounded foot was losing most of its swelling as his system absorbed the shafts of the quills and began to cover the insoluble points that lay flat against the bones in scar tissue. The fast decreasing cat population and his improving health were converging on a collision course, and something was bound to happen.

The rancher and his family were aware of the disappearance of their beloved felines, but the cause of their melting away was for some time a complete mystery. Nor were the two ranch dogs much help, for they were completely conditioned to the cat tribe. Early indulgence in the usual cat-and-dog mix-ups had resulted in punishment, causing them to ignore the cats almost completely. They became aware of Kleo shortly after he arrived, but after a few half-hearted barking sessions at night, they included him in the general cat-chasing taboo. So, for a while, Kleo enjoyed all the privacy of a veritable ghost.

One day the ten-year-old daughter of the family was out for a barefooted wade along the creek, playing in the delightfully cool water and overturning rocks to observe with fascination the wiggly creatures thus revealed. When she came to a point opposite the truck, for no particular reason she went up to it and climbed over the tailgate into the box. Idly, she went forward to the cab and peered into it through its rear window to find herself practically nose-to-nose with a huge cat. For a long, breath-catching moment both child and animal were frozen, then both broke and ran – the child on flying feet for the house, and Kleo out the window into the brush along the creek.

When the girl reached her father, who was working on a tractor in the yard, for several minutes he could not make head or tail of what she was trying to tell him, but when she calmed down enough to become reasonably articulate, he got his rifle and went with her to investigate. Of course, Kleo was long gone, but a few of his hairs clung to the nest on the truck seat, and then they located a big fresh track on some wet sand by the creek, further verifying her story. That find set off a chain of events that were to have some unusual, even traumatic consequences for the cougar.

Of course Kleo had no way of knowing this, or he would never have stopped travelling till he was on the other side of a large mountain. Sheer mischance had brought about a rare change of environment that he had used to bridge a painful period of his life. His indiscretion with the porcupine was nothing but a wave of the hand of fate.

Now that his foot was healing, and the hide in the truck was no longer secret, he was on the move, wandering down the creek towards its confluence with the river. It was too hot for travelling far, so he stretched out in the deep shade under some big cottonwoods, waiting for the cool of night. Like all his kind, he was a mostly nocturnal animal.

At first star-shine, he left the grove. But the hand of fate was not yet finished, and he had not gone far when his trail took him back to the edge of the hayfield just in time to see four yearling whitetail deer come frolicking out of the heavy cover into the open. There they began to gallop in a patternless romp in the pleasantly cool evening air – and pure luck brought one of them within two short jumps of Kleo, flattened out in the tall growth. The little deer was looking away when Kleo landed on it, his teeth coming together in its fragile neck, and his great hooked claws clinching into its head and back. Its death was almost instant, and for the first time in weeks, Kleo had an ample supply of fresh, warm venison. He fed till his belly bulged, rolled on his back nearby, and snoozed, then roused himself to feed again.

As morning light came, he cached his kill under grass and raked-up forest debris, and left. It was quiet as he padded off through the timber. Suddenly, from somewhere back up the creek towards the ranch buildings came the strange, long-drawn bawling of a hound, shortly joined by that of another. For a few moments he stopped, cocking his ears curiously. There was something ominous about that sound, and when he started travelling again, he was going at a lope.

On his back trail, not far from his bed of the previous afternoon, a man held back on the leashes of two big blue-tick hounds as they slowly worked out the scent still cling-ing to the damp growth under the big cottonwoods. He was a famous predator hunter, called to take care of a cougar with an appetite for house cats, a mountain lion that chose to hole up in an old truck, and let a little girl come right up to him before running away. The rancher had guessed that the presence of the cougar was somehow linked with the disappearance of the cats and had telephoned the hunter, who had driven most of the night, his dogs riding in an enclosed box in the back of the truck. Upon reaching the ranch, he had quickly picked up the cougar's trail. Now he held the hounds back on their leashes while they worked out the track as far as the deer kill, and there they went wild with excitement, filling the clear morning air with their steady baying. When he slipped their leashes, they shot away, bawling their heads off, their tails jerking and their big ears flying. Kleo heard the uproar behind him and put on speed, but a belly full of meat and a tender foot slowed his running, and in no time the dogs were ravening at his heels. In something of a panic he leapt up the trunk of the first big tree he came to – an old cottonwood with its top broken off. It was a short dead-end escape route that put him only about twice his length above the leaping hounds, their nerve-shattering racket keeping him there. Kleo flattened his ears at the bedlam and bared his formidable teeth in a snarl of anger mixed with not a little fear.

The hunter arrived and stood looking up at the big cougar. Many times in similar circumstances he had lifted a rifle to shoot the treed cat, but he had something else in mind for this one. He was not even carrying a gun. While he stood there sizing up the situation, he was joined by the rancher, who arrived on horseback, slipping out of the saddle and drawing his rifle from its scabbard in the same motion.

"We won't need the rifle," the hunter said. "Get your rope. I want this fellow alive. He don't know it yet, but he's going to be a movie star."

Kleo watched from his perch, flattened out in a crouch, and tensed as though about to jump, as the hunter walked slowly to his dogs. But he hesitated, perhaps because his foot was hurting, and the man snapped leashes onto the collars of the dogs to haul them back and tie them to a couple of small trees.

The hunter then slipped out of the shoulder straps of his small pack and took out a lariat and several shorter pieces of rope. As he carefully coiled the lariat and arranged the short noosed tie ropes by tucking them under his belt, he softly gave instructions. He was coolly unhurried, moving smoothly as he stepped towards the foot of the tree. Some tall fireweeds interfered with the loop trailing in his hands, so he deliberately tramped them flat. Then, with a long step forward and a lightning-fast flick of his wrist, he shot the loop towards its mark.

So quick it was hard to follow with the eye, Kleo reached out a paw and batted the rope to one side. Again, his muscles bunched under his hide as though he was getting set to jump, but again he hesitated.

"Easy, cat," intoned the hunter, as he recoiled the rope. Then he instructed the rancher, "This time when I get set to throw, toss your hat out to one side of the tree."

Again he stepped forward with wrist cocked; this time that hat went sailing out. The cougar's eyes were fastened on the hat when the rope struck to snap shut around his neck. The next instant, he jumped. The tightening rope threw him in a twisting somersault, but his feet were under him when he landed with a jarring thump, facing the man at the other end of it. Before the cat could move, the rope was around a tree. Every time he left the ground, the hunter dragged him towards the tree, until he was jammed up against its trunk, half-choked, but still snarling and fighting. The scene was one of bedlam, as the dogs yipped and bawled, turning handsprings at the end of their leashes. The rancher's lariat came into play, its loop snapping shut around the cougar's hind feet, and Kleo found himself stretched out, helpless to do much more than squirm and snarl.

Moving quickly, the hunter tied his rope around the tree; then taking one of the short ones from his belt, he stepped in close to snare one front paw. A half hitch flickered around the other and they were drawn together to be tied securely, immobilizing the dangerous, hooked claws. Pulling a short, stout stick from his hip pocket, he thrust it into the cougar's open mouth crosswise, and when the raging animal bit down on it, another short rope noosed its projecting end, to be quickly wrapped in a figure-eight design around the cat's nose and jaw, effectively muzzling him. When the remaining tie rope was used on his hind feet, Kleo was absolutely helpless, only his eyes giving away his anger and fear – they gleamed like hot, green-gold coals.

Later that morning, when his truck rolled out of the rancher's gate onto the highway, the hunter was whistling. Beside him the dogs sat looking out through the windshield, their tongues lolling. Behind them in the dog box, Kleo lay panting, still securely tied and feeling the wheels rolling under him. The man felt particularly satisfied for he had had a standing order for a cougar with a big Hollywood motion picture company that was presently located in the mountains about one hundred and fifty miles to the north. Pointing the truck that way, he bore down on the gas pedal. Kleo was suffering acutely from heat and thirst, his whole body throbbing and painfully cramped by the binding ropes. The unaccustomed sound and vibrations of the truck seemed to go on forever, clawing at his consciousness in an endless grinding nightmare. After what seemed a very long time, the truck slowed and finally stopped; the back door of the box opened, letting in a blinding flood of sunlight. Without making a move to fight or struggle in any way, Kleo felt himself being dragged out and picked up bodily to be carried a ways and set down. The thongs binding him were removed, but for a while he just lay there, reaching for breath, unable to comprehend that he was free. When something tugged his tail, he came to his feet, glanced back at the men standing behind him, and leapt away, promptly running into the ungiving barrier of steel-link fence. He swerved clumsily in another direction and collided with the steel barrier again. Kleo was confused and frightened, and it took him a while to realize that he was captive inside a big cage. For a while he kept on trying to find a way out, then he realized that the men were gone, and he came to a stand, looking at the details of his surroundings.

Everywhere he looked there were animals, some strange and some familiar: wolves, coyotes, wolverines, bears, even deer, which he looked at with none of his customary interest. They were all strangely mixed up, showing no recognition of each other's presence.

Some loafed in the sun, other slept, still others paced back and forth endlessly, whiling away their boredom in the confines of their cages. A big fat grizzly sat on his broad rump grasping his upturned hind feet with the long claws of his front ones, rocking back and forth ceaselessly.

Kleo snarled and reared against the restraining wall of his cage, suddenly leaping straight up in attempt to clear it, but he bumped his head hard on the heavy wire mesh top to fall back in an off-balance, ignominious scramble. Gathering himself up, he made another circle of the cage, for the first time becoming aware of a trough full of clear water, which he ignored for a couple of more circles. On the next circuit his thirst got the better of him, and he stopped to lap up some of the cooling liquid – his first concession to being captive.

A heavy box with an open end, containing a layer of loose straw, was sitting in one corner of the cage, but he paid it no heed as he continued to prowl, nervous, restless, and unable to comprehend the import of this great change.

All that night and the next day, he was continually in motion, his ears assailed by strange noises and his nose full of unusual smells. In the morning, the man who looked after the animals came and went quietly as he fed them. Finally he came close to the side of Kleo's cage trailing a hose, and the cougar faced him with an ugly snarl, exposing his teeth. The man did not back up, but only turned the hose on, filling the trough to the rim.

As he did so he admired the big cat, for this position was more than just a job to him; he loved animals, they fascinated him – especially this wild cougar with his blazing eyes and powerful muscles rippling with every move.

Sometimes he had trouble keeping quiet about how the animals in his care were used in the motion picture productions, for this company specialized in so-called nature pictures that were in many ways anything but natural. Too often, in order to film some dramatic sequences, the animals were forcibly subjected to situations that they would never encounter in the wilds. Sometimes, as a result, they were badly injured or even killed.

Kleo's predecessor had been fatally injured when he was forced to jump off a cliff into a river. The desperate leap was short, ending up on rocks, and he was so badly hurt that it was necessary to destroy him. In the making of another picture at a desert location far to the south, the script called for a boar javelina to chase a bobcat up a giant cactus, something a bobcat would never tackle in the wild. A compound was built around a tall cactus, and in it were put a javelina and a bobcat. They could not avoid each other and the cranky boar attacked the cat, finally killing it before it came anywhere near climbing the cactus. Before the required sequence was on film, the javelina had killed four bobcats. In the far north a polar bear cub was so badly injured that it died when it was pushed down a steep ice-covered slope so that its gyrations could be shot in slow motion.

Another time, during the filming of a squirrel picture, the keeper had been so filled with disgust when the teeth of two pine martens had been removed to prolong a killing scene, that he almost drew his pay and quit. The same operation had been conducted on the wolverine that he now fed hamburger every day, because it couldn't chew meat in chunks.

Of course, the people who saw the finished films never knew of the misery and cruelty suffered by the animals in them. They came in droves to applaud scenes that were beautifully filmed against spectacular backgrounds.

As he watched the big red-gold cougar turn away to pace along the far side of the cage, the keeper wondered what was in store for him.

For three days Kleo refused to eat the meat that was placed in his cage fresh every day. Never had he eaten anything he had not killed, but finally his hunger won out, and the keeper was happy when he saw that the proffered meat had been taken.

This acceptance of feed marked the beginning of a much improved relationship between the man and the big cat. Although always wary, Kleo began to accept the man to the point of even looking for his arrival. He also began to endure captivity without the endless prowling, sometimes taking shelter in the big nest box and sometimes lying on top of it half asleep, gazing off into the distance as though recalling the old, wild, free days on the slopes of the mountains.

So it went for several weeks. Kleo's paw was completely healed and his coat was beginning to shine again.

Meanwhile an elaborate compound had been built on a ridge top among some spectacular rock formations that stuck up out of picturesque timber against the high jagged peaks of the background. It was to be the stage for an epic sequence.

One day the director summoned the keeper to give him instructions involving the cougar. Kleo was to be placed in the compound. "When we get enough footage of the cougar moving around among the rocks and trees," the director told the keeper, "we'll put in a deer and wind it up with a killing sequence. It's a very important shot in this film and I hope that new cat will cooperate without holding things up. The producer's crying about expenses, so don't feed the cat for a couple of days. I want him hungry."

Grim-faced, the keeper asked, "What deer are you planning to use?"

"That big mule deer doe. We've already got some shots of her, and she might be big enough to last longer and make the scene interesting. Prolonged action is what we need in this kind of scene," came the reply.

"But she's a pet! Everybody knows her around here, and she'll eat out of anybody's hand. Anyway, she'll last about two seconds if the cougar jumps her. She'll likely think he wants to play!"

"Maybe we can clip the cat's claws and make the scene last longer," the director suggested. "I don't give a damn about the deer. We pay to keep these animals so we can use 'em."

"If we trim that cougar's claws, sure as hell he'll sulk," the keeper said angrily. "Don't forget, he was wild until we got him a month ago. Anyway, I'm sick and fed up to the neck with this trimming claws and pulling teeth business. One of these days the S.P.C.A. is going to drop on this out-fit like a ton of rock, and I'm not so sure I won't cheer when it happens!"

For a long, tense moment, the two men glared at each other on the brink of an angry blow-up, but then the direc-tor sagged back in his chair.

"Don't forget," he said wearily, "that I don't write the script. And I just follow orders like everyone else here. You have it your way about trimming the claws." Then he added, "But the rest of it goes. Shooting time is 10:00 A.M. two days from now if the weather is good. You just have the animals on location in time and you can go somewhere where you don't have to watch."

Feeling defeated and low, the keeper left to feed the ani-mals. That morning Kleo missed his fresh meat, and the keeper imagined he could see accusation in the cougar's green-gold eyes as they watched him fill the water trough.

When he came to feed the mule deer doe, he scratched her ears and murmured, "For two cents I'd turn you loose. But you poor old scrounger, you wouldn't leave if I did." His face was grim as he went on with his work.

That night he couldn't sleep; he lay listening to his alarm clock ticking away the seconds. Somehow it sounded louder than usual. He was angry and sad at the same time, berating himself for getting too involved with the animals in his care. For about the hundredth time, he considered quitting, but rejected the idea. The job paid well, he needed the money and besides, someone else would take his place and they might not treat the animals right. Then he snorted at that idea, hating himself and his helplessness.

Finally, sometime after midnight, he got up, slipped his feet into a pair of moccasins and went outside. Back of the trailer camp, the peaks were standing black against a clear sky full of stars. It was windless, very quiet and pleasantly cool as he stood still, slowly puffing a cigarette, letting the serenity soak into him.

Suddenly he threw the smoke down, stepped on it like he was killing some kind of objectionable bug and moved off towards the animal cages. Going into the cooling room where the meat was stored, he selected a choice chunk, which he carried to the cougar's cage, and opening the door, he threw it inside. He wasn't at all sure why feeding the cougar made him feel better, but it did. When he went back to his bed, he slept soundly for the rest of the night.

On time to the dot two mornings later, he drove the company four-wheel drive pick-up to the shooting location with the cougar and the deer in separate trap boxes in the back. Backing into the compound, he released Kleo, watching him streak away to disappear among the trees and rocks. Then he drove out the gate and carefully shut it before parking the truck out of sight and taking a position back of a tree to watch.

Kleo's first rush took him right across the compound and ended abruptly up against the fence. This fence was not only high, but was positioned to put any animal inclined to try to jump it at a disadvantage. To further discourage escape, three heavy barbed wire strands were strung in steel brackets projecting inward off the top of every post, forming an overhang. Kleo's exposure to wire had conditioned him to the futility of testing it, but even so he made a complete circle of the compound at the foot of the fence, before a man suddenly appeared to drive him away from it.

The enclosure was big and surrounded a heavily folded area of boulders, weather-worn turrets of rock and old, gnarled firs. Through this place, perhaps a hundred yards across, Kleo prowled back and forth, in and out, examining every detail of it, while six cameramen in hidden vantage points played their lenses on him as he moved.

The light was superb, and though unaware he was doing so, Kleo cooperated magnificently by posing here and there against the sky and mountains while the cameras rolled. The director hugged himself with delight, for what was being caught on film this day was rare and very valuable footage of an animal that normally chooses to move about only in the dark of the night.

Finally he lifted a bullhorn to his lips and called, "Cut!" This was the signal to take the deer into the compound as the cameramen reloaded their cameras, making ready for the epic grand finale.

The days of preparation and high expense were about to be justified, the director fervently hoped. The animals were in place and the real action about to start. The cougar was still restlessly prowling, but the doe was singularly unimpressed when she caught sight of him against the sky on top of a rock rib.

She was lonely and went poking slowly around here and there looking for company. Finally she located one of the cameramen and happily started to climb up to him hoping for a handout, but he shied a rock off her ribs, driving her away, and likely making her wonder what had gone wrong with her world.

The tension built up among the camera crew as the two animals moved about out of sight of each other. Finally they chose converging paths that would bring the doe into the top of a short, steep draw and the cougar cutting across its mouth from the side. When they saw each other, both animals froze, their eyes locked, at a distance of about ten yards. Then the hair rose on the deer's back and neck till she looked almost grotesque; her ears dropped, swinging loose on their sockets; she let out a sharp whistling snort and went completely beserk. In two high long jumps, she was over the surprised cougar and came down with her feet bunched in the middle of his back, knocking him flat.

Two cameramen with the view in their finders couldn't believe what they were seeing, as the cougar rolled away to the side under the onslaught, but they kept shooting anyway. Before Kleo could get his balance, the doe came down on him again, driving her weight like a piledriver, her sharp punishing feet making him squall. If Kleo had been cornered he might have fought back, but as it was, all he had in mind was getting away, so he came up running with the doe pounding along at his heels. Up and around and over the rocks they went, stirring up puffs of dust as they skidded in the turns. As he watched this astonishing mêlée, the keeper found himself silently cheering the big doe.

Kleo was hard pressed and desperate. When he came to a steep slope running down to the fence, he put on an inspired burst of speed and quit the rocks in a tremendous soaring leap – the highest and longest he had ever made in his life. His front feet caught the top, and there he clung, oblivious to the sharp barbs as he reached for a purchase with his hind feet. One of them found a toehold and the next instant he was over the top and down the other side, hightailing for open country at a wild run.

Behind him, the doe stood watching him go. Nobody knew it, but she had a history of such brawls. Picked up as a half-starved fawn, she had been raised on a ranch with a couple of dogs that, as she grew up, she treated as part of her life. But she absolutely refused to tolerate any other canines, and when a strange one showed, she instantly flew into a red-eyed rage. With typical deer tactics, she would leap high and come down on the surprised victim so effectively that she won every battle without exception. Finally a visitor's poodle was severely hurt by one of her onslaughts, and that was when she changed hands. She had treated Kleo as just another strange dog trespassing on her territory and did not share the general surprise at his retreat.

Her hair flattened out, and her ears came up as she stepped out sedately to find somebody for company – somebody who wouldn't shy rocks at her and would maybe provide a handout. Meanwhile, behind his tree, the keeper bent down with tears of suppressed laughter running down his face, and off to one side of him, the director chewed his cigar and savagely tramped his cap into the ground.

9

THE FRIENDLY OWL

Charlie found him on the ground under a big cotton-wood. How he came to be there will never be known. He was too small to have walked over the edge of the nest located thirty feet above. A look through binoculars from the top of a high bank on the other side of the creek showed another chick still in residence. Charlie considered putting him back in the nest, but the idea of braving the razor-sharp claws of a pair of belligerent parent great horned owls held small attraction. So he brought the little owl home; the small incongruous-looking ball of white fluff fitted easily into the palm of a hand, with small promise of ever looking like one of its big parents.

Thus Charlie became the godfather of a young horned owl, a turn of events that led to some mighty unexpected developments.

From the very beginning, we all agreed that if we were going to be responsible for raising this child of the wilds, it would not be confined in any way once it had learned to fly. If it ever chose to leave us, it would be free to go.

Charlie, having recently read some Greek mythology, named the little owl Achilles, which was taking something of a chance, for at that age even a biologist would have had a problem identifying its sex. There was a fifty-fifty chance that a lady owl might some day find herself wearing a name that didn't fit. However, that was of small consequence.

We all knew that owls eat meat, but our research into the subject of owl diet told us that just meat was not enough. To be healthy and happy, a great horned owl needs some fur and feathers mixed in, for these collect around small bones accumulated in what goes for an owl's stomach and are regurgitated. This process of throwing up pellets is an owl's way of putting out the garbage, and strangely enough they do not do well without it. With owls some very rough roughage is the name of the game.

Parent owls feed their young a wide variety of things, about everything in the small game line – even fish and reptiles on occasion. I once found the tail of a sucker on the ground below a nest, a big one that a parent owl had obviously taken from the shallow water on the edge of a beaver pond. So almost any animal is acceptable grist for young owls' digestive mills. For a start, Charlie set out a trapline for mice, which Achilles accepted with great enthusiasm.

For his size, his appetite was prodigious, and it grew with him. At first he was too small to tear up the mice into pieces to fit his gullet, so Charlie performed this chore for him. Achilles would eat till there wasn't room for another morsel, subside into a contented ball of white fluff until the process of digestion made room, then wake up to ask for more. The supply of mice barely kept ahead of the demand.

At the time, Charlie and his older brother, Dick, were going to high school in town twenty-five miles away and were boarding week days at a school dormitory. He wanted to take his adopted owl with him and look after it in the room he shared with several other boys. This posed obvious problems. We agreed to it as long as he got the necessary permission from the matron superintending the place, but we left the arranging up to him. With typical schoolboy philosophy, he concluded that what she didn't know wouldn't hurt her, so he smuggled Achilles into the dormitory.

Naturally, every boy in the place knew about the owl, and with uncompromising gallantry and allegiance to broken rules, they kept the secret. Achilles became a sort of instant mascot, spending five days a week in a dormitory subsidiary to the halls of learning, and his weekends at the ranch.

Charlie's responsibilities reached a bit farther than anticipated, for the duties of keeping the room clean and neat were ordinarily taken in turn – two boys for each week – but it was unanimously agreed that in view of Charlie's owl, he would serve a permanent position on the clean-up team. This was a development he could hardly complain about, for Achilles' burgeoning appetite meant that he contributed a horrendous amount of reasons for cleaning – an aspect of nature paramount over all attempts to housebreak him.

The only refinement of toilet he ever practised was to turn around when an urge of nature assaulted him while he was perched with his tail close to a wall. We were never quite sure if this was a habit learned or just instinctive. Maybe all owls practise this questionable amenity, but as he grew larger and developed an unbelievable range and velocity to his ejections, we were of mixed thoughts on whether it was anything to brag about. When he suddenly turned around and lifted his tail, anyone standing within ten feet had better take cover!

With everybody contributing to the food supply, Achilles never went hungry, and he rapidly grew out of the shoebox that was his original nest and was placed in a larger one. During classroom hours, he lived in a clothes closet, where his occasional chirps were sufficiently muffled not to carry to other parts of the house. The matron's inspection tours to check on the neatness of the room during the occupants' absence left her surprised at the unusual polish, but she did not find Achilles.

Achilles became more active as he grew. He rapidly learned to perch on things, and soon found the confines of a box annoying. When he was put out at something, he chirped loudly, a querulous complaining call very penetrating in its pitch, so Charlie worked hard to keep him happy. He got out of his box at every opportunity by hooking his beak over the edge and heaving himself up, with his claws scratching for a toehold. The hanger bar of the clothes closet made an ideal perch, so the clothing was pushed to one side to make room, and a makeshift partition made out of cardboard kept him from wandering on top of the apparel. A generous use of newspapers to accommodate the flotsam and jetsam that goes with a young owl helped in the house-keeping chores.

As the weeks passed, the problems of keeping him enlarged with him. One morning after breakfast, Charlie placed him on his perch in the clothes closet as usual and closed the door. But the catch did not quite engage, leaving a little crack of light showing, which undoubtedly intrigued Achilles. He leaned away over to inspect it and overbalanced, to come tumbling down onto the floor. Chirping loudly, he waddled over to the crack and pushed his beak into it; the door swung open, allowing him to go out into the room, where he rambled about. The door leading to the hall and the top of the stairs was invitingly open, and Achilles set out on a stroll.

Under the best of circumstances, an owl's feet are not designed for walking, and it moves in a mixture of steps and hops according to the footing and its frame of mind, but when Achilles came to the top of the stairs, he was faced with something of a dilemma. Undaunted, he stepped over the edge of the top step and fell to the next. Getting up, he shook himself, proceeded to the next drop-off, and launched himself again. His descent was rapid as well as unique, and he ultimately arrived at the bottom, somewhat ruffled but triumphant.

The good lady of the house was busy at her sink washing dishes, when her attention was drawn to strange noises coming from the stairway. She turned around just in time to see a very dishevelled young owl, with pin-feathers sticking out of his white fluff in every direction, come marching into her kitchen. She greeted him with a sharp exclamation of astonishment. He replied with a high-pitched chirp and came to a stand, swaying back and forth, his big eyes staring, and his round head swivelling from one side to the other on his skinny neck.

Some women would have gone into hysterics and yelled bloody murder for help, but not this one. She was the mother of several grown sons and immediately guessed how it was that she had an owl in the house. Having grown up on a country farm, she lost no time in getting a large box and placing Achilles in it.

Actually, she was more than a little intrigued with the young owl, but rules being rules, when Charlie and his volunteer conspirators came charging in for lunch, she sternly confronted them. The following weekend saw Achilles come back to the ranch for good.

It was not long before his pin-feathers were transformed into feathers, and he looked less like an animated cartoon and more like a great horned owl. Just as soon as the big primary feathers of his wings grew out, he began to fly – short hops at first to be sure, with take-offs much better than the tail-over-teakettle wrecks that wiped out many of his landings, but it was not long before he was doing much better and rapidly became a powerful and magnificently graceful flyer.

Although now a nearly full-grown bird with a certain imperious air when he chose – even with a fierce look about him on occasion – Achilles was at heart a very gentle character with a tendency to be a real clown. While still afoot, he had been installed on a perch on the veranda with plenty of old newspapers spread out under him to catch the inevitable droppings. Perhaps exposure to the written word triggered some kind of desire to amuse himself or whoever happened to be watching, but he learned to "read." He would jump down on a newspaper page and closely trace the letters across the columns with his beak in a way that was hilarious.

We were entertaining some guests one evening, and in due course they were introduced to Achilles. He came into our front room and perched on the back of a chair, regally looking at each of the strangers as though holding court. Then Charlie threw a newspaper down on the floor in front of him, and he immediately flew down to go through his routine. In the middle of the front page was a photo of a scantily clad beauty queen along with the account of her winning the contest. Achilles ran his beak along a line of print, and upon coming to the picture he reared back with a comical expression and then bent forward as though unable to believe what he saw. Ruffling up his feathers till he looked twice his normal size, he swung his head back and forth, peering at the picture as though it assaulted his sense of propriety to the breaking point. The whole room dissolved in a gale of laughter.

Although completely independent in his movements, he was totally dependent on us for feed. In the mornings he was always ravenous, and whoever showed up outside was immediately greeted with a series of cheeps and chirps (his repertoire did not include hoots, which are the call of a mature owl). So the first chore was to give him something to eat – a magpie or ground squirrel was best, for trying to fill him up on mice was next to impossible. He gulped them whole like so many raw oysters disappearing off a gourmet's plate, and we could not find enough to fill him. He tore up his own food now and would sometimes swallow astonishingly big pieces. We kept a supply of suitable things frozen in plastic bags in our freezer, which we thawed and gave to him as required.

One morning I gave him a magpie, whereupon he flew up to the peak of the gable on the end of our house and began to tear it up and devour it, feathers, bones and all. When he got to the wings, he did not separate them, but just ripped off the portion of the back to which they were attached and tried to try to swallow it. He got it down to a point where a wing was sticking up on each side of his face like a grotesque moustache, and there it stuck. He humped his back, ruffled his feathers, braced his feet, and gulped and gulped to no avail.

Finally he just stood still with his eyes almost closed, as though on the verge of death. Meanwhile I was watching from the lawn below, feeling helpless and wondering how long it would be before he came tumbling down from lack of oxygen. The question of how one would administer artificial respiration to an owl was crossing my mind, when he roused himself. Opening his eyes a bit, he reached up to grasp one of the protruding wings with a foot. He hauled the piece out and inspected it, then he put it down, pinning it against the roof, and began reducing it to more manageable pieces, pausing to give me a quizzical look when I burst into a roar of laughter.

He had a whole range of expressions – from extreme anger to sublime affection – according to his mood of the moment. Although he had associated with people exclusively, and undoubtedly related himself to us to some extent, as he grew older it became more and more apparent that he was all great horned owl and intended to remain so.

He and Seppi, our German shorthaired pointer, largely ignored each other, but he loved to tease our cat. Although the cat affected some tolerance, it was afraid of him. Achilles did nothing to reassure the cat, for one of his tricks was to fly at it from the rear as it crossed the lawn, planing in close on his incredibly silent wings. Becoming aware of the owl only when its widespread wings were directly overhead, the cat would let out an explosive hiss and hightail for the nearest cover. This seemed to amuse Achilles, for he would land on the nearest thing sticking up from the ground, and squawk as though inviting the cat out for more play.

From the moment he took to the air, we were aware of his absolutely phenomenal vision. One afternoon I was reading in a deck chair on the veranda with Achilles perched at my elbow. For a while he amused himself by "reading" the pages as they were turned, but then he subsided to sit with eyes almost closed. Suddenly he came fully awake, tense in every fibre as he looked up into the sky. The very slow turning of his head indicated that he was watching something on the move, but I could see nothing. Picking up my binoculars, I trained them on the seemingly empty sky where he was looking. At first I still couldn't see a thing, but then the nine-power lenses picked up a tiny moving dot – a golden eagle soaring at an altitude of thousands of feet.

Another day I was replacing a post in the yard fence while Achilles looked on from a convenient perch in a tree. When I got the new post set and had fastened the wire to it with staples, he flew down to land on it, peering this way and that in a comical fashion as though passing inspection on my work. Abruptly he tensed, looked off into the sky past the top of our hill, and before I could more than turn my head in that direction, he flopped down onto the ground on his back with every feather standing on end, his wings spread and his great talons extended upward. Almost instantly, a powerful goshawk spun by, barely missed the top of the post within six feet of me, shot up a hundred feet to turn, looking down at Achilles, then flew away over the trees out of sight. The goshawk had been in a sizzling stoop, likely going at a speed of over a hundred miles per hour – a strike that would have killed the owl immediately if it had connected. It was an electrifying and unusual opportunity to observe the violent interaction between two formidable predators.

Crows reacted violently to the owl's presence, and it was not unusual for us to wake early in the morning to the sounds of a riot going full swing, as a flock of them dived and swore at him where he sat perched in a tree. Beyond keeping an eye on them, he largely ignored them, but if one came too close, he would pop his beak angrily, loudly and rapidly. In the wilds it is evident that great horned owls prey on crows, probably at night, and they are implacable enemies. We never saw Achilles make any attempt to fight back when they harassed him, probably because they were on the wing most of the time. Horned owls do not take their prey on the wing as hawks and eagles occasionally do, but strike them from a tree or on the ground. In self-protection from the ear-shattering bedlam, one of us usually went to the rescue, our presence driving the attackers away, whereupon Achilles would look down, shake himself as though happy with the return of quiet, and squawk querulously.

Heat bothered him, and in the middle of summer days, he would sit in a shady place with his wings spread a little to let the air under them, and his beak half open. On such days he was almost completely inactive. But towards sunset, when it began to cool, Achilles would come planing in from some bower in the treetops to join us. He treated strangers with equal friendliness, but we always warned visitors of his presence. It is a bit unnerving to have a great horned owl appear unexpectedly, flying straight at you with his big yellow eyes gleaming, and land on the arm of your chair or on your shoulder. Even when visitors were alerted, Achilles' arrival never failed to give them a thrill, sometimes to our embarrassment.

One afternoon we were entertaining several VIPs – the president and top executive officers of a famous international conservation organization. After dinner, we all went out to sit on the big veranda to watch the sunset over the mountains spread out in front. I told them not to be surprised if a great horned owl flew in to join us, and not to jump away if he landed on a shoulder, for this would throw Achilles off balance, and if he used his talons to regain it the result might be painful.

I doubt that some of the group took me very seriously, but Achilles did not fail me; he suddenly showed up and set his wings to glide in for a landing on the president's shoulder. The gentleman from New York flinched involuntarily as Achilles spread his wicked-looking talons to land, throwing him a bit off balance. When Achilles reached out with a foot to steady himself, one of his razor-sharp talons cut a neat, shallow gash about an inch long on the side of our visitor's neck, just over his collar. For a moment we were all frozen, and then Achilles flew over onto the arm of my chair, happily chirping and twitching my sleeve playfully.

The president was understandably a bit incredulous and startled at this turn of events, but he was a good sport about it as we patched him up with some disinfectant and a small bandage.

Following the incident, Achilles and our five-year-old daughter entertained us with a game they regularly played. Wearing nothing more than a thin T-shirt and a pair of jeans, she ran down the slope below the front steps for a hundred feet or so and hid in the tall grass, whereupon Achilles launched himself high on a long swing over the hillside to look for her. Suddenly he peeled off into a fierce strike, coming down with claws fully extended as though to kill. But his landing on her little rump as she lay flattened out in the grass was as light as thistledown. With eyes half closed, squeaking happily, he walked up her back to gently pull her ponytail and tweak her ears with his beak as she giggled at his tickling. He left her to fly back up to the arm of my chair, while she hid somewhere else. As soon as she was still, he repeated the performance, and as always, it was a bit hair-raising to see the fierceness of his strike, even though it always ended in the gentlest possible contact. In spite of her thin clothing and the numerous times they played this game, he never marked her tender skin with his fearsome claws, indicating an incredible degree of control on his part.

Our visitors were so impressed that when they left, they were still talking about the experience. I heard later that the president made his scar a sort of conversation piece, showing it proudly to his friends.

As time went on, we were aware that Achilles was widening his range well outside the perimeter of our yard, even though his appearances at feeding time were prompt. This put him in some danger, for if he chose to fly up to a complete stranger, his friendliness might easily be mistaken for an attack – with dire results. It also became apparent that he would go back to the wilds if he could learn to feed himself.

Surprise could be in his favour. One day, shortly after noon lunch, I stepped out to look over a neighbour's field about half a mile down in the valley. Their new hired man was making a first cut around the edge of the hay crop with a power mower, the sound of the humming tractor coming very clearly on the still air. Achilles was sitting on the back of a chair nearby with his eyes rivetted on the moving machine, obviously interested in it.

Then something plugged the cutter bar, and the man stopped the tractor to clear the obstruction. At that point, Achilles took off in a long glide down over the treetops. Quickly picking up my binoculars, I watched as he arrived at the tractor and landed on the back of the seat. As always, his flight was absolutely silent and the man was unaware of him until he straightened up to climb onto the tractor, when he found himself eye to eye with a formidable-looking owl that squawked at him. He jumped straight back about three feet and it was lucky for Achilles that he didn't have some kind of weapon to throw or swing. For a long moment the tableau was frozen, and then Achilles took off to come winging back.

A couple of hours later I talked to the hired man, who was Danish and spoke with a heavy accent. He was still excited about his adventure and had some difficulty finding words to describe his encounter with the owl. He was even more astonished when I told him about Achilles and assured him that the big bird was very friendly, even if a bit sudden sometimes about introducing himself.

Achilles was very active at night. His favourite perch was on top of a power pole in our yard, where we could hear him squawk. It commanded a wide expanse of lawn and nearby open ground, and I wondered if he was catching mice.

One evening I decided to test him. Taking a light spin-fishing outfit, I coloured a white practice plug to a neutral grey and tied it on the end of the line. Then, standing out of Achilles' sight, I made a long cast out across the lawn. After a couple of slight twitches that moved the plug a bit in the short grass, Achilles came planing down off the top of the power pole to land on it and examine it with an expression of utter disbelief. What kind of nonsense was this? he seemed to ask, and I broke into laughter. This became a game between us, and always I was amazed at the keenness of his eyes. Rarely was it possible to more than twitch the lure before he saw it, even at a distance of well over a hundred feet. It was a sure thing that no mouse could move on the same ground without drawing his attention, although we never saw him take one.

As the fall progressed and the evenings became cooler, Achilles became more loquacious atop his favourite perch, giving forth raucous squawks in a very carrying pitch.

Occasionally we would hear the deep-throated hoots of mature owls somewhere off in the distance. The sound of his relatives excited Achilles, and he would snap his head around with his eyes fixed in the direction of the hoots.

Late one night when it was very dark, we became aware of two other owls in the trees around the house, and the yard was full of hoots and squawks. As suddenly as it began, the excited owl conversation subsided into silence, and in the morning Achilles did not show up for his feed. We wondered if we would ever see him again.

Forty-eight hours later, when I walked out into the yard at sunrise, I was greeted by an obviously starving Achilles. With a squawk, he flew down to land on my shoulder, followed by a whole series of animated squeaks and chirps. When I moved as though to go away from the house, he dropped down onto my boot and tugged at my pant leg with his beak. When I got him a chunk of raw meat, he wolfed it down in great gulps and asked for more.

He stayed with us for several days, then disappeared again. This time he was gone for nearly a week, and when he suddenly showed up one evening, there were two owls with him, calling from the shelter of the trees. Had his parents come back to claim him? There was no way of knowing, but most certainly the presence of the other owls was no coincidence. We noticed some changes in Achilles, for he had obviously found feed, and there was a marked aura of independence about him that told us he was returning to the wild. He accepted feed, but with a kind of diffidence, as though letting us know that he could now fare for himself.

When he left again, we thought he was gone forever. Late one night, as I was driving home through a new fall of snow, my car slipped off the shoulder of the road into the ditch. I left it and continued on foot in the moonlight. Within three hundred yards of the house, where the road wound through a grove of cottonwoods, a big owl came suddenly winging down to land on my shoulder. Achilles greeted me as always with a whole string of happy cheeps and chirps, and rode on my shoulder to the house, where I gave him a piece of raw steak. He tore it up and ate it with his usual gusto, demonstrating an unwavering appetite and an ability to swallow chunks that looked big enough to choke him.

In the morning he was still there, and I presented him with a fresh magpie. When the moon came up full and round that evening, lighting up the snow-draped hills and mountains spread out before our ranch buildings in glittering splendour, Achilles was perched atop his favourite post. Charlie and I were out in the yard, and we heard him give his raucous call. Faint and far off among the moonlit hills, another great horned owl hooted in reply. Then Achilles took off, a black silhouette moving against a star-filled sky, fading rapidly in the distance.

We never saw him again. But even now, fifteen years later, when we hear a great horned owl call, we are reminded of a friend we once knew, a gentle spirit of the wild country whom we loved.

10

SO THIS IS AFRICA

After twenty-five years of organizing many expeditions by packtrain involving as many as fifty horses, and a crew and adequate equipment to take parties of city-dwelling guests out into the Rocky Mountains for three weeks to a month, it was somewhat exciting to be offered the chance to lead a photo safari into Kenya, East Africa, by British Airlines and Air Canada.

They weren't just fooling around either. In due course, they gave me a sample of the brochure they had put together advertising the expedition. It was a magnificent example of this kind of tourist promotion, but it scared hell out of me. I was not exactly unknown in the world of tourism, and with that brochure circulating in travel agencies and airports around the world, we could be oversold by a country mile. I got on the phone pronto to remind the powers that be of our agreement to limit the guest list to fifteen people and was assured that they had everything under control. Some of the party was to leave with me from Calgary, and we would meet the rest in London, England. We were met at Heathrow Airport by a smiling representative of British Airlines, and with some misgiving I counted twenty-three people in our party. My frame of mind was not any better when I was further informed that six more people would be meeting us in Nairobi.

We flew into a blood-red dawn as we came to the coast of Africa. There were no clouds to obscure the view of the ground, which was too far away to make out any detail, but close enough to reveal the general layout of its geography. My personal fog of worry and concern melted like a snowflake hitting a warm wind. Let the airlines worry about their abundance of guests.

This was Africa!

When we landed at Nairobi, we were met by a very professional black lady who spoke faultless English and who proceeded to lead us through Customs without losing a step. Then, calling for our attention, she informed us that while we were in the air, Kenya and Tanzania had gotten into an argument over some fuel bills involving their jointly owned airline, which Kenya solved by seizing all the aircraft. Tanzania had retaliated by seizing sixty Kenyan tour buses in that country and putting all the drivers in jail, along with a number of tourists.

We couldn't complain about our luck, for if we had been a few hours earlier, we would have found out what it was like to be stranded in Tanzania while the two countries sorted out their differences. As it was, we now had the four days with no reservations for overnight accommodation – a somewhat daunting outlook in the view of a party of twenty-nine people that had to have beds and meals. I crossed my fingers and took a cue from the smiling lady in front of us. Then I found a young lady in my party I didn't know was there representing Air Canada. When she introduced herself, she told me that she had been to Africa before and would be glad to help in any way she could. I didn't say it out loud, but the way things were going it would have been fine with me if she had been born twins.

Kenya covers a large piece of very rugged geography, and for four days when we got up in the morning, we were never sure where we would be staying that night. But thanks to my helper and the woman with the tourist headquarters in Nairobi, who talked to each other at every opportunity by phones generally available at the scattered gas stations throughout the country, we found adequate accommodation, although we travelled eleven hours one day to get to it. The roads were narrow, crooked, and dusty. The weather was clear and about seventy to eighty degrees during the day, but cool at night, for in this region the equator cuts across high plains country between seven and nine thousand feet above sea level.

We were seeing wildlife every day. At Lake Nakuru in Aberdare National Park there was a flock of an estimated million and a half pink flamingos, which were no doubt attracted to this big shallow body of water by the freshwater shrimps and other kinds of aquatic life that teemed there. On a piece of marshy ground between the mass of birds and the heavy forest, a small herd of waterbucks was feeding – all males, and very handsome animals with their rich coats and graceful horns. When President Kenyata took Kenya out of British rule, one of the early and most important things he did was establish nine national parks in which hunting was forbidden and any kind of development was very limited.

It was through these parks that we travelled, for not only were the access roads better than average, but it was there that the Kenyan government had built lodges to accommodate tourists. A few of these were rustic with straw roofs, but these have largely been replaced with fully modern structures of concrete and quarried stone with swimming pools and carefully tended lawns. But raw Africa is not far away. At the Tsavo Park Lodge, a sign at the swimming pool said, "Pool closed at 5 p.m. The lions sometimes come here to drink."

Speaking of straw roofs, I have good reason to remember Salt Springs Lodge in the Tsavo Park, where the guest accommodation was built on concrete pillars high enough so the elephants had plenty of room to walk under them. The units were circular and two storeys high, and my wife and I had the storey under the roof. There were three big windows, and our view was truly magnificent. When we took stock of our quarters, we were intrigued by the built-in insect control – several well-fed looking lizards about a foot long. Buzzing up and down the glass of one window was the biggest wasp I have ever seen, about two inches long, a rich gun-metal blue, and altogether formidable.

Opening the window, I tried to herd it out, with no luck. Then with more bravery than good sense, I undertook to pin it down and throw it out, but by exercise of a double-jointed back, it stabbed me clear through the side of my index finger and ejected its venom on the window glass. For a minute or two my finger burned like it was red hot, then it tapered off to bearable, and I was happy that the wasp had missed me with most of its charge.

The sun had just dropped over the horizon when the parade of animals began to show up for water, led by a small group of warthogs followed closely by some Thomson's gazelles and impala. Then about a dozen elephants moved in through the scattered acacia trees to dominate the water-hole. It was a fascinating beginning to a continual but ever-changing promenade of wildlife lit up by a full moon. It went on all night and included two great herds of Cape buf-falo that totalled over seven hundred head.

Even the Africans were excited. It was one of those times that nature decided to put on a show – an extravaganza like nothing any of us ever expected to see.

11

THE LAND OF THE SKY

DON BRESTLER '98

T his day was blazing hot – much hotter than usual in early August, the sun pouring down and glinting off the facets of little waves stirring the surface of the lake in front of me. Sitting with my back comfortably propped against a small alpine fir tree in the cool shade of a bigger one, I idly watched a solitary sandpiper as it pirouetted and curtsied in pursuit of some tiny insects hatching among the water-washed pebbles of the beach a few feet ahead of my outstretched boots.

My fly rod leaned forgotten against the tree beside me. I had been out since early morning – just in time to see the beginning of a tremendous hatch of small black gnats that had brought the trout to the surface in a frenzy of feeding. The insects were so tiny, my fly box was hard pressed to match them, but a minute version of a parachute fly, simply tied, with no other dressing than three or four wraps of a single black hackle on a number sixteen long shank hook, proved adequate. It floated exactly like a miniature umbrella with the crook of its handle hanging below the surface, and while it in no way appeared to match the insects that were hatching, the trout took it with utter abandon. For two hours I had been fast to fish, some of them heavy enough to really work my light rod. Saving only enough to fill the frying pan, I had carefully released all the rest. Now I was sated with fishing, drowsy with the heat, and satisfied to just sit and watch the lake and the surrounding slopes.

Apart from the busy sandpiper, not a living thing moved. Across the basin on the shady side of a mountain beneath a ragged snowdrift, an elderly mountain billy goat lay on the flat top of a little outcrop projecting from a patch of broken boulders. Like me and every other animal in the basin, he was enjoying the coolness out of the reach of the blazing sun. Overhead the sky was a faultless blue, the kind of day when everything warm-blooded likes to hunt for a bed in the deep shade. Somewhere up among the terraces and patches of shintangle scrub to my right and a bit behind me were thirty-odd bighorn sheep – females, lambs, and young rams who had all been out feeding earlier in the morning, but now were so well hidden that the most careful combing with powerful binoculars revealed not so much as the tip of a horn.

For a while I dozed flat on my back with my hat over my face. A distant rumble of thunder brought me wide awake. Towering over the high ridge rimming the basin to the west, looking hard and white as carved ivory, a great mass of cloud was riding in on the southwest wind. As it came, the shape of it changed and it seemed to grow, the underside appearing a dirty greenish black. It was time for me to be heading for the tent. Then a flash of lightning struck the ridge top, followed instantly by a giant roar of thunder that bounced off the peaks and sent its echoes rolling down the canyon below, and I knew there wasn't time. Taking my rod apart, I left my fish cached under the flat rock at the water's edge and climbed to a niche under the rim of a low cliff a few yards above the lake just as the first big raindrops splashed the rocks. The place was barely big enough to sit in, but it was enough.

Again the lightning struck the mountain – closer this time, with an audible snap preceding the almost instant shattering blast of thunder. The vibration seemed to tear the bottom out of the thunderhead, for the rain came pouring down, streaming off everything, wetting the herbage and trees, bouncing in a fine spray where it hit the naked rock. Again and again the lightning played its hard bright fingers on the high places until it shook the mountains like a barrage of mighty guns. Water sprayed off the forward brim of my hat and my boot toes where they stuck out from under the overhang, but the rest of me was dry.

Then just as quickly as it began the storm was over. The sun came out warm and cheerful as it lit up myriad drops clinging to every grass blade and leaf. Down valley, the thunder continued to roll its drums, while the high arches of a double rainbow gleamed in contrast to the dark face of the retreating storm – so close it seemed possible to reach out and finger the brilliant colours.

Getting to my feet, I climbed up to a commanding point of rocks to sit and glass the slopes. A half hour before, the place had looked lifeless, but now it was moving with wild sheep gambolling and feeding on the lush green terraces just under the talus fans at the foot of the cliffs. They were mostly feeding, but the lambs were in a playful mood. About a dozen of these lighthearted young ones were in the company of an old ewe somewhat apart from the rest, a sort of babysitter for the bunch, keeping guard while the mothers fed. She was hungry and content to stay in one spot, but the light-footed little bighorns in her charge wanted no part of it. With a rush they left her to run towards the gnarled and weathered trunk of a huge old mountain larch lying dead among the rocks. There they began a sort of follow-the-leader game around and through its great broken branches, bounding ecstatically back and forth across the big trunk. The nurse ewe climbed slowly towards them, but she had scarcely arrived when they left her again to go at a high gallop down towards a big boulder on a bench meadow, beyond a little ridge. It lay half buried where it had halted ages before after a dizzy plunge off the cliffs above. It was covered with multicoloured rock lichen and weathered roughly in tiny ledges making footholds for the lambs as they climbed and played over it. After a few minutes, their energy seemed to flag and they stopped in various attitudes on this little mountain sticking up among a sea of wildflowers. One lamb saw the ewe coming over the swell of ground towards them and bleated. She answered, and so did its mother from farther down the slope, signals that seemingly reminded all the young ones that they were hungry, for they all began trotting back towards the main bunch, bleating as they went.

As each lamb reached its mother, it began to suckle vigorously, each tiny tail wiggling furiously in enthusiastic spurts of movement along with impatient bunting. The feeding was not prolonged. The ewes stood patiently while the pressure of accumulated milk was eased off their udders, and they terminated the suckling by simply lifting a hind foot over the necks of their lambs, fishing them away as they stepped ahead.

Now the lambs were scattered through the herd, but before long they were collected again, napping in the warm sun in beds up to their ears in brilliant blooms of monkey flowers, paintbrush, heliotrope, and many others. Their bedground was among a scattering of great, wide-branched larches in lightly dappled shade where the sun filtered down through the feathery green foliage. The breeze was cool now and the sheep were content.

When the binoculars swung back towards the old billy's hanging bedground across the basin, it was to find him feeding in a little pocket five hundred feet farther up among the sheer cliffs. The place was barely big enough to accommodate his angular frame; he seemed to stand on the edge of nothing, cropping busily on the lush green stuff growing where a little seep came out of a crack in the rock wall. The freezing and thawing of this water over countless seasons had eroded away the rock, forming a small pocket lined with a thin layer of soil sufficient to support the plant life growing there, mostly goat sorrel along with a thin scattering of fine tufted grass.

It did not take the billy long to get what was readily available, whereupon he moved casually, on up the cliff face, along a steeply inclining ledge, little more than a figment of imagination from where I sat. Short in the cannon bones, he could reach up and ahead for favourable places to put his hoofs and then lift himself with ease. Like all his kind, the slab-sided shape of his body with narrow hips and shoulders allowed easy passage close to the rock wall in places where a bighorn ram's roundness and thickness of horns and quarters would have pushed him off into space. As goats always do in a very steep going unless alarmed, this one climbed with a phlegmatic deliberation, very casual, yet placing each foot with the exactness of a real specialist.

And specialists they are in their own way, as are all animals to one degree or another. But this specialization is more noticeable among goats, for they choose to live, summer and winter, among high crags and cliff faces, rarely coming to lower ground except to cross over between the mountain ranges. Except for occasional licking at some mineral spring below the timberline, they stay among the crags. Their trails follow the broken ledges overlooking eagle thoroughfares where not even wolves, coyotes, or cougars often venture to challenge their mastery of mountains.

The billy was climbing steadily in the field of my glasses, pulled in close by the magnification in sharp contrast to the dark-coloured rock face behind, when an eagle suddenly appeared from somewhere up in the blue vault above falling like a javelin straight at him. The goat must have heard the roar of the wind in the eagle's pinion feathers, for it was his leap ahead towards a split in the rock that drew my attention to the eagle. He barely made it to the break where he had room to tuck in his hindquarters when the eagle struck at him. Facing out with his neck bowed, the billy parried with needle-sharp horns, forcing the big bird to veer off. The eagle let its momentum carry it up a hundred feet or so, rolled over and struck again, but again the goat bucked on his front feet with a lightning-fast thrust and once more the reaching talons missed. The eagle struck three times in almost as many seconds, but it had no chance in such a place, so it swooped away to leave the billy alone.

Here was another kind of specialist, not only as a species but as an individual, for comparatively few golden eagles will try to kill a fully grown mountain goat. Once, years before, away down among the high mountains of Idaho along the Salmon River, I had witnessed a similar attack. I was fishing directly across the Middle Fork from a sheer granite face about fifteen hundred feet high, when a big old billy appeared climbing laterally along a tiny ledge perhaps a hundred feet down from the top. The eagle came from somewhere thousands of feet above in a sizzling dive, with the wind a rising crescendo in its wing feathers. The goat likely heard the bird coming before he saw it, for he made about three quick jumps to a spot where a little chimney gave him room to turn and fight. Here with his long chin whiskers flying like a banner of defiance, he met the eagle in a short fierce battle where no contact was made, though the intent was obvious. Had the eagle reached him two seconds sooner, the goat would have undoubtedly been knocked off the ledge to a certain death on the jagged rocks far below – a well-pulped feed for the big winged predator.

It is not a common thing to observe, for having watched eagles in the vicinity of goats and sheep for uncounted hours over the years, I would say that very few individuals learn how to kill in this fashion. But seeing such a conflict between the winged and four-footed ones makes it apparent that these attacks are successful often enough to be encouraging. This one had failed, and now the billy was climbing again in his normal easygoing way, the incident forgotten.

The swinging glasses picked up the eagle and its mate riding a thermal high against the blue sky, circling on motionless outspread wings in a climbing spiral till almost lost from view. Somewhere beneath, hidden among the pinnacles and shelves of the mountain was a nest, but the fledglings therein would have to do with something other than goat this day.

The glasses continued their roving, pausing here and there to examine things that looked like animals but turned out to be something else. Then away up on the skyline to the west of the basin, from the direction the thunderstorm had come, black silhouettes appeared against the sky, the unmistakable shapes of bighorn rams. They were coming up onto the ridge crest from the far side, stopping one by one to look down towards me. There were ten of them in line, all mature animals but one; it was a fine bachelor's club, veterans of many seasons with only a single three- or four-year-old among them – a prince consort among kings. Although they were a long way off, there was no mistaking the full curled horns.

There are no animals in the mountains more dramatic. For these fit with the big sky and the rugged peaks of the Rockies, where clouds sail on the wings of the wind with shadows trailing swiftly below across hanging meadows, the open talus fans and the heavily timbered valleys. They live with the song of the wind in their ears, sometimes a soft caress of sound among rock spires and weather-bent timberline trees, sometimes a roaring full-throated crescendo, the background lyrics of wild sheep country. The two go together like northland lakes and loons, for one cannot really live without the other; it is the wind that whips the snow off the flanks and crests of the wintering grounds allowing the sheep to feed when the rest of the country is buried deep beneath the cover of the cold white blanket. The sound of it in summer is a reminder that one travels in sheep country, even though these animals may be out of sight.

For a few minutes the rams stood motionless, and then as though at a signal they all trailed the big leader at a tearing gallop down over a series of broken ledges and cliffs. One moment they were coming head-on and the next they had swapped ends in complete reverse to go streaking back towards the top. Without slacking stride, they turned again to come galloping recklessly down over a near-impossible place, sure on their nimble feet, rhythmic as dancers. When they came to the top of an almost perpendicular snowdrift, they did not check their headlong rush, but came down in a bounding glissade with slush flying from their hoofs high over their backs in glistening showers. They ran out on the top of a big talus fan, stopping there to gaze down over the hanging meadows below and then making their way sedately down to the first green growth as though something as undignified as play was completely beyond consideration. Fascinated as always with these curly-horned ones, I recalled another day in early May high on the slopes of Sheep Mountain above Kluane Lake in southwestern Yukon Territory. It was a brilliant morning with a vast sweep of mountains spread out beyond the still-frozen expanse of the lake. Perhaps four miles away there was a steep bluff dropping down to the far shore. It looked as though a giant snowball had been smashed against it, for shelves and cliffs were smeared with white. But the whiteness was Dall sheep. My binoculars were not nearly strong enough to make a count, but there must have been close to three hundred head in the bunch.

Directly in front of me, scattered in bunches for three-quarters of a mile were close to a hundred more, mostly ewes, new lambs, and yearlings. Not all the ewes had lambs with them yet, for lambing season had just begun. Not more than a hundred and fifty yards away, up at the foot of a broken cliff, five big herdmasters were loafing in the sun. Two of them were fine old rams with magnificent flaring horns, the tips perfect. They were paying me the compliment of ignoring me completely, although my perch was in plain view.

I wanted to get to the top of that cliff, for above it was a tableland of tundra, where there were likely more sheep, but I was not sure where to tackle it. Wondering if the rams would show the way, I climbed slowly towards them until barely fifty feet separated us. They stood bunched up, gazing curiously at me, and then one of the lesser ones nudged the old leader gently on the flank with a horn tip as though prompting him to move. He took the cue and in a very deliberate and dignified way led the bunch up along the foot of the cliff to a break and climbed up onto the shelves with me trailing along at a respectful hundred feet behind. Then, he showed us all a route up the rock face that was so easy I could have climbed it with both hands in my pockets. When we reached the top, they left me at a tearing gallop as though suddenly tired of my intrusion and wishing to be left alone.

From the mountains on the coast of Alaska to the Mackenzie Range to the east, and from the north slope of the Brooks Range south to the peaks within sight of the great Peace River, these northern thinhorn sheep, *Ovis dalli dalli* and *O. dalli stonei*, flourish. They go from snowy white in Alaska and western Yukon to almost black in certain individuals found among the mountains on the headwaters of the Halfway, Musqua, Prophet, and Prairie rivers. In between they run in every shade of grey. Some, like those found in the Snyder Mountains north of the Nahanni River, have black tails and black stripes on their shirts. The so-called Fannin sheep, with their blue-grey saddles, listed as a separate species by the early biological "splitters," are truly just another colour phase of Dall sheep. You can sit on a slope up near Teslin Lake near the Yukon–British Columbia border and see wild sheep that range from the next thing to pure white to iron blue in colour, all grazing on the same slopes and certainly all interbreeding.

The Peace River seems to have formed an effective fence that has kept the thinhorns and bighorns from mingling, for they likely would freely interbreed if they came together. There is a gap of about one hundred and fifty miles across where there are no sheep. South of the river and a bit east of Pine Pass is the northern limit of bighorn range. From there these are found all along the Rockies away south to the mountains of Sonora and Baiha in old Mexico. Over this vast reach of country the bighorn family tree divides itself into three main branches: *O. canadensis canadensis*, the Canada bighorn; *O. canadensis californi*, the California bighorn; and *O. canadensis nelsoni*, the desert bighorn. The California bighorn is found as far west as the Okanagan and Fraser valleys as well as in Washington State.

From the far north, where the winter night is six months long, and the mountains are whipped mercilessly by howling blizzards with a wind chill reaching an equivalent of one hundred fifty degrees below zero, to far south in the dry and equally merciless heat of the desert mountains, the sheep have adapted themselves remarkably well to the wide range of conditions they face. Only the grizzly bear matches their ability to adapt to climate, but it is not nearly so successful at meeting the pressures of men. The wild sheep have certainly suffered from human encroachment and much of their former ranges are no longer populated, but they still survive – often in good numbers where the country provides adequate shelter and feed.

Wonderfully intelligent, blithe creature that it is, the mountain sheep is the hallmark of the remaining mountain habitat in western North America, the one animal completely synonymous with the high rugged ranges – the land of the sky.

12

SAM LEE CAPTURES A WOLVERINE

DON BRESTLER '98

Sam Lee lived in the Okanagan Valley not far from the City of Kelowna. He was a trapper, professional guide, and orchard grower. His trapline was up in some high valleys spilling their creeks down into the Okanagan Lake. He had a pack of very good cougar hounds and was generally on call by the British Columbia Fish and Wildlife Department to eliminate problem cougars wherever they happened to show up.

I met Sam one winter when I was scheduled to show my wildlife films at the annual Fish and Wildlife Association's dinner. He had been on his trapline and caught a rather rare wolverine, which he had muzzled, loaded in his backpack, and brought down to his place a few miles from the city.

Sam knew exactly what he was going to do with that wolverine. He rounded up some pieces of steel construction rod and built a cage with his welding outfit on the concrete floor of his garage and shop. He turned the wolverine loose in it, and it would be fair to say by that time the animal was not exactly pleased. It squalled and growled and generally raised hell about the indignities that it had encountered and it was perfectly obvious to Sam that what the wolverine wanted most was to get at him and tear him all to shreds. He got some meat, left some of it in the cage, and then made a phone call to the Stanley Park Zoo in Vancouver to let them know that the following day he was bringing in the wolverine they had asked him to capture for them. Then he got cleaned up for the big dinner that night.

I heard about the wolverine and drove over to his place to have a look at his captive next morning. When I got there, it was in time to see that Sam was somewhat shook up.

Because of the long snowshoe trip the day before and the banquet following it, he had been slower than usual about getting up, and when he went out to check the wolverine, it was to find his six-year-old daughter feeding it some meat, which the animal was taking out of her bare hand. When the wolverine saw Sam, it let out a great snarling growl and jumped towards him. The little girl began to cry, and Sam's hair was standing on end.

Sam carried his daughter to the house. We had some breakfast, and then I helped him load the cage and the wolverine into his pickup truck. The last I saw of Sam that day, he was heading down the road for Vancouver. His little daughter was sobbing because he took the wolverine with him.

13

DANGEROUS GAME

The late Norman Luxton, an old acquaintance of mine and the founder of the famous Luxton Museum in Banff, had an experience one fall while hunting goats that was whisker-close to being his final one.

He and two of his friends were out in late October stalking a bunch of billies across a talus fan. There was a cliff fifteen hundred feet sheer falling away below and the rest of the mountain above and a foot of powder snow underfoot. Norman was behind his companions as they traversed a normally very easy and safe slope, when suddenly a dry slide let go somewhere above.

A dry snow avalanche can be a triple danger, for if you miss being buried or swept off a cliff, you can smother by breathing the flying powder snow accompanying it. The stuff gets into the lungs and melts, simply drowning the unlucky one.

Norman and his friends heard the slide coming and could see the great rolling cloud of snow coming towards them, and they began running to get out from under it. In seconds they were blinded by the fog of powder snow and crouched down to bury their heads in their jackets. When the slide had gone by and the air cleared, the two leading hunters found themselves alone. They looked for Norman, but he had completely disappeared. The slide had passed very close before plunging off the cliff below and they sadly concluded he had been caught in it and was lying somewhere far down the mountain, dead, for nobody could survive such a fall.

More or less in shock, they retraced their steps. Being experienced mountaineers, they were sure there was no chance of finding Norman alive. It was a long way to the bottom and darkness caught them before they could make a search, so they went to camp. There they built a fire and dug out the bottle of rum for a stiff toddy. They did not feel like eating, but they did have another drink. That one led to another as they discussed the sad demise of their partner, and somehow the night resolved itself into a kind of wake for the departed one.

But Norman was not dead. Caught in the slide, he had been swept over the lip of the cliff, but lodged in a little scrubby tree growing out of a crack in the rock just under the rim. Knocked unconscious, he had been hanging there covered with snow and his partners had missed finding him. After dark, he regained consciousness to find himself suspended over nothing, but somehow he managed to crawl to safe ground above. One arm was broken and he was battered and bruised, but he was a tough and determined man. Guessing why his partners had left, he slowly and painfully trailed them down the mountain under a late moon to camp.

Meanwhile the bottle had been emptied and the fire had gone out. The two mourners had crawled into their sleeping bags for warmth and were lying there suffering the depths of utter despair, while a couple of candles burned sombrely, lighting the inside of the tent.

Then from the night outside came the sound of groans in the distance and they thought they heard a voice say something.

"Dear Jesus!" one of the mourners exclaimed. "If I was a shuperstitious man, that would shound like a ghosht!"

"Must be the wind," said the other.

But the sounds came closer, accompanied by the crunching of feet in the snow, and then the tent flaps parted to reveal Norman tottering on his feet, splattered with dried blood from a deep scratch on his face – returned from the dead.

"Where is the goddam rum?" he gasped. "I need a drink!" – the understatement of his entire lifetime.

Shocked into complete sobriety, his friends helped him to a seat, and built a fire all the while trying to explain why there was nothing left to drink. At first they had trouble convincing Norman there was no rum, and when the fact got through to him, he became utterly furious, berating them for a couple of profanely described idiots. A pot of hot tea served to calm him down a bit and they attended to his arm.

They finally got him back to Banff and a doctor, and in due course he saw the funny side of the experience and forgave them. To his dying day, Norman proclaimed goats the most dangerous game in the world.

14

"CHALK ONE UP FOR US"

I remember spotting a fine trophy billy one bright October morning from the cook-tent door in a snug camp at the bottom of a deep narrow valley in British Columbia. I pointed it out to my friend Harry Jennings, and we decided to climb for him, although he was almost at the top of a high mountain.

Harry is a man with a built-in love of mountain hunting and wide experience, ranging from stalking Dall sheep and caribou in the Yukon to trailing goats, elk, and grizzlies down in my old hunting country. He is the sportsman's kind of sportsman, and before he retired was also one of the most skilled heart specialists in Canada's medical circles. In his own quiet, unassuming way, he has been one of the finest rifle shots I have ever known on both targets and game. He could afford good weapons and could use a rifle with skill under all kinds of conditions. I never had the feeling of being a guide while out with him, just a companion and friend privileged to enjoy his company. We rambled the mountains, savouring many things, sometimes taking a trophy, but just as often passing up an animal after looking it over.

This particular stalk was early in our acquaintance and was a kind of milestone in a long friendship. We climbed a long way over a steep slope out of bare rock into snow halfway to our knees and into the teeth of a wintry breeze. Finally about noon we came up onto a spur below a castle-shaped buttress of rock. When we reached the top of this, we would be within two hundred and fifty yards of the billy.

My leg muscles were tingling and I knew Harry was tired, so I suggested we eat lunch. Leading the way into a sheltered place against a sunlit face of rock, we ate our sandwiches and enjoyed our pipes. Then we climbed to the top of the rock buttress above. When I peeked over the skyline, it was to see the billy standing on a pinnacle exactly where I expected to find him.

He was a venerable old goat with his fall pelage heavy and thick, his pantaloons and beard waving gently in the wind. Standing broadside, he was a beautiful and unforgettable picture against the deep blue of the sky. Pushing my rucksack up onto a rock for an armrest, I signalled Harry to go ahead and shoot when he was ready.

He slid into a comfortable position, quietly sliding a cartridge into the breech of his rifle. I had my glasses up waiting for the shot, knowing just as surely as I stood there in my climbing boots that the goat was ours. Nothing happened and when I looked at Harry again, he was straightening up and opening his rifle breech.

Grinning at me, he asked softly, "Why should I kill that old fellow? I've already got a good head on my wall. What I came out here for was to get away from my telephone! Chalk one up for us."

The last we saw of that goat he was still standing there completely oblivious to our presence and gazing away off into the distance. We climbed back down to camp and a warm fire knowing the good feeling of having enjoyed a great day in the mountains.

15

Being Your Own Packhorse

DON BRESTLER '98

In the old days, many of the early trappers and prospectors who explored the interior of British Columbia and the Yukon went by means of their own two feet, carrying their food and equipment on their backs. It is a tough way to travel but has its advantages, for it allows a man to go where there is no horse feed and through country where the rivers are too swift for water craft.

Fifty-odd years ago, R.M. Patterson made an epic journey north from the Peace River to the fabled Nahanni River of the Yukon, spending months exploring the great canyons above and below the magnificent Virginia Falls. He was looking through the country called Headless Valley, so named because a party of prospectors disappeared there one winter, and later, when their skeletons were discovered scattered about in the vicinity of the rags of their tent, the skulls were all missing. A story of mysterious murder and intrigue was born. The real explanation is thought to be much less dramatic, for no evidence of foul play was ever found. The missing skulls are more likely explained as having been rolled into the stream by investigating bears and lost forever. However, the more sensational explanation remains a subject of much controversy.

Patterson spent most of a year rambling through the region discovering caves, hot springs, and a host of other interesting features that make this unique area one of the most interesting in North America. When he came out, he brought with him a collection of photographs as well as notebooks crammed with material later incorporated in his book *Dangerous River*.

Lord Tweedsmuir, at one time the Governor General of Canada, and a famous novelist who wrote under the name John Buchan, wove the story content of his novel *Sick Heart River* around this same fabled wilderness. In it he featured a backpacking wilderness traveller. His research was done firsthand, for he visited the Nahanni River country when it was still little known, in the company of Harry Snyder, the famous hunter and explorer. They were the first party to fly into the valley. It was on this expedition that Snyder discovered and hunted in a magnificent range of mountains that now bears his name.

Many of the early prospectors involved in the Klondike gold rush were no strangers to backpacks of various kinds. Some carried unbelievable loads up over Chilcote Pass in the dead of winter. A great uncle of mine, a tough Scot by the name of Neil McTavish, carried his food and possibles over trails reaching thousands of miles from Colorado to Alaska and northern British Columbia in his lifelong search for gold. I recall as a boy sitting around the fire in the evenings with him listening to the stories of his adventures, little realizing how much work and hardship had been absorbed by his tough, powerful body. He was near seventy then, but still straight and strong, his kindly face weathered by desert sun and arctic storms and laugh wrinkles curving away from eyes accustomed to looking across miles and miles of mountains. He died when well over eighty in a little town called Smithers up on the Bulkley River in northwestern British Columbia, still looking for the pot of gold at the end of the rainbow.

Backpacking in those old days of trapline and prospecting trails was not nearly as comfortable as it is today with modern pack frames designed with scientific precision and balance to fit one's back and shoulders. When I first packed my gear on my back on the trapline forty-odd years ago, the best equipment we could get was the Bergen Pack, manufactured in Norway. The bag was hung on a triangular tubular metal frame supposed to fit the wearer's back. I have a long back and never found one really comfortable on a long haul with a load. Inevitably I came in from such a trip with one thought uppermost in my mind: for the simple reason that I hurt in a number of places, how wonderful it was going to be to get that load on the ground – definitely the first thing to be done regardless of anything else that might be waiting.

My feeling about packs has a kind of parallel with a story about two Finnish soldiers skiing back from the Russian front to their home towns during the hostilities early in World War II.

They had been fighting on skis for months and were heading home across country, a journey of days and tough winter camps with a minimum of grub. Finally they topped a big hill looking down on their village, and paused there to savour the peaceful setting and the anticipation of warmth and food.

The older of the two men asked the other, "What is the first thing you are going to do when you get down there?"

"You know I was married just a few days before we went to the front," the other replied. "I haven't seen my wife for three months. The first thing I am going to do is fill up on one of her wonderful stews. Then I am going to take her to bed for a week!" Then he asked in turn, "What is the first thing you are going to do?"

"The first thing I am going to do is take off these god-dam skis!" came the positive reply.

Dissatisfied with the packs available in trading posts and outfitting stores, trappers began improvising their own. I recall being loaned one such pack frame made with two broken axe handles and quarter-inch iron rods for a trip in northern British Columbia. It was a comfortable pack, and it was designed with enough strength to withstand the trampling of an elephant, but it weighed enough to be a pretty fair kind of load without adding a pound of anything else. It was thus that the modern pack frame was born. The first really practical and comfortable pack I ever used was the Trapper Nelson, resin constructed of light canvas stretched with lacing over a light basswood frame on which a roomy bag was hung. It was a kind of pack saddle for human use, a vast improvement in its time, for it was light, protected the packer from any hard projections of equipment in the bag, and weighed only a few ounces.

It worked well in winter, but had its shortcomings for summer use. In warm weather there was little ventilation between the canvas and the wearer's back, and it could become scalding hot. I found out all about this uncomfortable drawback one summer in the Yukon.

The incident had some unique aspects, for after years of working with broncs, climbing, and travelling wild country without so much as cracking a bone, I fell through a scaffold while shingling my house and broke several ribs. Our family doctor taped me up with copious applications of adhesive to the point where I had trouble breathing. Shortly after, I took off on an expedition into the wilds of the western Yukon and during the course of events began climbing every day with a load of motion picture equipment. The weather was hot and soon I began feeling exactly like an old well-worn packhorse with a badly fitted saddle and a skimpy saddle blanket. My back began to itch and burn to an intolerable degree. Late one afternoon, my sons, Charlie and Dick, and I arrived back in camp dragging our shirttails after a long tough day in high country. My back felt like somebody had poured coal oil over it and set a match to it, so I pulled off my shirt and instructed my sons to remove the tape. This they did while I ground my teeth in agony, solemnly promising myself all the while that I would have some pointed conversation with my doctor on the shortcomings of using tape for correcting broken ribs plus some earthy comments on his ancestry thrown in for good measure.

The tape came off. Along with it came pieces of hide and bits of meat, for we found I had a whole assortment of little boils under it. The boys swore they could see into me clear to the bone in several places, but I suspected they exaggerated a bit for their own amusement, although I felt like the sun was shining clear through me. They swabbed off the raw places with a soft, clean handkerchief soaked in overproof rum, an operation that almost made me howl, and then rubbed in some bacon grease. Eventually my back healed and I have looked with deep compassion on every horse I have seen since with saddle sore marks on his back.

There is nothing like such personal experience to make a real impression on a man, and nothing more inclined to make him look for improved equipment. Owing to the demands of mountain climbers, hunters, hikers, and specialized military forces, outfitting firms designed and experimented with various combinations of light but strongly constructed pack frames made of aluminum and magnesium alloy tubing. There are many kinds, but the best has emerged in a type known around the world as the Kelty Pack, which incorporates about all the most favourable features of everything ever invented in the line plus sonic innovations of its own. It is a comparatively expensive piece of equipment, the frame being constructed of feather-light magnesium alloy tubing and coming in four sizes to fit anyone. It follows the contours of the back, riding on wide bands of nylon webbing that can be laced to varying degrees of tension and ensure that nothing can rub the wearer. A kind of padded bow rides over the packer's hips, and this is secured by a strong belly band, to avoid tipping and swinging when climbing. On the frame is slung a well-designed bag with inner compartments and outside zipper pockets for food and possibles. If one packs his gear so that heavy items ride fairly high on the shoulders, the balance can be adjusted to afford easy carrying. With the inclusion of a well-designed nylon mountain tent and a down-filled sleeping bag, it is possible to keep the load well under fifty pounds and still be reasonably comfortable for a couple of weeks. Of course one must take advantage of the very light, freeze-dried foods that are available. This combination is a high-country sheep hunter's dream come true, opening up a whole new horizon for the modern cameraman or hunter working country too rough for horses to negotiate.

Backpacking on a hunting trip for any kind of big game has its definite limitations. It is a specialist's way of going, and the "specialist" had better be in reasonably good physical condition. In any event, it is wise to take it easy for two or three days to give his muscles and feet a chance to tone up. It is profoundly important that his footgear be comfortable and afford the very best protection for his feet.

It's unlikely any backpacking hunter will ever be accused of being a game hog, for his bag will be confined to one animal and that nothing heavier than a mule deer, goat, or sheep. Even then he must be prepared to relay his meat and trophy out to more sophisticated transportation. Game such as moose and elk are out. A bull elk or moose is one of nature's most impressive animals on the hoof, but to kill one and then stand contemplating the inert mass of hide, flesh, and antlers, knowing that it has to be carried out piece by piece on a pack frame of any kind could be one of the most discouraging experiences of a hunter's life. Personally, I prefer shooting such animals with my camera in order to take the trophy home on film, then buy a side of beef. Any other way, the price of meat per pound gets unbelievably high before the job is done. As an Indian once remarked, it is much easier to camp by the moose and eat it where it falls.

After a lifetime of rambling through the mountains of Alberta and British Columbia with horses, I now find myself slinging a pack over my shoulders when I want to enjoy the remnants of what was once a vast wilderness of sheep country. It is the only way I can recapture the feeling of great freedom and spiritual rest that was once an everyday way of life. By climbing high up into the remote pockets and high basins, where cliffs and canyons defeat the persistence of the wasters, it is possible to camp beyond the sound of motors, where the air is sweet and clean as the mountain streams and the peaks look down across mantles of shining snow. I miss the cheery sound of Swiss bells on grazing horses and wonderful camaraderie of equine friends, but sometimes at night I still hear them, faint and far off, as I lie snug in my down robe with the smell of spruce and pine in my nose.

Every fall a young rancher and friend, Billy Morton, and I take off for a week of sheep hunting. We are very choosy, for while we have seen many sheep, we still have to find a suitable bighorn ram for him. He carries his rifle, but I go armed only with a camera. At first he was keen as a sharp hunting knife to kill a ram, but as time has passed he has become more and more the hunter for hunting's sake. Someday he will kill a ram, but when he does, I suspect he will feel a bit let down and wish perhaps that the search was not over.

Two years ago we drove his four-wheel drive up a creek along an oil prospect road to where a deep canyon cut it off not far from where I once camped in the old packtrain days. There, we left the vehicle and took off on foot. We climbed up over a mountain shoulder and down into a beautiful timberline basin just under the cliffs of the Continental Divide, where we set up our little mountain tent. From there we hunted the country up and down, then picked our outfit up and moved on to new ground.

It took us most of a week to comb country that could

easily have been covered in half the time with horses. We ate smoked venison saved from the preceding fall, cooked our meals over a tiny fire, and washed in ice cold streams. The weather was bad, with snow flying on the wind like winter and ice forming on the creeks sufficient to carry our weight. Our climbing boots were wet for days. We saw sheep, will-o'-the-wisps grazing high among stringers of fog and snow, but none with heavy horns. Three times we climbed to over eight thousand feet above sea level. Almost every night we dragged ourselves into camp after a long day of tough climbing in bad footing. But we enjoyed it, for there is a challenge to that kind of hunting like no other. Billy gained experience he could get no other way. I had the satisfaction of knowing that in spite of half a century of trails behind me, I could still ramble through high country when conditions were about as tough as they could get.

It is thus that a man can reacquaint himself with old familiar ground and relive the satisfaction of travelling along the rugged flanks of the shining mountains far from the ant heaps of noise and dirt we humans call civilization.

16

CAMERA HUNTING

There are many ways to get into trouble while pursuing big game with cameras, and sometimes misadventure has a way of sneaking up on one in a most unexpected way.

There was the time I was guiding a professional wildlife photographer, one of the earliest and most successful of his kind. He is retired now, living a long way from the mountains where this adventure occurred, and to spare him possible embarrassment I will leave him unnamed.

He was a big, lean, and powerful man well over six feet tall, good company on the trail, and very keen about what he was doing – namely, putting a film together portraying packtrain life and its association with various kinds of animals. Among other things, he was particularly anxious to get some good close-range sequences of mountain goats in their spectacular surroundings.

Mountain goats are not an easy subject for camera work because of the country they call home, and even though they are not unduly shy or difficult to approach, the very nature of their chosen habitat offers real challenge. Anyone attempting to get within close range of a goat sooner or later almost inevitably finds himself operating his camera with his hip pockets hanging out over a thousand feet or so of eagle thoroughfare, where if a slip occurs, it will not be the fall that hurts so much as the sudden stop at the bottom. It is no kind of country for a faint heart or shaky balance, for it can be exceedingly dangerous.

The danger is graded considerably by the experience and skill of the pursuing climber, but sometimes the best of cragsmen find themselves in a tight spot. When I was much younger and full of the stuff it takes to play with goats on their choice of ground, I was convinced that a man who was a good climber could follow them anywhere they chose to go. But one day I was trailing three of these whiskery mountaineers across a high face, where they led me down a ledge in a fairly steep incline. It took the goats around a bulge of the mountain, and when I followed it was to find myself close pressed from above by an overhang in a spot where the goats had passed with ease. They were fifty yards ahead of me at a place the ledge had been wiped out for a few feet by water and icefalls in a perpendicular chimney. Never hesitating, they blithely leapt the gap and proceeded on their way.

At this point I was beginning to feel that I would be much more comfortable somewhere else, but I was committed to follow for the pack on my back and the nature of the ledge combined with the overhang made going back extremely hazardous. The only way out was to trail the goats. When I came to the gap in the ledge and studied it, I knew very well why goats climb so much easier than a man – they have four feet to land on instead of two and those feet are specially designed to stick.

There was nothing to do but try to mimic their jump, which I did, landing on my hands and feet goat fashion. I skinned myself painfully in several spots but managed to stick to the rock. Then I climbed down out of there, a much wiser man. Now when I see one of the whiskery ones looking down at me from the top of some pinnacle, I am much inclined to say, "It's your mountain, friend, and you are welcome to it."

Falling is not the only risk, for goats often double back directly over the head of the pursuing climber and have the extremely nasty habit of knocking loose rock down. Having trailed and watched them innumerable times, I am tempted to believe they do it sometimes with malice aforethought, or with a kind of grim humour difficult to share. Any way you look at it, being on the bottom end of a rock fall is no joke and can be very final. In any event, wearing a hard hat is good insurance.

But guides and hunters are not normally morbid types or negative thinkers, and on this particular occasion my photographer friend and I were not giving a thought to the possibility of trouble as we stalked two big billies feeding in a shallow dip at the top of some talus fans beneath a precipitous mountain wall about two thousand feet high.

Our stalk took us up through a strip of shintangle into a little ravine. This bid us fairly well to the base of the cliffs, where a bulge of the mountain gave concealment in a traverse towards our quarry. When we came within range, my friend began to shoot film through the gate of his Eastman Special, but he had barely started when an eddy of wind gave us away. The billies instantly elevated their short tails and began to climb up and away across the broken ledges of the face.

I knew that mountain like the palm of my hand and was instantly aware of a possibility, for if the goats went in the direction of their retreat they might be pushed into an impossible place where they could be cornered. Ahead and above them was a chimney with a smooth semicircular wall and an overhang at its top. If they did not cross the chimney down low enough, they would be committed to climbing into a trap. The thing to do was push them, for if goats are pressed and keep looking back, it is possible to haze them into a place where the only way out is back past their pursuer.

I pointed out the possibility to my friend, quickly packed his camera equipment into my rucksack, shouldered the heavy tripod, and led the way up over the steep rock hot on the heels of the goats. My friend came on strong, his eyes shining with excitement, and knowing he had considerable climbing experience, I never gave him a second thought.

It was steep country but the rock was broken and rough enough to give good footing. Our Hungarian hobnails were clattering a merry tune as we scrambled in pursuit. The billies were out of sight, but pressing ahead I came within sight of them just as they were entering the chimney. Both looked back at me and obviously they were worried. Calling to my friend, I hurried, choosing a route carefully but swiftly as the billies dipped from view. Sure enough, when they came into view again, they were climbing into the blind chimney. Again I turned to urge my companion to hurry, but he was nowhere to be seen.

With a feeling of dread, I backtrailed around a steep buttress wondering if he had somehow slipped and gone over the drop-off below. Then I saw him – plastered spread-eagle fashion on the face of a steep place I had just passed at a scrambling run. His complexion was almost pale green and he was hanging on with every fingernail, his knuckles white with the effort. His eyes were tight shut, and it was instantly apparent he was in the frightening throes of vertigo, a kind of nervous sickness brought on by an awareness of height that can put a climber into a paralysing attack of fear. I had seen it happen before, and it was no fun for a guide and much less for the unfortunate victim.

Speaking to him quietly and reassuringly, I first found a place to safely stow my pack and the tripod. Taking a fifty-foot coil of rope out of the pack, I began to help my would-be goat photographer down onto more hospitable ground.

Tying the end of the rope around him with a bowline knot, I passed the rest of the rope around a stubby little tree anchored firmly in the rock, letting its free end hang down past him. Holding it to make sure he could not fall, I tried to talk him into moving but he only groaned and hung on all the harder. So I literally pried him loose and slid him down to a ledge below, letting the rope pay out as we went. He groaned some more and scraped his fingers trying to hang on, but I finally got him down to the limit of the doubled rope in spite of his best efforts to remain immovable. There was no tree for another belay at this point, but I found a projecting nubbin of rock that would do. Testing it carefully to be sure it would not crack loose, I placed my folded glove behind it to make a smooth bearing surface for the rope to slip on, and again slid the photographer down to the next available ledge, scraping all the way. He had me beat by forty pounds and was strong as a bull, which made the whole process somewhat complicated. I was sweating copiously in spite of a bitter cold breeze, when we came to rest a second time.

There another little tree gave me a third belay, and so we proceeded with me scrambling and cajoling. It was a tough, exasperating business, but by one means or another we finally made it to a nice, wide ledge maybe two feet across within a dozen or so feet of the top of the fine talus below. There I had no more belays, which did not matter much, for my friend could fall the rest of the way without doing himself much damage, the shale being pitched at a steep angle and lying deep and loose. So I left off being the solicitous diplomat and told him very shortly to open his goddam eyes and jump. But this he refused to do, still imagining himself halfway between sky and earth.

So I resorted to other tactics. One way to shake someone loose from vertigo is to make him or her so scorching angry that fright is forgotten. On another day I had deliberately done this when a lady climbing companion had frozen up in a tricky place. She had reacted so well, I thought for a moment she was about to pick up the nearest rock and brain me with it. Instead, she took off like a goat and I was hard-pressed to calm her down before she broke her neck. Then she realized why I had been so unpleasant, and we finished the climb good friends.

So without further argument I lit into the photographer, calling him every kind of yellow coward in a profound dissertation well spiced with some smoky, hide-peeling adjectives learned around cow camps over my youthful years. The therapy took effect and before long he was glaring at me in an extremely warlike fashion.

I wound up by telling him, "Look, you long-eared awkward string of misery! Either you climb down off here under your own steam or I'm going to kick you down! And if you think I'm bluffing just try me out!"

By this time he was livid with anger and with a withering look he turned his back and walked off that place as though it was fitted with stairs. A few steps down the shale slope, he looked back to see me coiling my rope and preparing to climb back up the face for his cameras. Realizing what I meant to do, he came back and begged me to leave the whole outfit – worth at least three or four thousand dollars – where it lay. Nobody, he told me, was going to risk his life to get that camera; to hell with it, there were lots more where that came from! I just grinned at him and headed up the mountain. By the time I got back, he was down where we had left our horses.

He was standing with his back to me, leaning against his horse, and did not even glance my way as I untied halter shanks in preparation for returning to camp. Then he turned with a lopsided grin and stuck out his hand in apology.

I told him to forget it, that he was not the first one who had come down with mountain sickness, nor would he be the last. He really had nothing to be ashamed about, for vertigo is a nasty thing and plays no favourites. Nor was I without blame, for I should never have taken him out on that face without some preliminary climbing to condition him. I learned something that day that has enabled me to avoid similar trouble since.

17

FIRST STEPS

DCB 98

Those first steps on the old ranch were a prelude to adventure – not altogether a unique thing, for life is an adventure for all of us. It matters not where we start it, for it is still an adventure. Whether or not we enjoy it depends on some luck, but perhaps more on one's desire to understand and enjoy even the pesky things with which we become inevitably entangled. It is then that the ordinary ceases to be ordinary and the dull takes on a shine, for all things have a story to tell if uncovered and understood.

If someone were to ask me what was the most valuable thing I have inherited from my forebears, I would certainly not list property, but rather an ingrown curiosity about living things and a built-in desire to respect and enjoy the adventure of living. My luck in having an environment in which to fully grasp the fun of being alive made itself manifest early in the game. The everyday happenings at the beginning showed me this before I had walked very far, leaving impressions that still stand paramount.

There was the time I stood on the perimeter of the yard in front of the house, a small figure on the edge of a vast rolling sea of grass, watching in fascination the flickering, ribbon-like gambolling of a weasel. No other animal moves quite like a weasel, for it never walks but always runs, and the running is with a silken poetry of motion – a cadence of muscle and gleaming fur in search of prey.

The weasel was all around me, prying and sniffing into every hole and tuft of grass, paying me not the slightest attention beyond a sharp-eyed stare or two, although it came several times within inches of my bare toes. I did not realize at first that the weasel was hungry and hunting for a meal. All of a sudden it must have run into a mouth-watering scent coming downward from a chicken coop between me and the house, for it paused with uplifted head and then streaked straight for it.

A fat old hen was living there with a clutch of newly hatched chicks, all placid and self-satisfied until hell arrived and the feathers began to fly. I ran to the coop to kneel and stare spellbound through its slatted front as the weasel began to massacre chicks with all the dispatch of a master killer.

My enchantment with this scene of murder and mayhem was suddenly interrupted by the indignant arrival of my mother carrying a broom. With an angry shriek, she up-ended the coop, turned the survivors loose, and in the same motion took a swipe at the weasel. The little animal dodged the blow with neatness and promptly ran down a gopher hole nearby. The vigour of the blow broke the broom handle, but when the weasel stuck its head out of the hole to shriek at Mother in return, she attacked it vigorously with what remained of the handle.

Now her weapon was much less unwieldy and her blows quick and accurate, but the weasel moved like flickering light, dodging every swing. The battle was resolved in a stalemate. In no way ready to give up, Mother gave me the club with instructions to keep the murdering little beast in the hole while she went for a bucket of water out of the rain barrel. Her strategy was to drown the weasel out into the open.

It took a lot of water before the hole filled up, leaving the weasel almost totally immersed except for its head and neck, but the little animal did not make the expected break for the open. It just stood eying us sharply and then opened its mouth to squall in defiance. Mother took a swift chop at him with her club. But as usual the weasel ducked like a flash, and the blow spent itself harmlessly. The animal's head came up again with a battle cry.

My father was out riding for stock that morning, so my mother was more or less left to her own devices for eliminating this raider of chicken coops. There is no telling which way the battle would have gone had not the hired man chosen this moment to unexpectedly appear.

It was his day off, and he was dressed in his Sunday best, complete with white shirt, blue serge suit, and polished boots – all ready for his visit to town. Taking in the situation at a glance, he volunteered his services.

"Just hold on a moment, ma'am," he said. "I'll get the boss's gun."

He went into the house and shortly reappeared, fumbling a fat red cartridge into the breech of the shotgun. Whatever his abilities as a hired man, they did not penetrate very far into the dynamics of ballistics and hydraulics, for without undue preamble, he walked right up to the hole. As Mother stepped quickly to one side taking me with her, he deliberately aimed at the weasel at a range of perhaps three feet and blazed away.

It might be truthfully said that he fired into the hole and the next split second the hole fired at him, for what happens when an ounce and a quarter of closely bunched birdshot goes into a gopher tunnel full of water at that range is most impressive, to say the very least. The hired man was transformed into a blinded, dripping mess of mud and water mixed with fragments of weasel. He stood in shock, pawing at his face. A piece of bloody skin to which was attached the bedraggled tail of the weasel hung over one ear. He was a total wreck from head to foot.

My mother and I stood paralysed, staring at him in wide-eyed astonishment. Then, as he began to partially recover, Mother suddenly covered her mouth with a corner of her apron and ran swiftly for the house. Meanwhile he had opened the gun and ejected the spent shell. I saw it lying in the grass and, curious, picked it up to examine it. It had an acrid smell of freshly burned powder – a somehow attractive odour that I sniffed with enjoyment as the hired man headed morosely for his quarters.

Ever since that day, when I see some uneducated pilgrim carelessly waving a gun around with no regard for himself or the innocent bystanders, I long to arrange for him to shoot at something in a gopher hole full of water. Nothing could possibly leave anyone with a more lasting impression of the destructive power of a loaded gun.

For some reason I sometimes still find myself sniffing absentmindedly at the open end of a fired shell with unexplainable enjoyment along with a vivid memory of the weasel that took shelter in a hole.

18

A Joke on Cap

It made a colourful story that has gone the rounds among old-timers for over seventy years. I heard it from an old cowboy forty years ago. This was frontier humour and entertainment, before people started writing implausible themes for western television shows. To be sure, somebody was usually the "goat," and the measure of a man was at least partly gauged by his ability to laugh at a joke on himself.

There was the time Cap Thomas and a friend joined in a poker game with a couple of strangers at an all-night session at Pincher Station, the station on the railroad about two miles north of the town of Pincher Creek. Because they were two miles from the police detachment, the boys were wearing their six-shooters, weapons usually confined to the open range on the Canadian side of the border, for the Mounted Police forbade wearing guns in town.

The game was going steadily against Cap and his partner. Cap was suspicious that the cards were being stacked, but he gave no hint of his distrust and kept on stubbornly and steadily losing money. Finally, in the small hours of the morning, one of the strangers made a slight slip in his dealing, whereupon the hot-tempered Cap pounced on him with an accusation of cheating. The man reared back in his chair as though reaching for his gun, which was a great mistake, for Cap promptly pulled his big six-shooter and shot the erring card player out of his chair.

The man never moved from where he hit the floor, and blood was running on the boards as Cap backed out the door with his smoking pistol in his hand. Sure that he had killed the man, shocked and scared, and knowing the police would soon be on his trail, Cap stepped up on his horse and burned the wind for his little ranch.

Cap was a young bachelor, slim and handsome – somewhat of a dandy, fond of well-tailored clothes. His boots were handmade. His saddle and horse jewellery ran to fine flower tooling and sterling inlays.

When he reached home shortly before sun-up, he paused only long enough to throw some grub in a sack, roll up a couple of blankets in a light tarp, and catch his top horse out of the pasture. Then he rode west and north to lose himself in the timbered breaks of the Porcupine Hills.

And so began a period in Cap's life when he learned something of the price a man can be forced to pay for freedom. Instead of a carefree and reckless young cowboy, who took his fun where he found it, he was now one of the hunted. At night he brooded and shivered beside a tiny fire built in some remote hole in the hills, where it was unlikely to be seen by anyone but himself. By day he lived on "the dodge," letting no man come close and being continually on the alert for police patrols.

He grew gaunt and hollow-eyed with a dark stubble of whiskers covering his usually clean-shaven face. His fine clothes became dirty and ragged. Only his ivory-handled Colt was kept clean and well oiled, and his horse stayed sleek and fat, for it was early summer and the feed was plentiful and lush.

Cap teetered precariously between giving himself up and going completely bad as he worked his way south to a remote timbered basin near the base of Old Chief Mountain not far from the international border. He was sitting his horse among sonic scrub pines on top of a butte one bright morning when he spotted a rider coming up along a little creek across a chain of open meadows. It was the familiar figure of his friend who had been with him on that fateful night of the shooting at Pincher Station. Unable to resist the opportunity for some talk, and also hoping for some food, Cap rode down to intercept him.

When they met, they just sat their horses for a while saying nothing, and then Cap's friend began to swear softly, fluently, and with great feeling. In language well spiced with adjectives reflecting on Cap's intelligence, his principles, and general ancestry for generations back, Cap was told how for weeks his friend had been searching for him to no avail, and how tired he was of looking after Cap's stock and ranch between sessions of looking. Finally he got around to telling Cap that all his running and hiding had been for naught, for he had not killed the man after all. The bullet had just creased him over an ear and knocked him unconscious. Upon some application of cold water, the man had recovered his senses and disappeared without reporting his wound to the police.

When Cap told me this story sixty years later, he remarked, "The joke was sure on me! But every time I tried to laugh about it for a long time after, my face ached." He opined, as a sort of conclusion, that a man was a damn fool to carry a gun unless somebody was threatening to shoot him.

19

NOTHING LIKE A MULE

A bachelor who lived on a small ranch a few miles from us had a team of small mules he used to pull a light wagon. They were as independent as animals can get and had about as much respect for a wire fence as elk do. Consequently they were well known to everyone in the country, since they regularly took off on a tour of the neighbourhood. They were particularly unpopular with the local housewives, who took a dim view of their sampling of vegetable gardens.

Forty miles farther north, another rancher had a team of huge mules, which he used for many years for all kinds of heavy draft work. Both were becoming old when one contracted a bad fistula and died. A lone mule is not much good to anybody, and the survivor of this team was no exception, for it never ceased looking for its mate. It became a sort of wandering long-eared hermit of the hills, disappearing for months at a time and then reappearing in the most unexpected places.

Many were the stories that went around concerning this mule. I had never seen it, and like a lot of people considered it more or less a sort of myth. Then one hot afternoon I was riding in the dust kicked up by fifty loose horses on the short end of a two-day drive to a base camp in the Oldman River up on the flats where Racehorse Creek joins the North Fork. I was making this drive alone, which kept me busy during the first day, when some of the bunch kept trying to find a way to get back to the home ranch. Fifty horses running free can make things interesting for a lone rider trailing them, but I was well mounted and had not lost one horse.

I was jogging along feeling tired but satisfied at pulling off a tough job. I was on the last fifteen miles of trail, going through the Livingstone Range at the Gap. It was blazing hot and streaks of muddy sweat showed dark on the dusty hides of the horses strung out ahead. Like me they were getting weary and anxious to get to camp. Most of the bunch had been there many times, a jumping-off point for pack trips through the mountains. They were reeling off the miles at a steady trot with the jingling of the Swiss bells of the pack horses accompanying their going.

Over the sound of the bells came a noise like nothing I had ever heard before. It had an eerie, unreal quality about it and seemed to come from nowhere in particular. My saddle horse, a bay gelding of somewhat nervous disposition heard it too, switched up his ears, and swung his head around to look up towards the top of a timbered ridge flanking the trail. Then the sound came again, a sort of awful hoarse scream ending in a coughing roar. It was unlike anything one would expect to hear on a sunny afternoon among the peaceful Alberta foothills. Had it been dark, the sound would have made a man's hair stand straight up, for it had a quality like something on the near slope of a very bad dream.

Then out of a fold in the hillside came the source of it, going at a light gallop – a monstrous bony old mule with a head like a wheelbarrow and a ridiculous string of a tail flowing in the breeze behind him. He had spotted my horse herd going up the valley and was bent on coming down off the hills for a visit, maybe hoping he would find his long-lost mate running with them. About every fourth jump he opened his great mouth and let out the most god-awful bray imaginable. He would have won no prizes in any kind of music festival.

By this time my saddle horse was fixing to throw a fit, and before I realized what was happening, he let out a sharp snort and bolted straight ahead through the bunch. That was all it took to spook my horses, and in two bounds every one of them was in full stampede. Rocks as big as eggs and chunks of sod were flying past me as those horses humped up and dug for toeholds to get out of there. My horse was fast, and before we had gone a quarter mile we were up with the leaders, burning a hole in the wind. The old mule veered in a swing along the hill to cut us off, but the horses did not give him much chance. He was braying steadily, trying to talk us all into stopping for a pow-wow, but none of the bunch understood his language. Those horses were never more inspired to run. They just left him as though he was tied – bawling and braying in their dust. When the procession slowed a bit, a mile or so up the valley, I eased back along one flank of the bunch to see if any were missing. They were all with me, but now their hides shone with sweat and their nostrils flared wide in their reach for more air. But the weariness was forgotten. We came into camp in record time, stepping lively. I had learned that range horses have a tendency not to recognize their relations on occasion – especially when they have never seen them before.

20

WILD VISITORS

DON BRESTLER 98

My house is on top of a hill within a mile and a half of the foot of the Rockies, which make a half-circle swing in front of my door that ends with the impressive bulk of Chief Mountain, a place the Blackfoot Indians consider to have great spiritual power. I am looking out at country protected by the Waterton-Glacier International

Peace Park, unique in the fact that it is the first international peace park in the entire world. Our ranch is wild
land adjoining the park, and we take great care to keep it
that way for wilderness country is becoming rare in Alberta,
where development for dollars has become a religion paramount to all others and to hell with the consequences. It is
virtually a part of the park, where wildlife is treated with
respect and care, and it is amazing how quickly birds and
animals come to recognize and enjoy it. There are grizzly,
black bear, moose, elk, mule and whitetail deer, as well as
coyotes, occasional wolves, cougars, lynx, beaver, and various other kinds of small animals, as well as a wide variety of
birds. The only competition they encounter through
human intrusion is cows, for we rent summer grazing. We
take our quota of wild meat in the fall, with the least possible disturbance.

Sharing the land with wildlife under circumstances in
which there is a minimum of stress and conflict between us
makes for some interesting observations that can be enjoyed
best when the ecosystem is left to take its natural form.
There is always change, and adjustments to change. A rise
in the deer population is generally followed by more pressure on them by cougars and coyotes. When conditions are
right for an explosion in the mouse population, hawks and
owls appear like magic to share the feast. Watching the various species is a never-ending source of interest and enjoyment. Sometimes the interaction that takes place between
the species leaves us wondering.

One March afternoon two years ago, my son Charlie and
I shared an experience that left us both guessing. It was a
mild day and we were in the house when we became aware
of the smell of a skunk. When we heard the squeal of a
skunk near the back door, we went to the kitchen window
just in time to see the animal run across the plank deck
closely pursued by a badger, which grabbed the skunk by

the neck and shook it vigorously, then turned it loose again. A badger is a tough fighter quite capable of killing a skunk with dispatch, but a skunk is a very smelly animal when aroused and this one was no exception. Even with all the doors and windows closed, the smell was very unpleasant inside the house. The badger must have been close to blind, for the skunk had sprayed him at close range several times and the essence is extremely caustic to the eyes of any animal. The skunk kept trying to get away, and the chase went on across the deep snow in the yard until it got to my car, whereupon it dived under it with the badger still in pursuit. I had no trouble imagining what was happening to my car at this point, but my fears proved to be unfounded for the skunk was running out of ammunition. The badger came back out from under the car, as did the skunk which ran down the road with the badger still in pursuit. Later, I followed their tracks for about half a mile and saw several places where the badger had grabbed the skunk, shook it, and turned it loose. We later saw both animals at different times in different places, so the story has a happy ending, even if why it happened is a mystery.

But I have wondered. Both animals belong to the weasel family along with wolverines, mink, otters and others, which breed in March. They all have one thing in common – scent glands of varying degrees of potency, firepower, and capacity, but the females may have some element of odour in common when they are coming into estrus, which could confuse an inexperienced young male badger. However, it is something not likely to be researched by even the most dedicated student of nature, for obvious reasons.

Moose, in spite of their size, can be very shy and difficult animals to approach. They can move through the heaviest forest growth with hardly a sound and they likely enjoy the most sensitive ears in all the North American wilds. So I was somewhat amazed one winter morning when I looked out of the kitchen window to see a two-year-old bull moose lying in the snow contentedly chewing his cud about fifty feet from the back door. He stood up finally and took a step, and it was plain to see that he was lame for his front foot was crumpled with the toes pointed back and the sole up. When he walked, he was lame; when he broke into a trot, he travelled in a normal fashion.

Towards spring he didn't show up for over a month. The grass was showing green when I saw him again one evening as he stepped out of the trees about fifty yards from the back door. I had a good chance to observe him and noticed he was standing with his foot crumpled up as usual. He stood for several minutes without moving and then suddenly began to play, dancing around on the lawn in a most lighthearted and astonishing fashion for an animal of his size, and I noted with interest that he held his right foot in normal fashion and stepped without limping while he was playing, but when he stopped and stood still, or walked, his foot crumpled and he limped. I can only guess that he had been tangled in a barbed wire fence as a small calf and was hurt but recovered. He doesn't show himself around the yard as often as he once did. He is a full-grown bull moose now, but it is easy to recognize his tracks for he still stands and walks with his right front foot inverted.

I have lived and worked in cougar country most of my life, but have had the chance to observe these big cats only four times on the ground. They prefer to hunt in the dark, are very shy, and are masters of camouflage, so I have often wondered if there haven't been times when I have been in plain sight of one and failed to see it. Though cougars tend to be scattered, even where they are not hunted, it is not uncommon for us to see their tracks. Indeed we have found their kills on several occasions, where one has taken a deer, an elk, or a moose.

Of all the big cats of the world, biologists generally agree that the cougar is the most efficient with a very high degree of skill, strength, and agility that is required for the killing of an animal generally much bigger and stronger than themselves. One winter day I was travelling on snowshoes when I came to a place where a female cougar with a pair of half-grown kittens trailing her had stalked and killed a cow elk bedded down in two feet of snow on a steep slope. When the mother cat made her initial jump on the elk, still in its bed, it plunged away with the cat on its back down the slope with such force that it broke off a four-foot diameter green aspen about a foot above snow level. It managed to make one more jump before it died of a broken neck. Every move that both animals made in that stalk and fight was plainly written in the snow. It was impressive.

Though there are records of cougar attacks on humans, they are very rare, so when we find cougar tracks on the ranch, we are never concerned for our safety. These big cats do a lot of travelling over a wide range and sometimes tend to visit certain places every time they make their rounds. One big male leaves his tracks in my yard when he makes his rounds and likes to cross my veranda. More than once I have got up in the morning to see the fresh pug marks of this special visitor on a fresh skiff of snow outside my door, and I am grateful for the amicable sharing of our territory, for the tracks indicate a powerful animal perhaps eight feet long from tip to tip and weighing close to one hundred and eighty pounds.

Two hundred years ago the Indian tribesmen of the Great Plains shared the peak of the life pyramid with the grizzly, and both species shared the food provided by nature in the forms of buffalo, berries, and various other vegetable growth. With millions upon millions of buffalo following their migration routes across the many rivers, there were casualties – sometimes heavy losses of life when herds got caught in the ice of spring breakups. At such times the bears feasted on carrion. At other times, they ate leftovers from the kills made by the Indians. There was little conflict between Indians and bears. But when the Europeans showed up with their muzzle-loading rifles, things changed. It was not long before the buffalo and bears were gone from the plains. Surviving grizzlies lived in the mountains of the west and it was there that I grew up sharing the Rocky Mountains of southwest Alberta with them.

Following the trails of a trapper, hunter, and professional big game guide, I was keenly aware of the big bears, but as time went on my feeling towards them changed. When one of my clients shot one, I could not help a feeling of sadness and regret. To be a successful guide, one must know a great deal about the animals being stalked but the more I learned, the less I wanted to be involved in killing them. So, when I got the chance to guide professional photographers and cinematographers, it was a welcome change as well as a greater challenge – as well as the fact that it offered a chance to learn about cameras from experts. From there it was only another step to producing my own films, and this eventually led to my making the first film featuring grizzlies ever made – a three-year research and filming program working in the best grizzly country of southeastern British Columbia, Yukon Territory, and Alaska.

The more I observed the big bears, the more I suspected that we had been overlooking a very important facet of their general character. To be sure, one must never forget that there is no fixed pattern in the character of bears, for, like people, they vary among individuals and I was convinced that most of them were inclined to be friendly.

We proceeded with caution and were rewarded with film sequences and photographs proving that we were on the right trail. Whatever the reason, the bears that travel through our ranch seem to know that they are on friendly ground.

In 1995 there was a very heavy crop of saskatoon berries with some clumps of bushes bending over with the weight of the fruit. Having stuffed themselves for weeks on this rich bonanza of food, the bears were going into den about as fat as they ever get and thoroughly contented. I have reason to remember this particular year.

About sundown one evening in late September, I heard a slight noise outside that I couldn't identify, and I went out onto the veranda for a look around. My car was parked on the driveway about even with the left end of the veranda. Suddenly a grizzly appeared from behind it and strolled in front of me about fifteen feet away without giving me so much as a glance. I was surprised, but I never moved a muscle as the bear came to a stop, turned her head, and looked me squarely in the face. There was another slight noise and to my complete amazement, two more grizzlies walked into view from behind a spruce and joined her on the driveway. They were her cubs almost full grown and, like her, were a deep bronze colour with gold-tipped guard hairs on their shining coats. They milled around quite casually as though they had known me all their lives – no threats or any sign of concern at my proximity. When I finally quietly told them that it was time they left, they stepped over the edge of the driveway and headed down the open slope towards the aspen forest and disappeared.

Right now I expect they are somewhere in the mountains back of the ranch preparing to go into den for the winter. They gave me a beautiful and unforgettable experience. I can only hope their friendly attitude and trust does not get them into trouble with my neighbours in the future.

21

GREEN ENGLISHMAN

My friend Butcher was the son of a British ship-owner who had quarrelled bitterly with his father over his desire to go to sea and become a merchant marine captain. As sometimes happens, the disagreement went past the point of no return, and Butcher left the home fires to come to Canada, where he eventually came to own a sizeable ranch just above our place on Drywood Creek. He was a fairly successful cattleman, albeit a bit eccentric on occasion. He was very impulsive and given to either effervescing in good spirits or wallowing in despair and self-pity. He had a sharp wit and a confessed antipathy towards women, which was really only a front to cover his shyness. He had a tremendous appreciation for good literature and music, and in the days preceding radio he had the finest gramophone money could buy and a collection of classical records numbering in the hundreds. He also owned a very fine library, including the complete works of such authors as Thackeray, Kipling, and Dickens in handsome calfskin-bound editions. Among the furnishings of his unique ranch house was the only player piano of the country, along with a considerable collection of music rolls for it. On occasion, although he could not read a note of music, he would sit down at this instrument and improvise by ear. At the Christmas concerts held at the local schoolhouse – a traditional entertainment enjoyed by all for more than a generation – he could be prevailed upon to play for the dance that inevitably followed the stage plays and recitations presented by the schoolchildren. With the help of a neighbour who played the fiddle and another who played a guitar, he would tease some lively music out of the ancient organ that would set the feet of the dancers going.

Butcher was a man of many parts, with a crusty exterior that camouflaged a heart of gold. His generosity was sometimes almost an embarrassment to his neighbours. If he entered into something of interest to him, it was in a whole-hearted fashion. There was no middle of the road for Butcher even if he did proclaim himself to be of a conservative nature.

Once or twice a year Butcher invited all his friends from near and far to a grand whist party held at his ranch house. This was something more than just a card party, for it provided him with a way to hold up his end in the social scheme of things. Because he was a dry-humoured, entertaining man with a great deal of charm when he chose to exercise it, he was a popular guest at the homes of the various ranchers in the country. And in many ways he was a brilliant host, who could mix a piano concerto, "improvised on the instant," with a positive genius for telling an amusing story. No one who ever attended one of these affairs went home with the feeling of having wasted an evening.

Shortly before Christmas it was his habit to take a team and sleigh to town. When I was a boy, he sometimes hired me to drive for him and accompany him everywhere, as he went up one side of the street and down the other, greeting all the storekeepers and neighbours encountered with cheerful compliments of the season and paying all his outstanding bills. On one particular occasion he met a lady, a friend's wife, who trilled happily at the sight of him.

"Oh, I'm so glad to see you, sir," she said with a bright smile. "We so much enjoyed your party last fall, and I meant to write you and thank you, but somehow never got around to it. I hope you will accept a turkey for a Christmas present."

Butcher graciously accepted and we all went on to the livery stable to transfer the turkey from their sleigh to ours. It proved to be a large one, all gaily wrapped with coloured paper and ribbons. Butcher was in a particularly fine humour as the team trotted briskly for home under the bright winter sun.

Every Christmas he put on a noonday dinner party for all his bachelor friends preceded by a gala Christmas Eve party, which was conducted while Butcher prepared for the big feed. His Christmas stag party menu was more or less fixed, for while Butcher was a fair kind of cook, he was not a particularly versatile one. The meal generally included roast turkey, cranberry sauce, mashed potatoes, canned tomatoes, lots of gravy, and finally, large portions of plum pudding prepared weeks before and kept frozen. There were very few variations.

On this occasion the gift turkey was popped into the oven early Christmas morning and by noon it was done to a rich golden turn. It held the place of honour on a huge platter at the head of the table. Lionel Brook, a perennial guest at the Christmas party, upon being requested to do the honours of carving, took his place and began to wield the carving knife. Slabs of well-done meat fell away from the keen edge of the blade, as plate after plate was passed to Butcher at the opposite end of the board to receive its portions of trimmings.

Finally only Butcher was left to be served. When he received his plate, he looked at it with a critical eye and said shortly, "Brook, I want some stuffing, if you please."

So the plate went back to Brook, who looked long and hard at Butcher and said, "Very well, Butch, old top, you shall have some stuffing!"

Whereupon he took the fork and gouged into the carcass of the turkey to come forth with a great load of gizzard and original plumbing natural to the bird, and set it in the middle of his host's plate.

For a few seconds there was silence as everyone at the table gazed at Butcher's "stuffing" with disbelief. Then came a great roar of laughter. They were a rough crew with hearts of gold and were not about to let such a small thing upset their appetites. Besides, there is nothing like a few tots of Christmas cheer to sharpen one's appreciation of a good joke.

Without a word, Butcher quietly removed the plate, got another, and loaded it. As he fell to with his guests to eat heartily, his only comment was, "Nobody but a woman would give you a Christmas turkey that had not been dressed!"

Actually, long habit and the previous evening's liquid refreshments had caught up to him, for ordinarily he bought a turkey at the butcher shop all drawn and ready to stuff. Because he had been unwrapping an oven-ready turkey for years, he had assumed this was already prepared for cooking. And no doubt he had not looked very closely through the alcoholic haze.

22

MEETING THE JUDGE

The first artificial trout fly I ever used was a snelled Royal Coachman wet fly, bought at the local hardware store more because it was very pretty than because I thought it could take trout. But the trout of my favourite beaver pond went hog wild over it, chewing it to rags in no time, but not before I had taken plenty of the biggest ones for a feed for the whole family. From then on I was a confirmed fly fisherman, although my steel rod was anything

DON BRESTLER 98

but delicate and my money supply did not include enough for a stock of store-bought flies. To solve this deficiency, for my first homemade fly, I pulled some feathers out of an outraged Plymouth Rock rooster and proceeded to tie something out of red wool, Christmas tree tinsel, and ordinary sewing thread. It was born looking like nothing ever seriously contemplated by a purist and made a splash like a drowning chicken. But, amazingly enough, it caught trout. As a matter of fact, the first time I used it, my heart missed a beat when a great Dolly Varden struck it hard, no doubt mistaking it for a small bird that had fallen into the creek. The big fish smashed into it in clear water within two feet of my toes as I stood on a low undercut bank rimming a deep pool, and I came within a whisker of falling in over my head. Thus a fly fisherman was born.

The first really good fly tackle I ever saw belonged to a circuit court judge, who spent his summer holiday for years camped by the creeks on our ranch or the adjoining one belonging to Butcher. The Judge, as everyone called him, was a Scotsman by descent, with a great love of camping alone in the midst of the wilds and with a taste for whisky. My first acquaintance with him got off to a very poor start, although my intentions were good and I very likely saved his life in the process, even if it was crudely done.

During July and August the big Dolly Vardens came up the mountain creeks from the rivers; their September spawning grounds were along the bars and riffles near the headwaters. Hunting and catching these beautifully coloured big fish was a never-ending source of excitement, and they were wonderful eating besides. So every evening when I rode down into the valley to bring in the milk cows, I went along the banks of the creek looking down into the pools to spot these fish as they lay on the bottom. The Dolly Varden, like its very near relative, the eastern brook trout, has a distinctive and sharply contrasting border of ivory-white along the leading edges of its pectoral and ventral fins, a colour that often gives it away to sharp eyes even when it is hidden by logs or overhanging ledges. If I located one or two of the big fish, I came back early the next morning properly armed for their capture.

One particular evening I came to a big pool at the forks, and as I rode up on a gravel bar dividing the creeks at their junction, a surprising sight confronted me. There in the middle of a fast riffle dropping into the pool sat a somewhat portly gentleman in long waders. The waders were awash, for the creek was running cheerfully over the top of them at the back, and the man was in grave danger of being swept down into deep water, where he would doubtless sink like a stone. It was the Judge.

For a moment or two I just sat there on my horse in astonishment, not fully aware that he was in real trouble. But when he turned to look at me, his expression gave away his fear, and it became instantly obvious that he was pinned down by the weight of water, virtually unable to move.

I was only a kid weighing perhaps ninety pounds, while the Judge in his present predicament with his waders full of water, likely weighed two hundred and fifty. To attempt to drag him out, as one would normally do, was just asking for trouble. Had I been afoot, the problem would have been near insurmountable, but I was astride a wiry little cow horse with a great love of snapping things on the end of a rope. Just as naturally as one would reach for his hat upon entering someone else's house, my hand dropped to the coiled lariat hanging on its strap on the fork of my saddle. Before the Judge was aware of my intent, the mare came splashing out towards him and a loop sailed out to drop over him and be jerked up snug around his arms and chest. In the same motion I dallied the rope around the saddle horn, and then with a great deal more enthusiasm than diplomacy my mount spun on her heels to head for dry ground. The Judge came sliding out of the creek backward, somehow managing to hold his rod out of harm's way, and when I checked my horse he came to a stop, head down in a hollow on the gravel bar. He was instantly inundated by a rushing flood issuing from his waders. He came up on his feet muttering thick Scottish words of import not found in courts or churches as he shook off the rope. My horse took one horrified look at him and bolted, which was probably just as well, for at that moment I doubt very much if the Judge was entirely cognizant of my good intentions.

The Judge's fine split-cane English fly rod had survived the action unscathed, but a few days later it met an incongruous end.

My friend Butcher, in a burst of enthusiastic extravagance that summer, had purchased a brand-new, magnificently appointed McLaughlin-Buick sedan – a grand car with an arrogant profile to its general outline and a powerful engine under its long bonnet. It was a favourite model of rum runners during prohibition, a famed "Whisky Six," a fast, rugged machine that would stand up to use on the sketchy roads of the times. It had one idiosyncrasy of design – the reverse-gear position was that of low gear in most other cars, so new owners who had learned to drive ordinary cars sometimes found themselves going backward instead of forward as expected.

Naturally Butcher was delighted with this new toy and drove it into our yard to show it off. Only my mother and I were at home, but we were a satisfactorily appreciative audience as he explained and pointed out all the finer points of his new car.

Finally Butcher turned to me. "Come along and open the gates for me. We'll go visit the Judge."

So I sat on the big leather-upholstered front seat beside him and away we went down a twisting wagon trail into the valley where the Judge had his tent pitched. The Judge was warm in his welcome and very interested in Butcher's new car. He uncorked a full bottle of whisky to celebrate the occasion as he and Butcher exchanged the latest accounts of happenings in the country, well laced with humorous comments. Being too young, I was not invited to join them in a drink, but I sat enthralled as they laughed and chuckled at various stories. As the talk proceeded, the bottle was passed freely back and forth, its portion being slightly diluted with creek water in large glasses. By the time Butcher was ready to leave for home, he was feeling no pain.

He shook the Judge's hand with decorum and settled himself with immense dignity behind the steering wheel of his car. The door banged shut as the starter whirred and the engine caught in a throaty purring of power that spoke of many horses waiting to be turned loose. Butcher threw the shift lever out of neutral into gear and let up on the clutch pedal, whereupon we began to go backward.

The Judge had been standing by the car as this happened, and he came trotting along beside the open window to pronounce with a certain judicial firmness of tone, "But Mr. Butcher, you are going backward!"

"Nonsense, Judge," Butcher replied, "I am in low gear."

About the time the Judge opened his mouth for some further comment on Butcher's mechanical misconceptions and direction, there was a vast clatter of various things, a ripping of canvas, and some lurching as the car went over a six-foot bank to land with a great crash in the creek. The engine stalled and Butcher opened the door to get out, but he changed his mind when he saw cold water lapping the floorboards of his vehicle. Somewhat sobered but still firmly in command of things in general, he started the motor again and drove straight down the bed of the stream to a low place in the bank where the trail crossed. There he swung the car back up on the beach and returned to what was left of the Judge's snug camp.

Together he and the Judge stood solemnly surveying the wreckage. The tent was flat and torn, the sheet-iron sheep herder's stove looked as though a very large elephant had stepped on it, and the rustic table and bench the Judge had so carefully constructed were all kindling wood. Sorrowfully, the Judge reached in among the rags of his recently nearly pitched tent and picked up the fragments of what had been a beautiful, very expensive fly rod. But the crowning touch to the gloom was the sight of an almost full case of fine Scotch whisky smashed as flat as a pancake with only a rich aroma left to remind them of its sweet potency.

With a typical rebound of good spirits, Butcher took the Judge's arm and said, "I'm dashed sorry, old man. Rotten luck, what?" And then he added with a Shakespearean flourish, "Come, we must not stand here mourning. Let us go repair the damage and celebrate in royal fashion a friendship welded even stronger by the whims of fate!"

We all got into the car and drove to my house, where I got out to watch them go on towards town in a swirling cloud of dust. The "repairing and celebration" lasted for three days, and their trail took them about a hundred and eighty miles north to Calgary. There Butcher bought the Judge an even better English fly rod, a new tent, and complete camp equipment of the very best quality, all of which was brought back and put into use at the site of the wreck.

One evening I rode past the Judge's camp on my way to get the cows. All traces of the wreckage had been removed and the place was again neat as a pin. The Judge invited me to get down and come into the tent. As he showed me the various items of his new equipment with obvious enjoyment, he was warm and friendly.

Finally he turned and drew himself up as though making some kind of dissertation in court, and his words poured out in a rich Scottish accent that still comes back to me forty-odd years later with clarity and poignancy.

"My boy," he said, "apart from the fact that I give you my belated thanks for possibly saving my life, albeit in a somewhat unusual and unexpected fashion, I welcome you as a friend. Let's you and I remember that clouds of adversity most generally melt into sunshine, given a bit of time, and that which may seem like disaster may well be the source of better things." And having got that statement of profound wisdom off his chest, he cleared his throat with a great harrumph, grinned like a boy at me, and invited me to share his supper.

Many times after that we met by the streams, and the Judge introduced me to the art of fly fishing for trout. His was the first real fly rod I ever held in my hand, and under his direction I learned how to let the smooth silk of a fine braided fly line go shooting on its own weight through the guides, so the fly came down lightly on the water with all the guile necessary for enticing the most wary fish. Thus he opened a door revealing something of worth and enjoyment in living – a door still open, which has led me to much adventure and exploration.

23

BUTTS LAKE

DON BRESTLER '98

The North Fork of the Flathead River heads in Canada just over the ridge south of Fernie, British Columbia. It was once a heavily forested area, but in 1928 a forest fire burned most of the timber, and in 1935 some of it burned again. I travelled through part of it in 1946, and it was a very wild country, hard to cross with horses because of the tangle of dead logs that covered most of it – big logs that could not be chopped out of the way with an axe or anything but a heavy power saw. There were miles of it where even the moose and elk could not travel.

In the summer of 1952 I got a contract to take a party of geologists through the valley, which involved a lot of hard labour for me and my crew of three and my horses. During the course of events, we were camped on an island where the river divided and ran around a lovely piece of the valley where the timber had not burned. We were only a few minutes' ride from Butts Creek, named after a man who had a small ranch nearby in the time prior to the big forest fires. He had maintained a sort of stopping place for travellers making their way up and down the valley across the international border, smugglers and horse thieves interested in hiding their tracks.

An old trapper who had lived in the valley for many years told me some of the history of the place and among other things mentioned Butts Lake, which was located on the head of the creek. He said it was a great place to fish for trout.

So one Sunday, I saddled a horse and headed that way. The old forestry trail that had been recently cleared of dead logs took me to what was left of Butts cabin. There I tied my horse in a shady place and headed up the creek on foot. It was rough mountain country and I don't remember ever touching to the ground on the way up to the small basin that held the lake. The easiest way to go was to walk the big dead logs that lay one on top of the other, feet deep in places.

The lake was small, very clear and most unusual in the fact that its bottom was white – a kind of marl. When I saw how shallow the water was, I was doubtful there were any fish in the place, but then I saw a good trout rise on the edge of what turned out to be a floating island, a hundred feet across on the far end. Some tentative exploration revealed that the lake was fed by a big spring gushing from the side of the mountain a hundred or so yards above the shore. Because the spring water was warm enough to prevent ice freezing over it, the fish did not smother for lack of oxygen in winter. I found a crude raft somebody had made tethered to a willow on shore and a long slim pole and set out to push the cumbersome, water-logged thing up the lake.

It was one of those times that one finds the joy of being alive. This was purely wild country, and wild country has always had a most stimulating effect on me. Fishing and hunting have been a major part of my life, though it is one and the same thing. Fishing is hunting; the only thing different is the weapon.

Instead of a gun, one carries a fishing rod, and my favourite is the fly rod. A fly rod is a truly beautiful instrument, agile, graceful and incredibly powerful for its weight. I have used a rod weighing only two and a half ounces to take a trout weighing ten pounds. It delivers a fly with the delicacy of thistledown landing on the water.

Because of the white bottom, it was possible to see fish a long way off. I poled the raft to a spit where the spring feeding the place spilled over the top of a beaver dam into the lake. The beaver had dug a ditch there and it was well marked by black leaf mould that had washed off the slope above.

A shadow moved out in deep water close to the floating island, and I watched as an enormous bull trout cruised up the ditch leaving a definite wake. Where the spring poured in, the fish turned and in a kind of majestic fashion went back to deep water at the same speed. My hands were shaking a bit as I tied a heavy leader on my line. I had a tiny Colorado spinner in my fly box with a polished copper blade. With more optimism than good sense, I tied this to the leader and cast it out to the ditch where it promptly sank to the bottom. Then I waited and watched.

A good hunter knows how to wait. His patience is assuaged by the ability to enjoy the waiting. Watch a blue heron fishing and you will see the art of patience and motionlessness being exercised to a perfection very difficult to emulate. Standing on two feet or only one, a blue heron sometimes will not move for an hour. For me, being completely quiet is not so demanding but it is never boring. Something is almost always going on. Birds call and flutter in the bushes; animals show up either swimming or travelling along the shore; insects come and go. Bull trout are predators that feed on other fish for the most part, so I was not watching insects with much attention. The drone of an aircraft came to my ears, and I saw a Beaver come over the mountains to fly down the creek towards a camp where a forestry crew was repairing a cabin. When the plane reached camp, a parachute blossomed under it as someone launched a package of supplies to float down to the ground.

Again out towards the island and the edge of deep water, the big fish showed up following the same route as before. It came into the channel and cruised towards me. When it was a few feet from my spinner, I picked it up and set it in motion by lifting the rod tip. The bull trout showed no excitement. It just swam up to the little lure, opened its mouth, and engulfed it. When I lifted the rod to set the hook, the fish showed no surprise. It just turned around and shot back towards deep water and the island. My reel screamed and howled, the rod bent almost double, and I had the feeling of being fastened to something completely beyond control. My line was rapidly running out, so I grabbed the reel to stop it and pointed the rod at the fish to break the leader. When the line went slack, I reeled it in to find the little lure still fastened to it, but the hook was straightened.

The raft had been drifting with the breeze towards the island, when I heard the drone of the plane coming back. Suddenly the engine died, and the plane sloped down straight at me. Suddenly that lake became very small and my raft absolutely huge. It was obvious to me that the plane and the raft were not going to fit that place together. I was poling furiously towards shore when the plane's engine came back to life and it flew over me, wagging its wings. The pilot was enjoying his little joke.

24

WAPITI LAND

DON BRESTLER 98

It was mid-morning on a fine July day when a friend and I rode up onto a ridge top overlooking a timberline basin in the heart of the Rockies. In front and below us, the creek draining the place was shrouded in green timber and bent in a curve under a solid unbroken wall of limestone two thousand feet high and a mile long, a part of the Continental Divide stretching away, peak after peak, until it faded into the haze of the distance.

Although not an animal was in sight, we knew there were elk here. The trails were full of fresh tracks, and every meadow we had ridden across had flattened-out places among the grass and flowers where the animals had bedded down between feeds. We had seen no signs of other humans for days, which meant the elk were undisturbed in the kind of country they always choose for summer range – high, wild, and quiet with an abundance of good grass and cold water.

We were hunting but not with steaks in mind, for my friend cradled a motion picture camera in the crook of his arm and was tasting his first excitement of filming animals in some of the finest big-game country left in the world. We rested our horses after the long, stiff climb, sitting our saddles in a screening clump of timberline pines as we played our glasses across the reaches of the basin. The trees were all bent and twisted from a lifetime of fighting wind and heavy snows. Down slope, three hundred yards away, the water of a little lake shone through the trees. Beside it a saddle-brown spot showing on the edge of a little green meadow suddenly disappeared from the field of my binoculars. I knew it was an elk.

I slipped out of the saddle and motioned for Frank to follow, and we left our horses ground-hitched as we eased down towards the lake.

This is the ultimate kind of hunting – stalking for the sake of stalking, pitting one's wits against the razor-sharp senses of animals keeping themselves alive by their noses, ears, eyes, and intelligence. When a man can slip in close to a herd in their choice of terrain without alarming them, he knows he is a hunter second to none, and he is aware of it without having to shed a drop of their blood. He can be as greedy as his skill allows without a qualm of conscience or any fear of bag limits or regulations, limited only by the quality of his patience and leg muscles. It is a sport loaded with excitement; anything can happen and sometimes does, usually without a moment's warning.

This was to be one of those times, for when we reached a spot in the timber perhaps a hundred yards from the lake, we found the place alive with elk. There were so many that we were instantly pinned down. To move another foot would certainly give us away. It was tantalizing because our position was impossible for photography. To make matters worse, two cows sprang out of cover into the lake. They leaped and spun in play, throwing showers of spray high over their backs. Between the intervening trees we could see just enough to know what we were missing. We were tempted to try to move to a better position, but we knew that if we did so the reason for moving would probably be gone. Finally we attempted it anyway and had taken barely three steps when a bull stepped out of a thicket thirty yards away. He looked squarely at us, every line of him triggered for instant flight. We froze, but it was too late. The next instant the timber began to crack as the herd went stampeding away, and we were suddenly aware of being very much alone.

"Now you see it, now you don't," I murmured ruefully. "I knew better but couldn't stay put."

"I was wishing I could reach out and pull some trees out of the way," Frank said, and then added wistfully, "Do you think we'll ever see anything like that again?"

One can never tell what is around the next bend of the trail or hidden by the next ridge. Only a couple of times through the years had I seen elk playing in water, but that did not say we would not see the same thing again in the next few days. It is the luck of the game that makes playing it doubly fascinating. About all I could promise was that we would see more elk – plenty of them – before this trip was over.

Three days later we were riding through a stretch of old glacial moraine under the face of a high peak farther along the range, in a place where emerald-green meadows spangled with alpine flowers lay trapped among the folds of the mountain. My horse put his head over a rise of ground, just where a game trail threaded its way between two piles of lichen-painted boulders, and suddenly stopped with his ears up and pointing at something in a hollow beyond. There, lying dead to the world in the warm sun, were a dozen cow elk with their calves. I eased my horse back and stepped down. A moment later Frank and I sneaked up behind a rock with the cameras ready. He ran his camera dry, reloaded, and was all set to shoot again when I stopped him, for this was enough of a record of what amounted to inanimate elk pie. Taking off my hat, I stood up, waved it, and whistled. One old cow sleepily raised her head. We could see her eyes widening in surprise as she came to her feet. A moment later they were all on the run out of there and over a hogback ridge beyond. Frank was about to go after them, but I stopped him.

"Let's lunch here," I suggested. "Give them a chance to settle down, and then I think I might show you something new. I have a hunch there's a big bunch somewhere close and maybe these have joined them."

It was one of those times when a guide can draw on his previous experience to call a shot before it is made. As it turned out, we were not disappointed.

An hour later we rode over a low ridge at the foot of a pass and reined in to overlook a great sweep of alpine meadow. The whole place was swarming with elk – bulls, cows, and calves – more than a hundred head of them. Against the striking mountain backdrop, it was a picture to remember, and we took full advantage of it.

First we shot them while they were still unaware of our presence, and then we got their reaction as they realized we were in the vicinity. The elk were wary, and I expected them to run over the pass, but instead they suddenly milled in a great running circle. It was a magnificent sight, like something from the days when the only human spectators would have been wearing paint and feathers. To add to the beauty and action, a small bunch of bighorn rams came flying down off the mountain to mingle with the elk, as though the excitement were more than they could stand without participating in it.

We shot film and more film and then some more until we were finally left standing looking at an empty place in the scenery, wondering if we had been dreaming.

So it goes when you fraternize with elk, the second largest and by far the most dramatic of the deer of the world.

When is an elk not an elk? This question can perhaps best be answered by saying when it is a wapiti, for although the Pilgrim fathers mistakenly called them elk after the European moose, their original Indian name is the correct one. But elk we still call them, and elk they will probably remain to most of us.

To those who have always known elk and watched them through the seasons from calving time through the bitter cold days of winter, they will always be symbolic of the high country of western North America. They are big, handsome animals, classically proportioned, proud, intelligent, and very enterprising when it comes to finding the best feed available. To those who have never seen deer bigger than whitetails, elk are indelibly impressive, especially in the fall, when the bulls, their antlers polished, fill the valleys with their bugling as they contest for the females.

Although I have seen thousands of them in about every condition possible, the sound of a big herdmaster bull bugling his challenge during the mating moon of September sends a thrill along my spine. My memory is still sharp with the dramatic picture of a scene witnessed one evening in early September years ago in a wild mountain valley.

It had been raining hard all day, a straight-down heavy rain that soaked everything and kept us in our tents close to the warmth of the sheet-iron stoves. When the rain quit an hour before sunset, I went alone for a walk up the river. A mile above camp, the trail took me to the edge of a meadow flanking a gravel bar. On either side, along the lower slopes of the mountains, big timber bordered the meadow. The weather had turned colder, and the clouds were breaking into lazy stringers of mist. High overhead, through a rift in the haze, the spire of a peak showed, all covered with new snow shining in the sun. It was a classic wilderness scene, and very quiet except for the gentle murmur of the river.

Then came a sound as wild as the picture before me – the challenging call of a bull elk echoing like organ notes off the slopes of a deep, twisted ravine running steeply down into the valley from the north, through parks of spruce and larch. A flicker of movement showed through the big timber, in a grove of western larches just turned to autumn gold, and my binoculars revealed a herd of twenty-odd cows and calves following a game trail down off the mountain. As I watched, another bull sounded off to one side. He was immediately answered by the first, a magnificent bull that came trotting into view, trailing the cows. His antlers were widespread, massive, and a rich mahogany brown. Six long points showed on each curved beam, their tips gleaming like burnished ivory. The great bull was in prime condition, his light buckskin coat darkening to deep brown and almost black on his neck ruff, legs, and belly.

Here was a typical herdmaster trailing with his cows, guarding his harem from the attentions of the other bulls now bugling steadily all over the slope.

As they dropped down the last steep pitch towards the valley floor, the cows broke into a run, but the bull walked proudly out on top of an outcrop of rock, laid his antlers back along his flanks, and bugled a reply to his rivals. First a deep note lifted through three higher ones into a long pealing whistle, then dropped to an explosive grunt that sent steam shooting from his open mouth. Finally he turned and trotted away out of sight after the cows.

The cow herd showed up on the edge of the meadow directly in front of me. They were obviously warming up after the cold, soaking rain. The big old dry lead cow wheeled out onto the flat, leading the bunch in a half circle at a gallop; then they all stopped, facing back towards the slope. Two cows reared, their noses pointed towards the sky, and almost touched briskets as they playfully pawed each other with their front hooves. Several calves bucked and gambolled around the herd. The big herd bull came trotting out of the timber with nose extended and antlers laid back. He went straight to a young smoky buckskin-coloured cow, but she sidestepped him with a playful flourish of her rear. Each animal had a plume of steam standing over its nose at each breath.

The herd bull stopped, lowered his head with nose thrust out, and gave a warbling series of low-pitched musical notes that seemed more like the call of a bird than the voice of a big animal – a liquid sound, like that of water poured from a big glass demijohn. He wound up this rendition with another great grunt, sending a shaft of steam shooting at least ten feet out from his mouth.

Four lesser bulls came out of the timber and circled the herd. The air was full of their bugling. The herdmaster charged one that dared approach the young cow. The usurper fled, but as he turned, the point of an antler cut from his rump a ribbon of hair that floated away to the side. The herdmaster circled the flat, driving away his rivals one by one. All had apparently tested him before, for none was inclined to fight. When the last one was driven back into the timber, he came striding arrogantly back into the herd with head low and antlers swinging in time to his strides.

He walked directly up to the young cow, now suddenly passive, reared, and covered her, while the rest of the herd grazed all around. It was an utterly beautiful and magnificent picture of procreation fitting to the wilds. Overhead the peak was lighted in deep rose over a silver collar of mist, while the river sang its soft song to the big trees beside it.

25

WILDERNESS ADVENTURE

Henry David Thoreau said, "We need the tonic of wildness – to wade sometimes in marshes here the bittern and the meadow-hen lurk, and hear the booming of the snipe; to smell the whispering sedge where only some wilder and more solitary fowl builds her nest, and the mink crawls with its belly close to the ground. At the same time that we are earnest to explore and learn all things, we require that all things be mysterious and unexplorable, that land and sea be infinitely wild, unsurveyed and unfathomed by us because unfathomable. We can never have enough of Nature. We must be refreshed by the sight of inexhaustible vigor, vast and Titanic features, the seacoast with its wrecks, the wilderness with its living and its decaying, trees, the thundercloud, and the rain which lasts three weeks and produces freshets. We need to witness our own limits transgressed, and some life pasturing freely where we never wander."

Thoreau spoke of his beloved New England country more than a century ago, but the principle and spirit of his words apply just as well to the mountain regions of the West today, for here, too, "the mink crawls with its belly close to the ground," and it is good for us to see our own limits transgressed. In mountains there is something grand that puts man in his true perspective, giving him a look at himself as just another warm-blooded thing, breathing and crawling across the face of an immensity, sharing an eco-system with bears, elk, wild sheep, and other wild things, including the little white-footed mouse and the mosquito.

If we are to call ourselves civilized, then we cannot look at a mountain in avarice and greed alone, reducing it to mere long tons and board feet, savouring it for what it might yield in fossil fuels, minerals, and lumber. We must see its beauty and stand in awe of its inexhaustible capacity to act as a storehouse for water to nurture the ever-demanding requirements of all living things; we must be aware of its function as a vault for the safekeeping of the riches it contains, a place where unfettered spirits can wander wild and free. In looking at the craggy features splitting the very clouds that blow across the sky, we need this reminder that we must weigh the destructive power of our technology and balance it with nature if we are to ensure our vital environmental needs. If we do these things, thinking with an open mind and heart, we will know that wilderness is truly a part of all life, where some things are measureless, mysterious and blue, deep to the ends of the universe. Otherwise we blight our bodies and our souls in a morass of destruction and filth with no hope for the future.

As one who has wandered in wild places all the years of his life, I have known firsthand the beauty, mystery, serenity, and utter savagery of nature throughout the vigorous seasons of this northern hemisphere.

I have ridden my horse, scouting ahead of a packtrain along the narrow trails of the Salmon River country in Idaho at greening-up time in spring – trails threading their way so precariously across cliffs above the boiling river that if two horsemen met at a blind corner, one would inevitably fall, for there would be no way to turn around. Indeed, there were places so narrow that a man could not even dismount in safety. If one chose to ride in those places, he stayed in the saddle till the trail widened again.

I remember one rider who tried to change his mind. He fell into the river and disappeared. The following spring I was fishing a deep run miles downstream and saw something flapping in the swift current six feet down or more. Waiting for a slick in the boiling current, I looked again and distinctly saw a stirrup waving on its leather – the rest of the saddle and perhaps the remains of the horse were buried out of sight in the gravel – the man long gone, his shell claimed by that merciless river.

The experience was stark, but the place was utterly magnificent. Snow-draped peaks gleamed high overhead, and the lower slopes were bright with new grass and the pastel shades of new leaves and bloom on scrub oak and sage. Mule deer grazed and browsed along the river in hundreds. Bighorn sheep threaded narrow trails across the lower rock battlements and the talus slides. Mountain lions prowled the thickets and broken rock, preying on the deer and sheep. We saw their tracks, heard them call, and counted their kills, but never laid eyes on one of the big cats, so secretive were they. At night flocks of bats emerged from cracks and caves on the rock faces to swoop and dart far and wide for insects, and great horned owls hooted among scattered groves of timber.

We slept on the ground with the muted roaring of the river always in our ears as it flowed swiftly down its water-carved way into a canyon so steep and wild that only the birds flew down its narrow cleft and mountain goats walked airy trails like bad dreams. No man could climb through that canyon, its walls overhanging in places, except on the river ice in winter, and then only at great risk. Its depths were inviolate.

Truly, this is wild country.

I have sat on top of a hump in a vast moraine in the St. Elias Mountains of the Yukon Territory, away back beyond the last faint sign of man, and watched the icefalls boom and cascade off hanging glaciers that cling to the almost sheer face of a peak cleaving the blue sky like a great white tooth. The cannonading of falling ice was punctuated by spurts of snow dust as great chunks hit unyielding rock and shattered. In spite of the impact, many pieces weighing tons reached the foot of the mountain intact. It was a salutary thing to see a mountain spitting out great masses of ice that it had grown tired of holding over the millennia it took to form, getting rid of a weight that had faulted itself past the angle of repose – masses exceeding the bulk of the small hills nearby.

A golden-crown sparrow perched on a sharp rock looked at me, paying not the slightest attention to the rumble and roar of the icefall. While his mate warmed eggs in a nest close by, he chirped with worry at my presence, a tiny, vibrantly alive thing in the midst of exceeding vastness.

I have rested on a dry cushion of tundra, comfortable in the warm sun, watching a trio of timber wolves trying a run at a bunch of caribou to see if there was one with some infirmity sufficient to warrant a successful catch. The wolves know that they cannot catch a caribou on such good footing simply for want of enough speed, so they will run a bunch long enough to spot a weakling. Three times they worked various small herds and every time gave up the chase, sitting with tongues lolling out of their mouths, frustrated. No easy lunch that day. Perhaps they settled for a meal of snowshoe hare or voles. Nature smiled benignly on the caribou after putting them through this test to find weaklings that needed to be weeded out. Thus vigorous strains are maintained within the wild, a play of genetics practised ages before man ever invented the word.

Cruel, you say? So is hunger gnawing at a wolf's belly.

My sons and I stood one night on the edge of the great valley where the mighty Peace River winds; we felt very small, like little boys standing behind darkened footlights in some vast, empty theatre, while a celestial stagehand amused himself with coloured lights and curtains overhead. The lights, green and red and opal, undulated in silken folds, sometimes lifting to the uttermost limits of the stars, then lowering so close that we were tempted to reach up and try to touch them. We stood in awe under the northern lights, for

> " – the skies of night were alive with light,
> with a throbbing thrilling flame;
> Amber and rose and violet, opal and gold it came.
> It swept the sky like a giant scythe,
> it quivered back to a wedge;
> Argently bright, it cleft the night
> with a wavy golden edge.
> Pennants of silver waved and streamed,
> lazy banners unfurled;
> Sudden splendors of sabres gleamed,
> lightning javelins were hurled.
> There in awe we crouched and saw with
> our wild, uplifted eyes
> Charge and retire the hosts of fire in the
> battlefield of the skies."

So said Robert W. Service, and he said it well.

The display faded to white and pale pink to march away back towards the curve of the polar rim and lose itself. Silent, we went to bed knowing we lay in the midst of wildness and were part of it, even if we did not fully understand.

26

MOUNTAIN STREAMS

DON BRESTLER '58

The song of wild mountain country is carried by tumbling waters running boisterous and free down rough wind- and ice-carved slopes on the first tumultuous bounds of their journey to the sea. The lyrics vary from full-throated roaring of river falls to the merry chuckling and tinkling of tiny rills, sometimes hidden and then revealed among the rocks. Springs bubble from secret reservoirs concealed in the sedimentary stone, leaping gaily, natural fountains playing in the sun among brilliant mountain flowers. Inevitably the small streams gather together to make creeks, and these follow the same pattern to form rivers winding like silver-blue ribbons down between cathedral groves of timber.

In the old days the Indians listened to the singing of the waters, and it was good. The streams were happy, they said, as they gathered across the face of the living earth; it was the marriage of the water, sun, and soil, making all life possible. Flowers and grass grew among the great trees beside them, joining with the wind to add their voices to the chorus. The Indians knew they were a part of it along with the buffalo, antelope, wild sheep, and deer they hunted. The sun was the great spirit, the earth was the mother, and the water was the juice that flowed between. For was it not the sun that brought rain, warmed the earth, and caused the winter snow to melt? To the Indians it was very simple to understand. They drank of the waters, bathed in them to cleanse themselves, worshipped the sun, and thus were a part of the pattern of life on the face of the earth. Because of the abundance of other life on the plains in front of the mountains and in the great valleys between the ranges, they were hunters.

The first white men who came working their way upstream from the east were hunters too. They came by boat till the streams became too small and swift, then they went on horseback and on foot up along the creeks in search of beaver. The beaver were so thick in many places that they choked the creeks with dams, laying one above the other like steps woven of mud and sticks, with ponds between. There the trappers, with old moccasins covering their feet, and with their buckskin leggings shortened to the knee, waded as they set their traps, cursing the icy water, and the only part of them that got bathed, short of accident, was their feet and legs. But they kept up the relentless search for skins, piling up the pelts till the beaver had all but disappeared.

The trappers were a breed set apart by their chosen environment, and they looked with some contempt and a reluctant awareness on the change in their wild free ways that came as white settlers wound their way slowly west by ox team and covered wagon, across the folds of great plains lifting and falling under their wheels like swells in a sea of grass. Buffeted by storms, sometimes attacked by hostile Indians or held back by the distances, they forded rivers and smaller streams, cursing when their wagons and stock bogged in quicksand and wheels broke on the steep, rocky pitches of the banks. Sometimes men and animals drowned in the swift waters, but others fought their way on west, following their destiny towards a land of riches somewhere yonder beneath the setting sun.

When they came to deserts, they fought their way across them, too; no detours for them, no bending to the forces of nature; it was fight and fight some more – defeat the wilderness – every step of the way, while the pitiless sun shone down and the shining sand was like the floor of a red-hot oven. There were no waters singing here, and many died of thirst.

One group had come west to escape persecution in the eastern settlements. The Saints, they called themselves;

their leader was Brigham Young and their guide the famed Jim Bridger, mountain man turned trader and guide for these wagon trains. He brought the Saints to a huge, wild, and inhospitable basin between the mountain ranges overlooking the glistening reaches of Great Salt Lake and stopped. He sat his horse, with the long fringes of his greasy buckskins stirring slightly in the hot wind. Taciturn for the moment, he silently contemplated these travel-worn, sunscorched, but grimly determined people who had followed him to this place. Out of long ingrained habit, his eyes were on the move, making note of every detail near and far, reading things completely hidden to the others, signs as lightly written as the soft brush of owl feathers in the dust, where the bird had taken a desert mouse. His gaze swept out across the dry, parched earth past a lone cottonwood tree to the distant blue sheen of the lake so salty a fresh egg would float on it, then swung back up a watercourse along a river in a valley debauching from the mountains back of the wagons. Even the river lost itself in the sand and gravel beds before it reached the lake. It was tough, inhospitable country, where roving Indians did not tarry long.

Why would these people want to settle here? Brigham Young had answered that question by stating it was his instruction from God; they would settle in this spot because it was far enough away and hard enough to reach that nobody else would want it. How would they stay alive? They would use the streams coming down from the mountains to irrigate this land and bring it to life. The mountain man reputedly scoffed at that and offered the Mormon leader one thousand dollars for the first bushel of corn grown in this place. But Bridger had not reckoned with the know-how of these people or with their determination. For in due course they harvested their first crop of corn. History does not record if Brigham Young was ever paid, but the recollection of Jim Bridger's offer amused him and he was fond of telling about it in the years that followed.

Apart from the Spanish settlements in California, where irrigation had been used in the previous century, and some early efforts of farmers and ranchers in the plains of north-eastern Colorado, this was perhaps the first time settlers utilized the streams in western North America on such a scale. But they and the horde of settlers to follow thought of water as something put there for man to use. They did not relate its presence to the life it supported in this great new land, for their fight to stay alive in the wilderness had become an ingrained thing, a characteristic still evident in our use of resources, and one that has proved to be short-sighted and very wasteful. Too many have looked on the great trees growing in the valleys and along the flanks of the mountains, their roots set deep in the water-moistened earth, as only something to be cut into planks and boards. They have not paused to see the beauty. If any of those early settlers loved the streams purely for their freshness and beauty, it was the children who played beside the crystal-clear cold water, fished for trout, and swam in them. They heard and began to understand the song.

Up along the foot of the Canadian Rockies, I grew up on a ranch on the edge of the frontier, exploring and fishing the creeks. One of them I came to think of as mine. It was the Drywood, and it nurtured me.

We lived in a comfortable home overlooking the forks where the creek swept down past the rugged flanks of Drywood Mountain, which stood with its great shoulders lifted in a never-ending shrug of patience with time, the elements, and the vagaries of men. The clear, icy water pro-vided me with a playground – a place to fish for the softly coloured cutthroat and Dolly Varden trout and to swim in its deep pools. I left tracks on the sandbars with those of deer, bear, beaver, mink, and many other wild creatures, large and small, which shared their secrets with me, each of us adding a sentence to this story of the wilds. It was there on the edge of a beaver pond, by the gnarled feet of some giant cottonwoods, that I met my first grizzly face to face. The great bear towered at full height over me while I stood frozen in my tracks, scared, small, and very much impressed by this huge beast that chose to turn and leave without a hostile move.

It was there I heard and listened to the song telling me of the mysteries of life supported by this stream, life that ranged from the tiniest of larvae to great Dolly Varden trout as long as my leg, the one dependent on the other. For I caught the Dolly Varden and learned from looking in the stomachs of the smaller fish in its belly that my feeding on its delicious pink flesh had started with caddis larvae, fresh-water shrimp, and other bugs eaten by the trout's prey, all forming a part of the mysterious and intricately woven life pattern of the creek.

In winter the creek ran under ice frozen on its surface; then my tracks mingled with those of the things I hunted while the water murmured sleepily in its bed, shackled by the elements. Sometimes storms tore at the trees growing along its banks. In spring the ice thawed, and the creek roared with boisterous delight at being free and fed copiously on the run-off from melting snow. Then it was dangerous to fawns, cub bears, and small boys. Sometimes tragedy struck among the snags and rocks where the fierce waters flung manes of spray into the air and roared with utter savagery. In summer it was serene and lovely, harbouring hordes of tiny fish fresh-hatched from its colourful gravel beds, feeding them the minute things needed in their struggle to grow big enough for boys to catch. In the process, some of them in turn fed the great Dolly Vardens.

All life is wonderful and beautiful, said the song, and to the boy, watching sometimes in awe and listening to its music, wondering and waiting for what would happen next, a day seemed short. Time was something that began when the sun came up and ended when he fell asleep. To the stream and its foster parent, the mountain, time was as endless as its patience with all things – the fierce storms, the wind, heat, and cold. But there was no way of accounting for the ambitions of men who had never heard the song.

One day they came – men who had no feeling for what it means to live on the face of the land and be part of it, relating to the life patterns there. They knew only how to tear riches from it, leaving scars that could never heal – festering, scrofulous scars. They neither knew nor cared about the virtue and rewards of patience; otherwise they could have taken what they wanted without leaving hideous marks along their trails. They drilled holes down past millennia of rock, two miles or more towards the very heart of the earth, and there found residues of things long dead. They hurried, breathing hard in their excitement, for this was gold – black gold – poison gold laden with sulphur, the smell of Hades, gases and minerals to throw away or offer on the marketplaces of the world. In their tearing hurry to refine the valuables, they had no time for caution. They took what they wanted, released the stink to putrefy and poison the air, and poured deadly effluents into Drywood Creek. These killed every living thing within its waters for miles, even the old trees I had known along its banks. They transformed the stream from a thing of wondrous beauty into a twisted, tortured wreck as dead and lifeless as the body of a snake rotting in the sun. Even a dead snake supports some kinds of life, but the creek now supported nothing except a grey-green algae that turned the coloured rocks in its bed into featureless lumps of slime.

It is dead, this stream – as dead as anything can be and still have hope of being restored to life. As it stands, there is no way this can be done, for there is nothing in it for anything to eat; the once pure waters stink.

Can the Drywood and others like it be revived? It is a question of how soon we learn to care and understand and how much we are willing to pay. The price of such carelessness is high. But there is really no choice. If we can claim the intelligence to create our technocracy, we must also find the way to manage it and repair the damages, thus returning the dead to the living, restoring the wasted waters so they again belong to nature – a place where trout swim and bright-hued dragonflies dip and dance on delicate wings as a prelude to laying their eggs.

Only then will the song resume.

27

WINGS OVER THE MOUNTAINS

DON BRESTLER '98

We had been climbing all day, revelling in the keen, clear air and the challenge of pitting our wits and leg muscles against steep rock. Not just one but two peaks were behind us where the mountains pitch tall and craggy on the west slope of the Continental Divide, and our tortuous trail had kept us high above timberline since sunrise.

Now we were tired – bone weary is the better term for it – as we stood on the rim of a cliff overlooking the valley where our tent was pitched five thousand vertical feet below the soles of our climbing boots. My partner and I stood looking down, silently wondering if we had enough steam left in our frames to reach it, and knowing that if we didn't it was going to be a long, cold, hungry night without sleeping bags or grub – a siwash camp where one covers an empty belly with a tired back. The sun rolled below the horizon to the west, leaving a rosy halo in the clear sky along a rim of jagged skyline fifty miles away. It was an evening without a breath of wind, the silent hush of twilight dropping around us like a soft blanket.

Then came an electrifying sound, faint and faraway, of wild geese calling, and we lifted our eyes to see two great ragged Vs of snow geese heading southwest overhead. They were high enough to be still in the sun, their white feathers looking rosy pink against the blue of the sky, and their wings heliographing in time with their steady beat. We stood there a mile and a half above sea level, with the geese another five thousand feet over our heads as they winged their way down across the Rocky Mountain flyway on their journey to California and Mexico for the winter. These were the leaders of the legions to follow, birds that had hatched down on the oozy tundra of Canada's cold north rim where the great barren lands slope into the sea, or out on the Arctic islands beyond. Now they were a bit more than halfway on their four-thousand-mile journey to the balmy climate of their wintering grounds.

Just seeing them was exhilarating, and as we climbed swiftly down the steep pitches towards camp, racing the night to a hot supper and warm sleeping robes, I was thinking of these birds and marvelling at their spectacular and unerring navigation of this flyway. One does not ordinarily look at mountains cleaving the sky with waterfowl in mind, but here they are at times during their migratory passage, sometimes flying in perfect weather like this, but more often beating their way through turbulent storms.

The greater part of their kind swim east and south from the northern nesting grounds to go along the Mississippi and Atlantic flyways, but a good portion of them choose this sky road – a flight line crossing the Rockies near the 49th parallel. It is a spectacular flyway shared by hundreds of thousands of other migrants – Canada geese, whistling swans, mallards, pintails, gadwalls, goldeneyes, bluebills, and even the dusky-coloured coots, to name a few. Following the nesting season and moult, all these gather into great flocks across the parklands and prairies. The snow geese come from farthest north, winging south on the breath of the first cold blast of Arctic storms heralding the coming of winter, and they gather on the larger lakes in thousands.

There they mingle with other wildfowl that have learned to glean grain from the stubble of wheat and barley fields – the Canada geese, mallards, and pintails, all fattening on the rich food. It is a dramatic pause, for each day they fly a gauntlet of guns in hidden blinds deceptively surrounded by various kinds of decoys set out to lure the birds within range – subterfuges sometimes astonishingly elaborate, contrived by men caught in the spell and excitement of the sound of whistling wings. Though they kill the birds, they love them, a love well illustrated, for it was at their insistence that an international law was passed in the dried-out hungry 1930s to save the birds from extinction and ensure the continued flight of these feathered travellers down the length of the continent. Since then, the hunters themselves have dipped deep in their pockets every year for the money to reclaim wetlands, improve nesting grounds, and provide protection.

On down the plains on the eastern side of the Rockies the birds slowly make their way from one choice feeding ground to another. The slough ducks, such as teal, spoonbills, and gadwalls, join the divers – the redheads, scaup, goldeneyes, and others of their kind – in the procession south. Then the pintails – Hollywood mallards, as some hunters call them – take their leave. Only the mallards and geese linger as the smaller lakes freeze over. As colder weather begins to clamp down, thousands gather overnight on Waterton Lakes for a rest before they take the high flight across the mountains.

Because these lakes are protected by the boundaries of a national park, the guns no longer boom, but feathered and furred hunters are on the prowl. Very early one morning, I came out onto a point near the mouth of the river at the top of the lower lake. In the darkness, I felt my way out through a stand of willows into a natural blind among the weather-bleached roots of a couple of big old cottonwoods washed up and stranded here in a previous spring flood. It was still and frosty as I readied my camera on the tripod and made myself as comfortable as possible to wait for light, listening all the while to the gabbling of geese and ducks directly in front of me along the silty shore of the lake.

As dawn began to break, some of the birds became visible, resting on the water amid wraiths of rising mist that lay close to the surface. Beyond the lake a snow-streaked mountain slanted down over a steep slope of yellow grass to a golden footstool of aspen-covered bluffs. The birds and I shared a scene of utter serenity, but we were not alone.

Directly in front of me on the tip of a sandspit jutting a few yards out into the lake, a dozen honkers were resting, big and black against the silvery surface of the water. Between us in a scattering of little willows and grass something moved. At first I could not make it out, but a cautious peek through the binoculars revealed a big grey coyote crouched as still as a stone image, calculating the next move that would put him within charging distance of the geese. So well did his coat blend with the surroundings that I could blink my eyes and lose sight of him – a kind of visual sleight-of-hand that made me wonder if the light was playing tricks. Here was drama in the making if the action would only wait until the light got strong enough to expose film. My fingers shook a little as my hand slid towards the camera trigger. But it was not to be.

From behind me a trio of mallards came flying down the river through a corridor of big cottonwoods. They swung, set their flaps, and swooped down so close overhead that I could almost feel the wind off them. The sudden swoosh of feathers caused the coyote to move, and the motion caught the keen eye of a goose. The big bird stretched its neck, gave a low honk, and then, as though at command, all the geese just walked into the lake and swam away. The expression of undiluted chagrin on the coyote's countenance almost made me chuckle aloud. By sheer chance the ducks had robbed us both.

Another day I stood in a grove of scattered snow-draped aspens watching a flock of Canada geese flying towards me at a thousand-foot altitude. It was an undulating formation of no particular pattern, for the birds seemed to be winging along with no destination in mind, loafing carefree on the air currents.

Suddenly, from far above, a golden eagle swooped down like a feathered spear hurled by angry gods. It struck one of the geese with such force that the air around it was filled with a great burst of feathers, and the hapless bird came down to earth dead as a stone. The eagle followed it and fed on it where it fell, for it was far too heavy to be carried away.

The lives of the wild flocks are full of drama, often with tragedy darkening the picture of an otherwise idyllic life of changing scenes and great freedom. For here are birds whose ranges stretch across thousands of miles of tundra, prairie, and mountains, the pattern of their lives changing with the seasons as they follow their destinies back and forth between Arctic barrens and warm subtropics.

Yet their lives are not without moments of natural comedy wrought by the circumstance of the moment – some unusual condition not normally encountered.

On a clear, windless morning following a short, sharp freeze, the water of the lakes above the outlet of the river was frozen in a skim of ice as clear as plate glass. A hundred yards out in the lake was an open hole completely crammed with mallards sitting in the water and on the ice around it. A few yards beyond them, a small flock of Canada geese were resting with a lone whistling swan among them. I was sitting with my glasses glued to my eyes, watching these birds, when the bugle of a swan drew my attention to a flock of these big white birds flying at low altitude up the river. Whistling swans are birds of beauty and immense dignity, much taller and heavier than almost any other wildfowl – their size and beauty are equated only by the much rarer trumpeter swans they closely resemble. Indeed, they look so proud and dignified in comparison to other birds that one is reminded of slightly stuffy society types, very class-conscious and somewhat impressed by their own fine feathers. These are the aristocrats, and they appear to know it.

The approaching flock of a dozen birds came within sight of the ducks and geese and honked a couple of times, a call that was immediately answered by the lone member of their own kind. They began sloping down for a landing, setting their feet and wings for a touchdown a few yards short of the ducks, apparently not realizing that they were dealing with glare ice. What followed was an absolutely hilarious burlesque of what was intended to be a dignified and graceful landing. The instant their feet touched the ice, they were transformed from a group of decorous and elegant birds into a bunch of ridiculous clowns completely out of control. One of them tried to abort the landing with a great thrashing of wings, but it was too late; its feet slid forward past its beak and it went over backwards, with feet paddling futilely in the air. The rest ground-looped and scrambled, flapping their wings and scratching desperately to check their speed, folding themselves together and then unfolding in a wild spectacle of lost balance. Half of them went ploughing into the ducks, causing a great burst of flapping wings and startled quacks. The rest ended up strung out raggedly across the ice, gingerly coming to their feet and trying to regain their composure. While various birds sorted themselves out, the geese and the first swan looked on unmoved, but I wondered if they, too, had not landed earlier in the same unexpected fashion.

Sometimes on a clear day after this kind of cold, sharp storm, it is possible to lie back with binoculars trained on the sky and see three distinct layers of migrants flying in three directions at this eastern take-off point of the mountain crossing. The lower layer will be sloping in to land and rest on the lakes. Not all of these birds cross the mountains here, and the middle layer will be heading directly south past the projecting tip of the Great Lewis Overthrust, where Chief Mountain stands looking out across the prairie. These flights point towards the headwaters of the Missouri and a mountain crossing farther south. The top formations, thousands of feet up, will be headed in non-stop flight southwest over the Continental Divide.

It is seeing the sky full of warm-blooded life, all headed for the same general destination by different routes, that makes one's spirit soar, sharing in imagination the adventure and grandeur of migration.

28

RELATIVE TO RICHES

On the edge of a meadow, alone with three coyotes and a mountain, I stood by a frozen beaver pond. Up on the rim of the peak at the head of the creek, January frost and new snow glittered in the dying rays of the sun, but down in the valley the light had turned sombre grey. A bite in the breeze made me hunker down into the warmth of my jacket collar. A hundred yards away, the coyotes were going through a patch of heavy grass like a trio of pickpockets. They were hunting mice, taking their time about it and treading softly, alert and listening. Now and again one would freeze and then pounce, with front paws held closely together on something rustling in the grass. With

DON BRESTLER

infinite finesse born of long practice, the coyote would extract the mouse from where it was trapped, then chew and swallow it. So went the hunt until the whole grass patch had been worked out.

Two coyotes came together and touched noses, and perhaps as a signal of approval for an idea expressed, one of them pointed its nose to the sky and howled a long-drawn song – a salute that the mountain answered with an echo. The coyote had just finished its wild paean when another joined in, then the third, until the whole valley rang and echoed. The trio wound up their cantata with a yapping chorus, a tricky blending of voices sounding like three times as many – fierce, wild sounds telling of the chill, the coming night, and a unique kind of freedom. Then all three trotted away to lose themselves like wraiths of smoke among the willows, leaving a profound silence between me and the mountain.

Coyotes are innovative, enterprising, and exceedingly cunning hunters. On my way home while the first pale stars were showing overhead, I thought about them, remembering times when their playfulness, intelligence, and cruelty had been demonstrated.

From the top of a rocky bluff overlooking an open slope below, I once saw four coyotes come streaking out of a grove of aspens. The leader was carrying a dead magpie, and the others were pursuing in a sort of tag game. Suddenly the bird carrier threw it high in the air, and another picked it up, to be in turn pursued. Back and forth and around and around they went, making the snow fly on their quick turns, until finally their enthusiasm ran out and they just stood looking at one another, panting in the warm sun.

I recalled a frosty morning in late fall when I trotted a bush trail on the way back to school after a weekend holiday. The trail passed a willow-ringed slough, where an old emaciated cow was bogged deep in the muck along its edge.

A day or two before, she had walked out on the frozen mud for a drink, but the ice had thwarted her, and when she turned to come back, the frozen crust had broken under her, letting her down in the soft stuff underneath, trapped and helpless, unable to move an inch. Sometime during the night before, the coyotes had found her. Unable to kill her or even tear her tough hide, they had improvised by coming up close behind her to eat their way into her pelvic aperture. When I came, she was still incredibly alive. Her owner was duly summoned, and he put a merciful end to her suffering, with a bullet through the head, softly cursing coyotes all the while. Right then I felt that all coyotes should be killed on sight, but as the years passed and my experience grew with me, I came to know that all nature is starkly cruel at times and that this is also a trait of men. The little grey yodeller is a part of the wilds where hunters and hunted contest, and in this I too am responsible.

For many winters I pursued coyotes for their pelts, with rifle, traps, snares, and sometimes hounds. Because some coyotes develop a taste for sheep and poultry, a few of my neighbours resorted to poison. This is a method with no conscience, for poison plays no favourites, killing anything that happens to eat it. It is a means of control I have hated ever since a favourite collie came staggering home, glassy-eyed and retching, to die miserably in convulsions begging for help we could not give.

Finally the killing palled completely, and I found myself watching and admiring this animal that had foiled me so many times and had also managed to survive everything man had contrived to wipe it out. It is amazing how versatile coyotes are when it comes to finding food; only a small percentage learn to kill poultry and sheep.

On a fine October day my wife and I watched four coyotes as they stalked and caught grasshoppers. I have seen them picking and eating saskatoons and huckleberries when the fruit was hanging lush and ripe on the bushes. But they are basically hunters, and there are times in the hard days of winter when they go in small packs after deer. Sometimes they are not successful, but if the snow is deep and crusted enough to carry their weight but lets the deer down belly deep, the killing will be frequent and bloody. It is nature's way of trimming the deer herds to fit the life-sustaining capacity of limited winter feed.

A hunting pair will sometimes relay a jackrabbit – one hiding while the other runs the prey in a wide circle – and when the big hare passes close by, the hidden one takes over, allowing its mate to rest. I once saw two coyotes course a jack around a butte on the prairie, and after they had taken turns running the hare for a mile or so, both coyotes joined in a final dash for dinner. When the lead coyote drew close to the frantic animal, the hare made a lightning-fast dodge of sheer desperation, a long twisting jump back over the nearer pursuer. But it landed squarely under the nose of the second one and was dead in the wink of an eye.

Though formidably armed, neither the skunk nor the porcupine is safe from a hungry coyote. It will brave the frightful stench of a skunk, picking it up and shaking it to death in a horrible halo of its spray, and then eat it with enthusiasm. Almost every coyote, eager for action on its first hunts, runs into a porcupine and gets a painful lesson, but occasionally a mated pair learns how to handle the quilly creature safely.

One spring evening at greening-up time, I was sitting with binoculars trained on a porcupine feeding on new grass out in the middle of a meadow. Two coyotes suddenly appeared on the edge of some thick-growing aspens beyond, and it was evident that they had spotted the porcupine too. Very businesslike, they trotted out towards the unsuspecting animal, but when they came within range of its shortsighted eyes, it swung around, presenting its heavily armed back and tail. With its head tucked in close to its front feet, it looked like a quilly ball fringed with yellow hair.

The coyotes were not impressed, for the male split away from his mate to circle the porcupine. This put the unfortunate animal in a quandary, for in no way could it keep its back to two animals at once, and it spun around, frantically switching its tail. With perfect timing, the male shot in close, flicked his jaws low to the ground to grab the porcupine by the nose, then threw it flat on its back right in front of the female. She clamped down on its unprotected belly, killing it in a few seconds. Both animals fed until there was nothing left but the hide lying flesh side up on the ground. As they turned to leave, the male went to a little cinquefoil shrub and cocked his leg, then turned to make arrogant scratches with his hind feet, throwing dead grass over the shrub, thus endorsing his calling card.

The female was heavy with young, and a couple of weeks later I found their den. Curious to see the pups, I did not approach too closely, for to do so would have caused the parents to move their family to a new location. One evening after a shower, when the sun was warm on the slope, I finally saw all four pups out of the den. It was probably their first adventure out in the bright new world, for they were still small and quite wobbly on their legs. The female sat looking on while they ventured a few steps this way and that, nuzzling each other and falling over their feet. Finally they found their father curled up asleep among some yellow Indian turnip flowers a bit down the slope and crawled all over him in a squirming heap. He woke but did not move, obviously enjoying their attention. One of the parents at last must have given some signal inaudible to me, for the pups scrambled back to the den and disappeared. A few seconds later both parents got to their feet, stretched, and trotted away for some hunting.

Ground squirrels and young snowshoe hares were the major prey of this pair as the pups grew and flourished. Now the pups were outside the den much of the time, and the grass and other herbage around its mouth were flattened from their rolling and romping. When one of the old coyotes showed up with some food, the play routine changed in a flash to one of fierce competition that was equally comical, for they would grab hold of a squirrel or a hare all at once, tugging and hauling in every direction until it was reduced to little but a memory.

The male coyote was a specialist at catching ground squirrels – his technique usually flawless, to a point bordering on art. There were hundreds of these animals on the flats along the creek below the den – easy pickings, it would seem, but each squirrel had two sharp eyes and a penetrating squeaking whistle to warn of an intruder. When the male coyote did not want to be seen, he expertly made use of every bit of cover. Belly-crawling through the greenery, taking advantage of every fold of ground, he would contrive to get himself within charging distance of a squirrel without alarming it or any of its neighbours. Then he would freeze, patiently waiting for his prey to feed away from its hole, watching its every move till it looked away. When everything was right, he burst into a grey streak of action. He rarely missed adding a luckless victim to the string of groceries carried to the den.

Once I saw him frustrated in an unexpected way. He came out of a grove of aspens to thread slowly through a bunch of cows grazing and loafing with their calves in a meadow. Apparently they were accustomed to seeing him, for they paid scant attention, and he was very diplomatic about not irritating the mothers by getting too close to

their calves. Using them for a screen, he stalked a fat squirrel sitting bolt upright on the dirt mound in front of its den.
Closer and closer he crept until he finally slid into position
behind a camouflaging tuft of grass, and there he froze with
feet all drawn up, waiting for the squirrel to begin to feed.
The squirrel finally moved, and so keen was the coyote's
concentration that he did not notice a curious calf tiptoeing
up behind him. Just as he was about to launch himself in a
charge, the calf sniffed the end of his outstretched tail. He
was so startled that he leaped straight up onto his feet. But
the squirrel had not seen him, so he turned his attention
back to it, flattening out and getting ready for a rush. Again,
when he was just ready to explode into action, the mischie-
vous calf sneaked up to sniff his tail. This time the coyote
did not look back, but streaked towards his intended victim.
But his timing was now off, and the squirrel dodged him
and escaped into its hole. As he stood looking back towards
the calf, that coyote's expression was one of pure disgust and
frustration. Then he trotted away, doubtless looking for a
place where the interference was less nerve-racking.

Again, when I was watching the pups outside their den
from a screen of brush on top of a knoll a hundred yards
away, the female came up behind me and got my wind. She
barked in alarm and instantly every pup shot out of sight
into the den. When I came back a couple of days later, the
whole family had moved to a new location. In spite of careful searching, I could not find them.

But I still saw the parents hunting on occasion. Then,
one day as I was sitting on the veranda looking down over a
neighbour's fresh-cut hayfield where the swaths were curing in the sun in preparation for baling, out of a stringer of
cottonwoods along a fence line came my acquaintances, the
coyotes – both parents and three pups. One of the pups had
disappeared since I had last seen them. The remaining three

were almost full grown now, and they were slipping through the scenery, evidently taking one of their first hunting lessons, for when they came to the swaths, the parents began to hunt mice. Trotting along a swath, the male stopped and lifted a paw, with his nose pointed into the loose hay, every line of him a study of concentration. Then he pounced and shortly came up with a fat vole dangling from his jaws, which he speedily ate. The mother caught another, and she also promptly ate it, with no more than a glance at the nearest pup.

It was a lesson by example, and before long the pups were all imitating their parents. Their enthusiasm was much greater than their skill, for several opportunities were missed, but two of the pups managed to catch a mouse before they all moved out of my sight into a hollow.

In a few weeks they would all be wearing heavy winter coats, hunting regularly, living off the land by their wits, sharing a valley and mountain with me, and lifting their voices to the stars on clear frosty evenings. They are a part of the wilds, and so am I – all partaking of a host of riches.

29

A Frontier Woman's Solution

Nita Tolway rode up to the gate in front of her house, wrapped her bridle reins around the hitching rail, and busied herself as she watched the rider approaching across the flat. When he was close enough to see her, she slid the Winchester rifle out of its scabbard on the near side of her saddle and carried it through the gate, across the yard, and up the three steps onto the veranda of her house, where she leaned it against the back of the big rustic armchair there. Then, as though seeing him for the first time, she watched the man ride to her hitching rail, step down, and move to her gate.

She had been expecting him. The last time she had been in town she had heard that he was serving notices of seizure for the bank. The bank held a note on a loan she had obtained from them to buy a tractor. Through no fault of hers, she was behind on her payments. She had gone to see the bank manager, but he hadn't been very friendly, probably because he was new and maybe because she was a woman.

Whatever the reason, here was Jake Smith all dolled up like a cowboy, complete with hat, shirt, and high-top riding boots that he wore over the cuffs of his pants. The last time he had been close to a cow was when he cleaned out his father's dairy barn back in Ontario. Undeterred by Nita's inhospitable refusal to let him come through the gate, he was talking in his grating unpleasant voice about the endless rain, the muddy condition of the roads, his horse and its lineage for three generations back. Then hardly pausing to take a fresh breath, Jake asked for a drink of water, opened the gate, and started up the walk towards her.

Nita stepped back, picked up her rifle, and sat down in her chair with it lying across her knees.

"Jake," she said. "That's a beautiful shirt you are wearing. It ain't going to look so good with holes in it. Now you get back through that gate and close it after you. Get on your horse and get off my ranch!"

Jake did as he was told and he never came back. He was not the smartest man around, but he knew better than to argue with a woman with a Winchester. Nita paid for her tractor in good time with no further argument with her bank. She is eighty-five years young and glows with the love of life. Like me, she has seen the time when her only means of transport was horses. Now she rolls on wheels or flies in a jet airplane.

30

ADVENTURES WITH SUSIE

DON BRESTLER '08

Anybody who has had any experience with training horses knows that, like people, no two are exactly alike. They vary in physical characteristics but even more in their likes and dislikes, their general attitude towards people, and their tendencies towards cooperation with them.

Away back, when I was very much younger, I cut Susie out of the wild bunch one day to begin training her for work on a mountain packtrain. She was born and raised in the brushy hills between the prairies and the mountains and was no stranger to wild country. She had a strong background of original cayuse and enough thoroughbred blood to put some fire in her make-up. By way of description she was an unremarkable bay with black points, easy gaited, with big ears and a back like a mule.

By the time I got her leading well, I figured we had come to be friends. She put her nose against my chest, nuzzled me with both ears standing up, then opened her mouth and bit me hard. I naturally backed off, and her teeth made an audible click when they came together. Everybody who works with horses gets nipped once in a while, and generally the horse registers anger by pulling its ears back. Susie was different. She put her ears up and looked anything but mean and it felt like she had taken a piece out of me.

When I saddled her and led her around the corral, she registered indifference. When I booted a stirrup and swung my leg over the saddle, she acted like she had been ridden before. After a couple of short reining sessions, I took her out for a ride in a big pasture where there were cattle and horses. Not once did she show any sign of wanting to buck. It was that indifference that made me wonder.

Next morning I took her out for a long ride. It was a nice June day, warm and sunny; we crossed a creek valley and climbed up a steep slope on the other side. Up near the top, one of those little twisters common in the mountain foothills in spring came roaring along the slope in front of us and met us head on. It picked up my batwing chaps and slapped Susie on both shoulders with them.

She turned and jumped, bucking straight down the hill. Around the second jump, I knew I was in trouble for she was sucking back under me every time she hit the ground, and about the third jump she shed me and the saddle over her ears. I had a horsehair macatte on my hackamore with the long tag end tucked under my chap belt, which I grabbed as I hit the ground, but I went clear off the end of it and knew I was afoot.

I looked around for Susie and saw that she had lost her footing and was down. She had slid on top of the hair rope, which had pulled her nose back against her chest so she could not get up. It didn't take me long to get her back on her feet and saddled.

Susie had come awake; for the rest of that ride she snorted and shied at nearly anything that gave her an excuse. She had about as bad a case of rollers in her nose as I have ever known. When I rode her past a slough, she turned towards it, obviously wanting to drink, so I let her go. She walked out into it, drinking as she went, and suddenly she just collapsed into it. There was nothing wrong with her except that she wanted a bath. I was wet to the ears and my boots were full to the top by the time we got back on dry ground. I was learning about Susie.

She had bit me, bucked me off, and tried to drown me, yet she looked about as innocent as a horse can get as I turned her out to pasture. When we rounded up the pack strand to trail them cross-country to the base camp, Susie was travelling loose in the bunch with the rest. We made camp that night beside the Castle River after a thirty-mile ride.

Next morning I caught Susie for my mount and noticed that her ears were drooping a bit as I pulled the last slack out of the cinch. When I stepped up on her, she bogged her head in a storm of bucking. When that was over, I figured the rest of the morning would be peaceful, but I was wrong. Susie had cooked up a big mad, and she was not about to quit. She would try to buck me off and then would rest a while to get her wind back before having another try. Twice she slammed into the barbed wire fences along the road allowance we were following. Even though I was wearing heavy chaps, I was cut on both knees. About noon, she bucked down a steep slope that was covered with badger holes. Somehow she managed to keep her feet out of them, and we arrived on the flat ground at the bottom right side up. At that point my patience was gone, and I whipped her with the leather tag on the end of the maccate on the tender part of her belly. She came to a stop and seemed to be giving the whole question some thought, then shook herself and trotted after the horses.

I roped a fresh mount, changed my saddle, and let Susie run free. Never again did she buck with anyone. As time went on, she showed a definite fondness for kids and women and became one of our most trusted horses. But she never did learn that taking a bath with a rider on her back was not good manners. We warned the people who rode her to keep a tight rein when we went through water, but more than one found themselves taking a dip with her.

Susie was more than just another horse; she was a character.

31

THERE MY STICK FLOATS

DON BRESTLER '98.

One of the west's wild rivers, a magnificent stream full of mystery and beauty, strong in its current, placid in its pools, and still reasonably pure in its waters, winds down between folded hills, blue and silver in the sun, alternating fast white water and slick runs with quiet holes. Beyond the hills the Rockies rise, tall and craggy, their expressions strong in profile, enduring since the earth's crust split to heave them slowly up towards the sky.

For two hours I had been fishing, standing thigh-deep in the river and enjoying the powerful tugging of its current against my legs – soothing medicine to wipe away the tension. There are few things as satisfying as plying a finely balanced fly rod and line in presenting a hand-dressed fly to feeding trout. While a full creel has no part in the witchery, mine hung comfortably heavy on my shoulder – sufficient promise of a delicious breakfast when the sun rose again.

The fishing was only part of the river's wealth. There were signs of mink and beaver along the edges of sandbars. Elk, moose, and deer tracks showed here and there, and in one place the big paw marks of a black bear were printed deep in the mud beside a spring. Earlier in the evening, while the sun was still up and the world still warm after a long hot day, I had come down a steep bank along a little trail. It led me through a pocket close by the river and filled with berry brush higher than my head. As I made my way into it through a patch of tall fireweed, the leaves rustled noisily in the breeze, muffling my footsteps. There was a sudden explosive snort and a great crash as a huge whitetail buck with antlers like a rocking chair leaped from his bed into flight, so close I could have touched him with the tip of my rod. My thoughts had been somewhere else, and the suddenness of it made my pulse jump a bit, but doubtless less than his at having me almost walk on his tail. Later, as the evening cooled and I was standing knee-deep in water at the tail of a pool, I watched a doe browsing delicately among some saskatoon bushes, alternating choosy nibbles of leaves and twigs with enthusiastic mouthfuls of the luscious ripe fruit.

The sun dipped down onto the far rim of the mountains to the northwest, throwing long shadows of trees and promontories along the opposite bank. I shot my line upstream to drop a tiny fly where an eddy curled by some big rocks. There it danced, light-footed as a mayfly, when suddenly the kerplop and splash of a diving beaver sounded behind me. Swinging my head to look, I let the fly drift unattended for a moment and missed the strike of a good trout. The beaver surfaced to swim towards me, full of curiosity, his whiskers working on each side of his face like an animated moustache as he tried to get my scent. My chuckle triggered another great tail-smacking dive that threw water in all directions.

My attention to my fishing had been broken again, but such is a love affair with a beautiful river, and now I stood contemplating it, full of wonder at all the life it had known over the long reaches of time before I was born. It was to places like this that the first white men came, some of the old mountain men – free trappers adventuring in search of beaver. They may have stood here braving the dangers of wrathful Blackfeet just for the privilege of looking at new territory and taking some skins. They had seen the ancestors of my beaver, the deer, and other game, their spirits lifting as mine did at the sight of a flaming sunset over the mountains.

For a few mystic moments the shadows of Old Bill Williams, Jedediah Smith, John Fitzgerald, and others like them stood close beside me, contemplating the river, leaning on their long rifles with the breeze stirring the fringes of buckskins redolent with the smoke of a thousand campfires. A peeled beaver stick floated by in the lazy current, bringing to mind something just beyond the edge of recall – something heard or read long ago.

Then a great horned owl suddenly broke the silence from some cottonwoods across the river. "Who? Who? Who?" it called as though questioning my thoughts.

Then I remembered. It was Old Bill Williams, of course! When something pleased him or he liked a place, he would say, "Thar my stick floats!" And come to think of it, there my stick floats too.

32

THE SPEEDSTER AND THE SLOWPOKE

Nature is fond of developing specialists of one kind or another in the animal world, species specially adapted to their surroundings in ways that make them unique. Two such animals found on the plains and in the high country of the west are almost complete opposites in choice of range and in certain physical attributes, yet they are relatives. They are the pronghorn antelope and the mountain goat.

ON BRESTLER

Incongruously enough, the pronghorn is more of a goat than an antelope, and the mountain goat is more closely related to the antelope. If one were to draw a geographic comparison, with Africa representing the antelope family and North America the family of goats, the mountain goat would be located somewhere in the vicinity of the Canary Islands. The mountain goat is a link between the two species but is much closer to the antelope family.

The pronghorn antelope of North America's plains and plateaus is one of nature's most refined achievements among the cloven-hoofed animals in its adaptation to life on the open prairies. Its frame and muscular development are superbly constructed for fleetness of foot, and it depends largely on speed to protect itself from enemies – it has been clocked at sixty miles per hour. It is the only cloven-hoofed animal of the entire world that has no dewclaws – the secondary toes, or, more correctly, heels, that project from the back of the hoofs of all other ruminants. Perhaps these were lost over many thousands of years of evolutionary process by being repeatedly torn off when the antelopes turned at high speed on rough ground. The pronghorn is the only animal wearing true horns that sheds them annually; each year the bucks shed the outer shells of their weapons and grow new ones.

The colour of the pronghorn is a rich tan and white with pelage of the same nature as the deer: the hair is tubular and offers very effective insulation against both heat and cold. The rump patch of snow-white is very pronounced and can be fanned out in moments of alarm to form a flashing, danger-signalling heliograph that other pronghorns can see for miles. From the front, or quartering on from the side, a pronghorn is difficult to see against the natural background of tawny plains grass, but when it turns to go, its rump patch flashes like a mirror.

By contrast, its relative the mountain goat lives in the standing-on-end country of the mountains, walking with utter unconcern along airy ledges. With characteristic deliberation it can climb places where it would seem a fly would have trouble sticking to the rock. Its feet are specially designed, with soft rubbery pads on the soles cupped in rims of hard horn. These stick well to almost any surface, enabling the animal to defy what would appear to be the inevitable law of gravity. The goats' cannon bones are very short, allowing them to reach up, place a foot in a tiny crevice, and then lift their weight. Phlegmatic by nature, they out-climb enemies more than they run from them. Understandably enough, nobody has clocked their speed, but it is doubtful that a mountain goat can achieve more than twenty miles an hour on the most ideal footing.

The whole frame and muscle structure of the mountain goat is put together for climbing and living on high rock terrain. Mountain goats are narrow and slab-sided, with horns that do not project to the side, and thus they are able to traverse narrow ledges without danger of being tipped off into space by their own bulk. Their coats are long and creamy white, with fairly coarse guard hair covering an undercoat of fine wool. When fully haired-out for winter, they present a rugged picture that is in sharp contrast to bare rock or that blends with the snow. A billy and nanny are hard to tell apart, for both have baggy pantaloons hanging to the knees, thick coats, pronounced neck ruffs, and long flowing beards. Both sexes wear short, curved, and very sharp black horns that they keep honed like the points of stilettos, sharpening them on the rocks. The horns of the females are often longer than those of males of similar age but are much slimmer at the base.

When the white man came to the west about one hundred and fifty years ago, he encountered pronghorns and mountain goats for the first time. He had little interest in the goats, for he was travelling by boat or on horseback and had no ambition to spend the time and energy pursuing these climbers of the crags. The pronghorns were the "lunch meat" of the frontiersman – they were everywhere on the Great Plains, could be killed with relative ease, and were easy to handle. Even the biggest bucks weigh only about eighty pounds hog-dressed. Consequently, when the settlers came pouring in, the pronghorns were killed off or further reduced by disruption of their environment. Today only a comparative handful remains.

When wire fences began cutting up the prairies, the antelope were in trouble. At first they were afraid of the wire. The only way they could get through a fence was by crawling under it, something rather difficult to do at high speed. In spite of their nimble feet, they are not jumpers. But with the passing of time, they have adapted to the wire. I recall sitting on a low knoll in the extreme southeast corner of Alberta one November day, watching about forty antelope running across country. A stout barbed wire fence was dead ahead of them, marking the boundary between Alberta and Saskatchewan, and when the band came to it at a leisurely forty miles an hour or so, they just flipped on their sides and passed between the strands, scarcely touching them and not losing a stride. Occasionally the bucks tangle their horns during this manoeuvre and pull off the shells.

Again, in this same region, I had the chance to test their speed while driving a station wagon along a country road. A bunch of about fifty head came pouring across a flat, quartering to me with the obvious intention of crossing in front of the car, as they love to do. I stepped up my speed to fifty miles an hour, about the limit for the condition of the road, and for perhaps half a mile the pronghorns cruised along beside me, running effortlessly. Then they tired of my company and speeded up. When I was going fifty-five miles an hour, they passed in front of me, then tore up a draw with plumes of dust at their heels and disappeared among some hills. They had to be going more than sixty miles an hour to make such a move. The only other animals of the world that can match their speed are the cheetah of Africa and the black buck of the plains of India.

Their eyes and those of the mountain goat are superbly keen, probably eight times better than those of an average human. While the pronghorn pays strict attention to any intruder who might threaten, the goat may choose to ignore the approach of a man or a predator if it feels safe on some dizzy height.

The pronghorn often seems to delight in the slightest excuse to burst into a run for the sheer exuberance of it, while the goat is more inclined to make use of the logistics of its inaccessible terrain for protection. The pronghorn has a wide streak of curiosity built into its nature, a characteristic that can get it into trouble with hunters, who sometimes lure it within range of their rifles by tying a handkerchief on a stick and letting it flutter in the breeze. No such decoy will get more than a look from a mountain goat. Its reaction to danger is usually remarkably phlegmatic. Unless closely pressed, it will rarely break into a gallop.

The pronghorn occupies a land of distant flat horizons where the sun lights up the golden savannas for miles and miles. Sometimes its range penetrates big valleys and plateaus close to the mountains, like those in parts of Montana and Wyoming. Occasionally one sees them setting sail across the great flats where mirages lift and curl, creating an illusion of animals running over water or completely detached from the ground like some sort of speedsters of the sky.

The mountain goat is symbolic of high mountains, where glaciers hang trapped between cliffs, and pinnacles cleave the sky – a land of harsh and varied climate ranging from benign sun to fierce storms. They are born, live out their lives, and die where no other kind of cloven-hoofed game can exist. In summer they sometimes share their range with wild sheep, but often they winter where sheep could not possibly stay alive. For all its austere harshness and violent topography, their world is a magnificence of peaks, an Olympian land fitting a brave and enduring spirit.

33

AUTUMN GOLD

DON BRESTLER

This is the time of year when all nature seems to celebrate the end of a long, fruitful spring and summer by decorating the face of the land with colour, ripening the grass and splashing the leaves of the trees with gold, yellow, red, orange, and rich brown along with about every shade in between thrown in for good measure. Away up at timberline on the faces of the mountains, the September larches stand like golden spires among the evergreens; the larch is the only conifer that sheds its leaves for winter. Down along the valley bottoms where clear creeks wind, banks of majestic cottonwoods stand dressed in gold, their branches hanging over the water. Hidden among the branches of the trees are the abandoned nests of birds, their summer's sheltering of eggs and fledglings done. Some of these will blow away in the wind with the leaves, but others will sturdily defy the elements to gather caps of snow – a reminder of the craft and care taken in their building.

No longer do the timber and brush thickets resound with bird song; the sounds are now muted chirps and restless trills, along with the rush and whisper of flashing wings. My binoculars pick up a flock of several hundred crossbills working through a grove of wind-twisted white pines to find seeds. Not far from them a smaller flock of Bohemian waxwings move through the blood-red leaves of a patch of saskatoon brush, feeding on the dry berries still clinging thickly to the twigs. It is snowing slightly, the first flags of winter signalling the cold to come. With a rush of sound, a flock of nearly two hundred robins sweeps overhead only a few feet above the treetops, heading south. Most of the other thrushes and small songbirds have already gone.

The first flocks of migrating sooty-grey coots are showing up on the bigger lakes. From nesting grounds farther north they are winging their way south on this first winter squall, splitting the wind with their sharp ivory-white beaks and beating their way with short wing strokes as though the effort were almost too much for them. Much more at home on the water, they dive deep for food, using their wings for this, too, although in slower and easier tempo. Without a head wind to aid them, they are hard pushed to take off into the air, but in diving they are in their element, graceful and astonishingly long-winded. While resting on the surface, they are wont to flock up in thick masses, sometimes numbering in the thousands, seeming to take comfort in togetherness for social warmth and comfort. Although they are unobtrusive, meek, helpless-looking birds, I have seen them bunch suddenly in a thick mass, their beaks upraised, their frantic feet stirring up a flurry of flying water, in their attempt to stand off the attack of a stooping eagle by sheer weight of numbers. Unloved and unadmired by most men, they are rarely pursued as a game bird; they need fear only the winged predators or the occasional mink or coyote that might sneak in close while they rest on shore.

The hawks are also on the move; sparrow hawks, redtails, marsh hawks, prairie falcons, duck hawks, and other predatory birds work their way south towards lands less harsh in winter. They hunt as they go, sometimes perching in tall trees or on ridge-top snags to rest. Sometimes a dozen will be in sight at once with several species represented among them. Their flight is rarely straight, but a progressive series of interlocking circles as they drift from one thermal to another, riding the wind currents, wild and free, always on the watch for prey, and beautiful to observe. Among them all, only the tough, powerful goshawks will linger here for the winter, stalking their prey with deadly efficiency over deep snow, scouting in low flight through the timber groves.

My roving binoculars pick up black bears on the prowl, stuffing themselves with berries to the point of utter gluttony, their outlines glossy and rolling with accumulated fat. Carefree, jolly animals, they revel in the berry harvest, following their searching noses from one patch to another. A black mother crosses an opening between two patches. Her yearling cubs, still busy stuffing themselves behind her, are slow to follow, but they finally take off at a rolling gallop in pursuit of her fast-vanishing rear. One is so exuberant that it puts its nose down and does a complete somersault, coming up on its feet without missing a stride, as rhythmic and smooth as a trained gymnast.

Towards evening, as the lazy clouds part and lift around the crest of the peaks, I come to a stand in the timber of a wild valley between towering mountain walls and listen to the exciting music of rutting bull elk. Peal upon peal of whistling calls that wind up in deeper tones and gusty grunts echo off the cliffs, making three or four bulls sound like legions as they challenge each other for the favours of the cows. Right in front of me, moving like grey ghosts, silent and unconcerned, are two mule deer bucks. Their antlers are clean and polished like those of the elk, but they are still two months away from their mating season.

Where the creek pours out of a canyon to go meandering across a flat stretch of swamp all red and yellow with the leaves of scrub birch and willow, a bull and cow moose loom huge and jet-black. They look ponderous, but when they move it is with a joy of grace and power like none other of the deer tribe of the world. For they are the biggest of all deer and move with ease across bogs where any of the bigger animals would be in trouble. Their blood is also stirring with the first flush and heat of the mating season. The bull eases close to her, shouldering her on the flank, grunting and whining low in his throat, but she shies away, unready to accept him.

The dark closes in, reducing the colours to shades of grey among the brush, and the moose blend into the deeper shadows till my binoculars are hard pressed to pick them out. I turn away towards home, tired, hungry, but soothed and happy after a long, productive day afield. Like true gold, the richness and throbbing life of autumn lie deeper than surface colour.

34

THE WAY THINGS WERE

The man sat with his back to a clump of stunted birch high up near the brow of a ridge among the Porcupine Hills in what is now Alberta. His eyes missed nothing that moved across the vast stretch of brush- and grass-covered country below him. A herd of horses suddenly galloped into view pursued by a pack of wolves, but he gave them only a fleeting glance as they ran past a hundred Athabascan bison feeding on a bluff. The man had his eyes on a partially hidden hollow at the bottom of a sloping basin half a mile below and to one side of him. Birch and aspen grew thick there and every few minutes one or two of the trees waved and jerked, giving away something big feeding out of his sight.

The brush suddenly began to ripple and sway in a line pointing to the near edge of the hollow. Suddenly a big bull hairy mammoth broke into view, the ivory of his great twelve-foot tusks framing his head and trunk in a gleaming curved outline that contrasted sharply with the dark-brown hair and wool covering his entire body. He was a sight to make any hunter's heart pick up a beat.

Right behind him came an old cow, not as large, but massive just the same. The big bones of her hips and shoulders showed through the new growth of her coat, which still included the old bleached-out patches of unshed hair and wool here and there that spoke of her years and of a long, tough preceding winter. At her heels came a first-year calf. Then one by one followed a line of twenty-odd mammoths of various sizes and ages, young bulls and cows, two or three more mature cows with calves, and, a bit behind the string, another big bull. At a steady walk and in a long angle, they filed up a grassy slope and finally swung directly towards the watching man, whose eyes were fastened on the last bull. They came over a saddle on the near side of a ridge and slanted down another slope to the edge of a steep-sided gully, where a whitewater creek ran down towards the river.

There the lead bull stopped, as though contemplating the way down the steeply pitched bank of gravel and loose rock. Swinging his trunk and rocking his tusks, he sidestepped down off the edge and went ploughing towards the stream at an angle. Every animal followed him, and by the time the last of the line came to the top, the herd's feet had crushed the gravel into a smooth pathway. The last bull paused at the top of the bank, watching the rest of the big animals lining up shoulder to shoulder for a drink, before following to take his position lower down.

He was a young animal, though fully grown, his new coat deep brown and his tusks massive, though not as big as those of the lead bull. On one flank the man's keen eyes could see a long scar almost grown over with wool and hair, a severe brand that the older bull had no doubt inflicted for his brashness in challenging him for the favours of a cow in heat earlier in the summer. A painful wound, it did nothing to improve his temper, which, the man knew, was none too sweet at the best of times.

Almost directly above them now, the man stood up, slung the carrying strap of his pouch across his shoulders, and picked up a matched trio of spears and his throwing-stick. Leaning on the spear shafts, he continued to watch. Like all good hunters, he was a man of great patience. Lean, well-muscled, and powerful, his every line was as wild and free as the peregrine falcon perched on the tip of the rocky point behind him, lit up in the early-morning sun. His name was Big Tooth. The time was summer, thirty thousand years before the present.

Big Tooth knew every animal in this herd very well, for he had been watching them for days, studying their feeding patterns, and testing their reaction to the sight and smell of him, sometimes at very close range. They had become so accustomed to his presence that they scarcely paid any attention any more – all but the young bull wearing the scar, who showed fight every time he saw the hunter. Once the bull had almost caught him, when in escaping from a charge he failed to see a boggy spot in time and landed in it up to his knees. Big Tooth bared his teeth in a wolfish grin as he remembered the narrow escape. There was a score to settle and a dream to complete, a dream that had told him that he and this scarred bull were destined to fight to the death.

Four summers before, when he had been a stripling keen to join the hunters of his band, the medicine man had sent him off alone, as was the way of his people when the time came for a young man to seek his naming dream. He had climbed up to a big tree growing on a ledge on a cliff many miles from here, close to the ice, where peaks sticking up from it overlooked a lake in the corridor farther north, a favourite spot for the big white-headed eagles to nest. Following the medicine man's directions, he had nothing to eat or drink, carried only his spear, and wore nothing but his breech-clout. If the spirits so willed, they would bring him water, but he could not move away from the tree in search of it.

He had never known time to move so slowly. During the day, when it was baking hot, with little shade, he stood or sat with his back to the tree, watching its shadow swing as the sun moved slowly across the sky. He saw a pair of eagles fly out from their nest atop another tree farther up the cliff, as they swung and climbed on the thermals hunting for food for their young. They were the friends of old Eagle Speaker, the medicine man, and told him many things: the best herb roots and leaves for healing wounds and curing bellyaches and fever. The boy watched one of the eagles stoop like a falling spear out of the clouds and kill a marmot

in a patch of boulders and carry it up to the nest. He eyed
the marmot hungrily, his stomach growling, and worked
out a route to climb up and steal what was left of it, but then
put the thought resolutely from his mind. At night he
curled up in a kind of nest he had made from green twigs
broken from the tree and a little grass he had gathered from
around its base. It was cold there when the sun went down,
with the smell of glacier ice on the night air. Fortunately
the nights were short at that time of year. On the third
morning he watched the sun come up hotter than ever,
wondering if the spirits meant him to die here without giving him a dream. Then a black cloud shot through with
lightning bolts blotted out the sun, the thunder came with
deafening explosions, and the lightning struck the top of
the cliff over his head, along with rain that fell in great
sheets. The boy caught it in his cupped hands and sucked it
up, feeling it spread deliciously through his parched body.
Then a great blinding shaft of lightning shivered atop the
eagles' nesting tree, followed by an ear-splitting crack.
When his eyes came back into focus, the nest was gone; the
tree smoked and steamed with a new white scar showing
from its top to its roots. The sun came out again, warm and
lovely, soothing away his shivering as he watched the towering cloud of the storm moving up the valley, the lightning
still dancing to the rolling of its receding thunder drums.

That night the air was uncommonly balmy and the boy
slept deeply for the first time under a brilliant canopy of
stars in a cloudless sky. Suddenly it was there facing him, so
close he could smell its fetid breath – a great mammoth bull
with tusks red with blood and eyes that glowed like coals
fresh from the campfire. It towered over him, blotting out
the sky and trapping him against the cliff. He reached for
his spear, to find it grown so big that he could scarcely lift
it, then swung it around with its tip pointing at the bull, its

butt against the solid rock. The monster spread its great ears, blew a blast of rank-smelling air at him, rolled up its trunk between its eyes, and came at him. The stone spear point glanced off the base of a tusk, skidded through the wool of its shoulder, and opened a bloody gash along its flank. Then the spear broke off and the bull screamed, rearing high over him – to suddenly fall backward off the cliff. The boy woke to his own scream, his eyes blinded by the rising sun and his body drenched with sweat.

On shaking legs he climbed down off the cliff to the forest and the trail that would lead him to camp. When he arrived there, the people all greeted him as he tried to walk proud and tall, drawing on his innermost strength to keep from tottering.

Eagle Speaker came to him, his fierce old eyes reading him at a glance, and taking him by the arm he led him across to the fire, where they sat down, sharing the same skin. Reaching into his pouch, the old man mixed various things in a hollowed-out rock, grinding them up with another stone. Taking a horn ladle, he dipped some soup from the trough by the fire and mixed the concoction into it by stirring with a stick. Handing it to the youngster, he bade him drink it. The taste was sharp, but not unpleasant, and the feel of it spread like a glow until it seemed to make his very fingers and toes tingle. He looked longingly at the meat in the trough, but Eagle Speaker took the ladle back and shook his head. So for a while the boy just sat there enjoying the warmth of the potion till his eyes became heavy and he could no longer keep them open. Then he rolled over on his side and slept.

When he woke, it was sunset. He felt enormously refreshed and utterly ravenous. His mother, Shining Star, a strong woman with a purposeful way about her and a wide smile, handed him a slab of bark piled with steaming meat, which he ate like a hungry wolf. Then he helped himself to some more. His father, Bear Paw, the chief of this band, came and invited him to join the council at his dome-shaped wickiup of hides supported by mammoth ribs. The council formed a ring around a fire built in front of it and the people circled them.

Eagle Speaker took his place by the chief, then rose and extracted from his pouch certain herbs and grass, which he burnt on the fire. Holding his hands to the smoke, he went to Bear Paw and rubbed his fingertips on his forehead, before doing the same for every member of the council. After a considerable pause, during which there was no sound except the crackling of the fire, Bear Paw rose to his feet and made a short speech.

Reaching down, he took the boy by the arm and said, "You have been on the first hunt. Tell us about it." Then he sat down.

At first the boy was hesitant, but then he recalled how other hunters told their stories around evening fires, and he warmed up and his voice expressed excitement. When he told about the storm and how the lightning bolt came down to wipe out the eagles' nest and blast the bark from the tree, there was a ripple of exclamations around the fire and some of the council covered their mouths with their hands, the sign of great astonishment. After a pause, the boy told of his dream, not losing anything in the telling, as the vivid recollection of his dream animated his voice and made his eyes shine. Suddenly conscious of being carried away by his own story, he sat down, his head bowed, looking at his feet.

Old Eagle Speaker stood up again, quiet for a while, then he reached down into that marvellous pouch of his and took out a small leather bag dark with grease, untied the top of it, and signalled the boy to rise to his feet. Holding the bag aloft, he intoned a powerful prayer calling on all the spirits of the sky and earth to witness this great medicine and to give the boy all the power and protection needed by a mighty hunter. Finally, dipping his fingers into the bag he proceeded with deft art to draw across the boy's forehead a jagged line in red paint depicting the lightning, then the sign of the sun on either cheek, strength signs on his shoulders, and other equally significant symbols on his back and legs. On the chest he drew a very fair sketch of a mammoth bull coming head-on with outstretched ears and great tusks. Then, placing both hands on top of the boy's head, he said, "You have met the spirits. You are now a man. I give you the name of Big Tooth."

That had been four summers ago, and now Big Tooth was in the prime of manhood. He was taller than most of his peers, his finely muscled body wide in the shoulders and narrow at the hips, with a deep chest from running across this rugged land, sometimes for hours without a break. He was an experienced hunter, recognized as a leader. He was a scout who ranged alone much of the time, keeping track of the herds of animals sharing this territory with his band, as well as acting as a messenger between his people and others scattered across this country, which would one day be drained by the Oldman River.

Now he watched as the mammoths crossed the stream to climb the opposite bank up onto a bench, where they bunched up in the sun to digest their morning's feed. He set off down the slope at a long, striding walk towards the massive animals. They paid him no attention, for as usual he wove an indirect pattern of approach, never looking at them directly for more than a moment, pausing here and there, and giving the impression that they were of no interest to him.

As he came up to them, the big bull with the scar was on the far side of the herd, the herd bull was in the middle of the group, and nearest him were some cows. The hunter circled with casual motions that were smooth as silk, and when he passed within a few steps of a dry cow, she flapped her ears and blew at him but did not move her feet. As he expected, the scarred one was slightly separated from the herd, so he circled wide to come to a stop directly in front of the animal about fifty steps away. For a while they eyed each other without moving, then the bull raised his trunk and blew angrily. Big Tooth set about deliberately taunting him by dancing forward and back. The huge animal spread its ears and glared. Then suddenly it charged in a deceptively fast rush. Big Tooth stood poised, absolutely still till the last moment, before leaping to the side, allowing the bull's momentum to carry him past. Without losing a step he shot across behind the bull, giving him a solid blow across the flat of his rump with the shafts of his spears. When the bull swung around, Big Tooth was gone, hidden in a clump of brush. The bull charged back towards the herd, stopped, and turned to see the hated two-legged one once more taunting him on the edge of the drop-off towards the creek. His eyes red and bulging with rage, the bull charged again with a speed and agility amazing for such sheer bulk.

Again, just a split second ahead of utter destruction, the hunter dodged aside and the bull's speed carried him over the edge, to go skidding down with a great clatter of stones towards the water. This time Big Tooth followed him closely, stabbing his victim several times on his exposed rear, until the monster found some traction at the bottom and swung around screaming with fury. As usual, his tormentor was gone. Several of the herd had come to stand on the rim, no doubt trying to figure out what was causing the uproar.

Then Big Tooth appeared again, running easily on a slant up the far side of the gully back along the mammoths' trail. At the top of the saddle he looked back and saw the bull climbing back up towards the bench, and his teeth gleamed again. This one was ready. There was a fine line to be drawn in this game, and he knew that overdoing the taunting would go against his plans, for the bull would learn the folly of blind rushes and become very difficult, if not impossible, to handle.

The morning was still young as he set out at a long trot for camp several miles up a river. The sun was still only halfway to its zenith overhead when he walked into the camp of his people, and headed for the fire smouldering in front of his father's wickiup, where the chief was sitting talking to old Eagle Speaker. As he approached, Eagle Speaker's sharp, deep-set brown eyes studied him from under a headband of fur decorated with little bones that rattled when he moved.

"I have seen him," Big Tooth told them. "The bull with the scar on his flank – the one of my dream."

His father covered his mouth with his hand, his eyes widening with surprise. Eagle Speaker grunted, as though confirming that this was not news to him.

"I have been with him and his herd for seven suns," Big Tooth told them. "He is ready. I am going to kill him. It is my dream."

Again Eagle Speaker grunted and his father said, "When the sun goes behind the mountains we will talk."

Big Tooth leaned his spear against the side of the wicki-up, set down his pouch, and turned to the fire, where he ladled a chunk of elk meat out of the steaming trough heated by hot rocks. He squatted on his heels, his eyes roving around the camp as he ate ravenously.

Between him and the river he saw Sun Gazer, the band's flintknapper, his squat, powerful body straddling a log as he studied a rock in front of him. At long intervals, he turned the rock a bit and studied it from a different angle. Standing back to one side, leaning on their spears, a small group of hunters stood patiently waiting. After demolishing another chunk of meat, Big Tooth wiped his hand across his mouth, tossed away a bone, and walked over to join them. They greeted him quietly, careful not to disturb the concentration of the man on the log.

It was not till the sun was directly overhead that Sun Gazer picked up the stone in both hands to lift it high and slowly turn it in final examination of its every minute detail. Then he set it down again on the log directly in front of him. Picking up the specially shaped striking-stone that fitted the palm of his big hand, he lifted it and brought it down sharply but with the utmost precision on top of the rock at its edge. Like magic, a long, flat sliver of flint fell away. Slightly turning the stone each time, he struck it with exactly the same rhythm and tempo again and again, and just as often a flake of the flint was knocked free. By the time he had turned it a full three hundred and sixty degrees, the stone was the shape of an inverted cone sitting on its small end, perfectly balanced.

For a few minutes he studied it. Then, with a grunt of satisfaction, he struck it again, and a long, perfectly tapered flake dropped, which he picked up and set to one side. Again and again the striking stone came down, shearing off flakes, until all that was left of the original rock was a circular-shaped tapered core. Picking up the flakes, he held them up and examined them one by one against the sun. They were opaque – almost clear towards the edges in places. Only one of them showed a flaw and he discarded it.

Picking up a curiously shaped tool made of deer horn, he began to work on one of the flakes. Sometimes tapping the horn into gripping the flint, sometimes aided by gentle taps of the hammer, he deftly twisted off tiny flakes, quickly shaping the long, double-edged point of a spear. He flattened it at the base, chipped two notches on each side of it to hold the binding thongs, and carefully smoothed these so they would not cut the rawhide. Then he worked in the distinctive groove running from the base up the blade a third of its length which would accommodate the shaped shaft tip. Finally he smoothed the edges, drawing them down to a fine point. When he was finished, it was much more than just a utilitarian spear point – it was a beautifully crafted object of real art, a Clovis point, as it would become known.

Sun Gazer then passed the point to a waiting hunter and began to work on another. Big Tooth slipped away up the slope back of the camp where there was a projecting sandstone ledge. Reaching under it, he drew forth a long pole, three times as long and heavy as a throwing spear, which had been cut from a carefully selected green birch with only a few small knots. It had been scraped, smoothed, straightened, and cured slowly where the sun never shone on it. He had kept the making of it secret.

Carrying it out, he rejoined the group still standing near Sun Gazer, balanced it on end, and waited. The length of the shaft brought some grunts of astonishment from several of the hunters, but the artist on the log paid no attention. Finally, when the time came, he looked inquiringly at Big Tooth, who pointed to the circular core of the flint stone that had been left when the flakes had been chipped away. Lowering the long shaft, he indicated how he wanted it fitted to the already shaped tip. Sun Gazer examined it, turning the stone first one way and then the other before beginning to chip away at it, drawing the taper of the flint core down to a sharp point. His fingers flew and the thing seemed to grow in his hands almost as though it was soft instead of being among the hardest stones found on earth. Finally, he shaped the base carefully, keeping it square to the centre line of the rounded point. When he was satisfied, he handed it to Big Tooth, who grinned when he held it against the socketed tip of the longest, heaviest lance any hunter had ever seen.

He took the shaft and point down to the spring, where some rawhide thongs were tied under water to a submerged willow root. Being wet, the thongs were pliable and easily stretched to fit the contours of the point and shaft tip. Selecting a long thong and a shorter and wider piece, he carried the components for his mighty weapon down the stream to a long, low bank and sat down. Behind him several of the women were working with skins, but beyond a curious glance or two, they paid him scant attention.

Using a pointed flint knife with a marvellously keen edge, Big Tooth cut a hole in the middle of the wider piece of rawhide, slipped it over the point, and snugged it down around the base over the socket. Trimming the hanging ends so they would sandwich the shaft with no overlap, he then cut small holes along the edges. He took a piece of thong, stretched it carefully till it was thin, and stitched the rawhide around the wood, forming a snug sleeve. He wound the rest of the thong around the base of the point, pulling it up hard at every turn as he wove it on down the shaft twice the width of his hand, where he tied it off. Then, with the remaining length of rawhide, he started at the top again and repeated the process, taking it even farther down the shaft. When that was done, he leaned the spear up against a tall sapling growing nearby to dry the rawhide in the sun, before he rubbed some grease into it. The drying would shrink it and set it as hard as the wood.

That evening there was excitement at the sunset, for the word had got around that Big Tooth had made an enormous spear. When the council gathered, Eagle Speaker began with the usual opening smoke ritual. Bear Paw stood up and paused for a long time, silently looking at the sky. Then he asked his son to speak.

So Big Tooth told them what he had been doing for seven suns. He told them about the bad-tempered bull mammoth and how he had watched and prepared him. "He is the one of my dream – he wears the scar. Tomorrow I will go with five hunters. It would please me, O Chief, if you would pick them. When we come to the long-nosed ones, I will fight him and kill him – alone. No one will throw a spear unless he kills me. Then the hunters can let his blood run out on the ground."

"He will kill you," snarled one of the hunters, a tall man standing at the back of the council ring. "He will kill you," he repeated. "No hunter has ever killed a long-nosed one alone!"

The tall hunter, who had a terrible scar on his face from a fight with an enraged bear, then shook his head and said nothing more.

For a while the council sat unmoving, then one by one they placed their hands palm-down on the tops of their heads, signifying that they granted their permission. The hunters were chosen, among them the fierce-looking Scarface. That night there was no storytelling, no drums or dancing. Everyone went to their sleeping skins quietly, for this was an unheard-of thing. As he flattened out his bed of soft tanned furs, Scarface shook his head again, for Big Tooth was the one who had saved him from the bear. He knew that if it hadn't been for the dream, the council might have stopped this foolishness.

At dawn the whole camp was stirring with preparations for the hunt. The hunters would go ahead, but every person in camp able to travel would follow, not just to see the fight, if possible, but to carry back meat.

The hunters took three spears apiece and their spear-throwers. Big Tooth carried only the long one. Dressed in moccasins and breech-clouts, their hair tied back at the nape of the neck with a cord, they left camp at a fast walk

heading for high ground before turning downriver following the slope. Big Tooth was in the lead and he chose a way
along a high bench overlooking the country below. By mid-
morning they were on a rocky point not far from where he
had last seen the mammoths. There was no sign of them, so
the hunters strung out, heading for a jutting shoulder
ahead. Again there was nothing to be seen of the quarry, so
they moved on. This time they had not gone far when Big
Tooth stopped and pointed with his spear. Down in a grassy
basin surrounded on three sides by brushy slopes, the
mammoths were taking their morning rest after filling their
bellies with feed.

Big Tooth led the hunters down the slope. When they
came to the rim of an open shelf just over the floor of the
basin, he motioned to the others to wait there and then went
down towards the huge beasts to scout casually along the
open edge of the meadow. The herd was about one hundred
and fifty steps away, all lazing in the sun flapping their ears on
occasion. As usual, the bull wearing the scar was separated a
bit to one side. If he was to have a fair chance of making
the kill, Big Tooth had not only to lure the bull away from the
herd, but also to pick a spot to meet it with the spear.

In front of him a shallow channel made by spring melt-
water, but now dry, swung in a curve; it was rimmed by a
low bank with a gently sloping gravel bar opposite. Big
Tooth looked it over and found it just what he wanted. He
crossed the dry wash and laid his spear flat on the gravel
with its stone tip pointing at the bull.

Then, as casually as he would stroll into camp, he walked
towards the bull, which was standing with its tail squarely
to him, swaying gently on its feet, apparently sound asleep.
If any of the rest of the herd saw him, they paid no attention, and Big Tooth finally came to a stop barely twenty
steps from the sleeping bull. For a few moments he stood

motionless, then turned to check the spear before letting his eyes swing up onto the ridge. Up above, some of the people were already lined up watching, and others were filing into view. Turning again, he looked around him, and spotting an arm-length stick as thick as his wrist, he stepped sideways to pick it up. Winding up, he flung it hard and caught the bull squarely across the root of the tail.

For a moment the bull didn't move, then the great animal turned broadside and froze. With seeming casualness Big Tooth turned his back towards it, bent over, and flipped the rear flap of his breech-clout up and down. The bull blew an angry blast as it came around to face him, then spread its ears and raised its trunk. But it froze again, seeming to doubt what it saw. The hunter danced backward towards it, still flapping the breech-clout, while he watched over his shoulder. When he had gone three or four steps, the bull suddenly blew another great trumpeting blast and Big Tooth leapt away as it charged.

The hunter dug in his toes and sprinted straight for his waiting spear, gaining a little ground, then holding it. When he reached the spear, he came to a sliding halt, grasped the middle of the shaft, and slid the butt back against the bank. Centring the point, he barely had time to aim it low under the bull's jaw for the hollow at the base of the neck, just over the brisket bone. At the impact, Big Tooth braced himself, with all his weight on the upward straining bow of the tough, seasoned shaft. The spear went deep into the bull's chest – deeper than he had expected, for he was almost under that mighty trunk and the sharp tusks curled over his head. Then the spear shaft broke and he leapt sideways just in time. The bull pivoted towards him, blowing a great blast of air and blood that turned Big Tooth crimson from head to foot, momentarily blinding him. With the broken shaft standing out from its chest, the bull followed him. As the hunter dodged, pawing blood out of his eyes, he slipped on the gravel and went down. Rolling sideways, he barely missed being trampled under the raging animal's great feet, but he recovered in time to regain his footing and grab the bull's tail. The mammoth swung in a full circle, screaming and bellowing, showering blood in every direction, with the man joining in with a war cry of his own as he clung grimly to the tail, off the ground more than he was on it.

Then the rest of the herd arrived, and Big Tooth found himself surrounded by the great, blood-crazed beasts, their feet thundering and tusks clashing as they trumpeted and milled around in confusion. Spotting an opening, he let go and dashed for the brush, only to have a half-grown cow almost run him down. He grabbed a double handful of its long hair and vaulted up onto its back, whereupon it squealed like a great pig and spun in its own length, but he had a good grip and stuck like a burr. The cow carried him clear around the milling herd with the stricken bull in its middle, and when it came through a tongue of brush, he leapt off, to instantly disappear.

When Big Tooth had climbed through the brush high enough to be clear and able to see, the bull was down on its hindquarters, sitting propped up by its forelegs, its breath coming with great heaves. The ground was red with blood and it showed copiously on the flanks of the animals still milling around him and shattering the clear mountain air with their trumpeting. Suddenly the mighty animal lifted its head high, pointing its trunk and tusks at the sky, then it sagged, rolling over on its side to lie still.

Scarface arrived through the brush to grasp the hunter's shoulder, his face twisted in a lopsided grin. Then the other four hunters came on the run to join him, their eyes blazing with excitement. Their blood was up, and it was obvious that they wanted to try for another kill. But Big Tooth shook his head. "Enough," he said. "The spirit of all hunters says no more this sun." And they complied, for he was the chosen leader of this hunt, though they showed their disappointment.

The rest of the people began to arrive, chattering and exclaiming; Sun Gazer, Bear Paw, and even old grey-haired Eagle Speaker placed their hands on his shoulders in the age-old tribute of one hunter to another.

Their frenzy spent, the mammoths suddenly stopped their wild milling and tore away at a gallop, leaving the scarred bull, ten thousand pounds of dead meat, bone, and hide, behind them. Big Tooth led the way to the huge carcass. Reaching down to grasp the stub of the spear protruding from the chest, with difficulty he tugged it clear. It had penetrated almost a third of its length, and the stone tip was broken.

Now the butchering began. Using their razor-sharp flint knives, some with the blades lashed in a cleft stick, others held in the hand, the people took that huge carcass apart with amazing speed. By the time the sun was halfway down to the western horizon, all that was left was the big bones, the tusks, and a huge pile of offal surrounded by heaps of red meat. As a long line of people strung out carrying big loads, smoky green-wood fires were lit all around the spot to keep off scavengers till all the meat could be relayed into camp, where it would be cut up and dried.

Back at camp it was a time of celebration, of feasting and joyful dancing in homage to the successful hunter. The full moon lit up the council circle around the fire in front of Bear Paw's lodge, where the trough was full of rich soup, seasoned with herbs, and boiled meat. The stars of the Big Bear swung and the eastern horizon was lightening when Bear Paw rose to his feet, lifting his hands for silence.

"My son," he said. "You have made a dream live for all of us. You have shown us a new way to kill the long-nosed ones. It is for you to have a gift from us – any gift you ask for. Choose now!" Big Tooth stood up. "O Chief, I am grateful. I will choose!"

His eyes roved around the circle and then fastened on the slim form of a girl standing just on the edge of the fire-light. Walking over, he took her by the arm and led her away to his sleeping-skins, while the people returned to their singing and dancing.

So it was on a summer night thirty thousand years ago in the Porcupine Hills, when the people celebrated the first single-handed killing of a giant hairy mammoth.

Pure fiction, you say? Maybe – but also maybe not. You will have a very rough time proving it, while I will smile, for I know that this part of the world, south of Calgary and just east of the Rockies and the foothills, didn't ice up until very late in the time of the glaciers, and I have seen unmistak-able evidence that mammoths and many other animals ranged here and were hunted by the people of that period. From up high on the mountains, I have sat alone under the shimmering, hissing curtains of the aurora borealis and communed with the spirits of the people who were here ages ago – the early descendants of those enterprising ones who came across from Asia on the land bridge into Alaska. They left indelible tracks in the form of their stone tools and the knife-scarred bones and ivory still preserved in the middens of their old camps. And, as you will hear, at a dig near Taber, Alberta, archaeologists have found a skeleton fully forty thousand years old.

So before you get too set in your opinion, listen for a while to an old modern-day hunter, who knows what it is to eat and feed his family with the meat taken with his weapons. He has only been in spirit with those old Clovis people who populated and hunted in what is now southern Alberta as early as forty thousand or more years ago. We haven't found all the tracks yet by any means, but we have found enough to outline a picture – a fascinating part of the history of North America.

But first you have to be able to look at a river and see something more than water sliding down from the top of the Continental Divide to its juncture with the sea. For those with eyes to see, a river can be a living link with our past.

35

HORSE AND BUFFALO

What had been a way of life for thousands of years began feeling the first touch of the winds of change – for the horse had come back to North America in the ships of Spanish explorers, who were settling in Mexico. Where the Blackfoot first encountered the horse is something hidden by time, but it almost certainly occurred to the south. Legend has it that a party of Blackfoot warriors was attacked by a party of mounted Shoshonis, who suddenly

swooped in on them firing their arrows from horseback, to the utter amazement and no doubt embarrassment of these fierce tribesmen. It is not difficult to imagine the excitement and dismay back in camp when the Blackfoot warriors returned with their stories of this big medicine of the Shoshonis. The news was likely carried fast to every camp in the Blackfoot hunting country by the moccasin telegraph. Since there was no word for horse in their language, they may have identified these amazing animals by calling them "medicine dogs," or something akin to the only domesticated animal they knew.

Sometime between 1700 and 1725, however, the Blackfoot acquired horses. How they obtained them is not known, but it was likely by trade, perhaps with the Mandans to the southeast on the Missouri River, who knew about and traded with the Spanish. All it would take to give them a start in raising horses would be a stallion and a couple of mares, for they lived on the finest kind of horse range in the entire world. In a relatively short time the Blackfoot were mounted, and the cultural change in their lives was instant.

Now they found themselves incredibly mobile, able to move easily from place to place; journeys that once took weeks were now possible in a few days, and when they arrived, they were fresh and ready for anything. Always fierce and proud in their bearing, the men now had that certain arrogance that goes with sitting tall on the back of a horse. No longer did the women have to labour over the prairies on foot when they moved camp, carrying backbreaking loads. The tipi poles made fine travois, enabling her to ride the horse that pulled a much bigger load. Extra possessions were packed on the backs of other horses, for now they counted their wealth in horses.

Tipis could be made bigger, requiring twelve to fourteen buffalo skins and as many as twenty-three lodge poles.

Some wealthy men had lodges that were palatial, sewn from thirty skins, and with two doors and two fireplaces. They were constructed in two pieces, each forming a single travois load. To anyone who has had experience putting up a tipi, pitching such a lodge was an amazing feat of ingenuity, for they were about thirty feet high and required about thirty-two poles of sufficient length. It was here that the advantages of having at least four wives to do the necessary work became very evident! Such a lodge-owner's status in the hierarchy of the band as a hunter, leader, or warrior was assured and marked him as having done something outstanding in war.

With a little imagination, we can see this man at night, reclining against a willow backrest, telling stories to visiting relatives and friends, eating and smoking with them while the flames from the fires lit up the towering cone of poles overhead in golden hues. The liner, tied on the inside of the poles to a head-high level, decorated with designs and figures painted by the women, made a colourful backdrop. Up through the smoke-hole, a bright star looked down, while outside, a favourite horse or two, tied close by, occasionally stamped and whinnied gently. It was very pleasant, and even the dogs must have enjoyed the new life, for now only the poorest people still used them as beasts of burden.

But wealth generates envy, and now the Blackfoot warriors were at war much of the time. The Crees to the north were hungry to acquire horses and came to raid their herds, along with the Assiniboines, and both tribes wished to hunt on their buffalo-rich hunting grounds. When the Blackfoot were not out driving away these intruders from the north, they were busy raiding the horse-rich Crows and Shoshonis to the south. Occasionally they tangled with the mighty Sioux to the southeast, whose descendants were to teach General Custer a terrible lesson.

The Blackfoot went to war either to capture enemy horses and other possible loot, or for revenge. A raiding party of young warriors would usually go on foot, sometimes for very long distances, to an enemy village, with considerable risk of discovery. Carefully they would prowl around the outskirts to discover where the horse herd grazed, and how many guards were in attendance, and to learn the details of the ground. Then, at the darkest point in the night, the warriors crept in close. It was no easy task to elude the guards, get in among the horses, and catch mounts, for horses are skittish and noisy in the darkness. But sometimes a daring and skilful young man would sneak up on a dozing guard, cut the lead rope of his horse, and lead it away without his being aware of it until too late. When everybody had a horse, they vaulted up onto their backs, and with fiendish yells shattered the stillness of the night to stampede the whole herd into a wild run.

They almost never got them all, so it wasn't long before pursuing enemy riders were hot on their trail. Then it was a race through the night, and the dawn, and on through the daylight hours, the pursued trying to keep the herd together and the pursuers doing their best to catch up. The Blackfoot were noted for their ability to keep stolen horses from scattering, thus depriving their enemies of relatively fresh mounts. If they contrived to hold their horses together for the first day, they had a distinct advantage, for by that time they knew which horses were the leaders and which ones were the most likely to break back. When darkness fell, they could change direction, thus slowing up pursuit, for it is almost impossible to trail even a large number of horses at night. After a long run, a loose bunch of driven horses is easier to manage, and with luck even half a dozen well-mounted riders can put them anywhere they wish them to go. With some luck in the general geography of the country and perhaps a downpour of rain to erase the tracks, they could get away from their pursuers. When they finally arrived back at their home camp, it was time to celebrate. Young men who had left more or less in poverty could come back rich, with the means of making gifts for the hand of the girl of their dreams.

Much honour could be gained at home by a young raider who could sneak in alone among enemy tipis at night and get away with two or three choice mounts without having to kill anyone. It was not considered necessary to kill an enemy; to touch him with a pipe or a coup stick and get away with his horses was far more daring. To collect a scalp for a trophy was a secondary thing. It was a game for the youngsters eager to make a name for themselves and to acquire some horses. Most warriors retired from it before reaching middle age to raise papooses and to look after their horses.

When, for reasons of revenge, it was decided to mount a big attack on an enemy tribe, the campaign was very carefully planned by the war chief and his councillors. He could call on any camp for men, and when he took the lead on his favourite war horse, he might have two or three hundred superbly mounted men with him, all rigged with their best weapons. Surprise was always something they strove to have in their favour as they swooped in to attack. But that was not always possible, for a large party of warriors was hard to conceal. Quite often they found themselves facing an equally strong war party, and it was then that great feats of daring sometimes unfolded in the clouds of dust stirred up by whirling, plunging horsemen bent on killing adversaries. To show their bravery, some warriors would sometimes ride out between the opposing lines, dismount, and tie themselves with a short piece of rope to a stake driven in the ground. There they would stay until killed or until the enemy was defeated, defiantly staging their fight on foot within the confines of the tether.

Such set-piece battles were always wild and often bloody, frequently with heavy casualties. When the Blackfoot warriors returned to their camps, there was generally wailing of wives mourning husbands and relatives lost in such battles. Bodies of all dead warriors were brought back if possible, and, following the funeral ceremonies, the camp was abandoned. It must have been a melancholy moment for the surviving warriors to look back and see the burial platforms, or perhaps the lodges containing the bodies of their friends, with dead horses, their favourite mounts, stretched out alongside, and to hear the wailing of their women, sad under the prairie sun.

The wounded from such a battle were cared for with skill, for these people knew how to treat wounds and set broken bones and splint them with rawhide to hold them until they healed. Their knowledge of the use of medicinal herbs and the roots of certain plants, picked from the foothill slopes and prairies or the banks of the Oldman, was extensive. They had medicine for just about every ailment they knew. The women had potions for birth control and abortions, and skilled individuals among them acted as midwives administering to difficult births. For the most part, the women had little trouble having babies and generally were up and going about their duties the very same day.

They were children of the earth. This was the golden era of the Blackfoot people, rich with horses and endowed with hordes of buffalo in a hunting country so big that to climb a hill and look was to see forever. Vengeful and fierce as they could be, they were also sensitive to the world of the spirits and had a full understanding of the world in which they lived. They were the product of a dramatic prehistoric time covering eons of uncounted winters; their time of destiny was now, their position unchallenged as among the most attractive and free of all Stone Age cultures.

It was during this time of horse raiding and hard riding that a daring raiding party of young Crows set out from a camp far to the south heading north. Nobody knows who their leader was, but he must have been something of an explorer as well as a man with a powerful urge to acquire Blackfoot horses. Probably travelling at night and sleeping by day in some well-hidden spot, he led them on foot close to five hundred miles. In the valley of the Oldman River not far from the slopes of the Porcupine Hills, they crept into a large camp of Peigans and proceeded to abscond with a bunch of their horses. But the Peigans discovered them in time to pursue them closely and cut off their escape route south, whereupon the Crows changed direction and headed west up the Middle Fork, probably hoping to get over the mountains into friendly Kutenai country. The pursuing Peigans caught up to them, however, near the foot of a precipitous cone-shaped mountain that jutted out on the edge of the valley.

There the Crows abandoned their horses, took to the cover of the boulder-strewn lower slopes of the peak, and fought the Peigans fiercely. Reinforced with more warriors, the Peigans threw a ring around the entire mountain, determined to wipe out these cheeky horse thieves from the south. Unable to get out, the Crows climbed the mountain under a cover of mist that blew in on a north wind. The following morning was clear and the Peigans could see them moving around against the sky. After a short period of siege, some of the young Peigan warriors climbed the peak – only to find the enemy gone. The astonished Peigans believed that their enemies had changed themselves into crows to fly away. They called the mountain Crow's Nest, and so a

Rocky Mountain pass, a lake, and a river running out of it acquired a name.

No longer was the famous Head-Smashed-In buffalo jump in regular use, for, with horses, the Blackfoot found that they could ride up close beside the big animals and bury their deadly arrows clear to the feathers. At first the buffalo must have been confused by contact with horses, but they rapidly came to fear and hate them. Hunting buffalo on horseback was exciting and often dangerous, for, as many braves and their horses discovered, buffalo were incredibly quick on their feet and could whirl in the wink of an eye to catch a horse on their horns and toss it high over their backs. A good hunting horse had not only to keep its feet out of badger and gopher holes, when a stumble could mean death, but also to know when to dodge an angry charge.

Generally a group of hunters rode as close as possible to a grazing herd and then coursed them at a high gallop, and when it was over, dead buffalo were sometimes strung out for miles. When conditions were right and the size of the herd was manageable, mounted Indians could make a ring forcing the buffalo into a milling mass in the centre. Then they pressed in close, running the outside rim of the circle, firing their arrows into the panicked animals until there were no more to fire. Every man's arrows carried his personal mark, so when the hunt was over, the women, who always did the skinning and butchering, knew which dead animals were killed by their husbands. Yet this information was for reasons of claiming and bragging only; the meat itself was fairly distributed among the members of the whole camp. The hunters could claim the robes, but a good hunter often gave most of them away. The Blackfoot were a truly communal society.

When they came to the Oldman River valley in summer, it could be to afford the women the chance to pick berries, or it might be to meet with people of another band for a visit. Whatever the reason, it was always an opportunity for the braves to join in competitions of various kinds, like the wheel-and-arrow game. This was a simple game involving a little wheel made of willow, which was rolled past the contestant, who attempted to throw or shoot an arrow through it as it passed.

Since the Blackfoot were a very physical people proud of their strength, the youngsters as well as the mature warriors competed in all sorts of games, including foot races and wrestling matches. There were two kinds of wrestling, one conducted between two contestants on the ground and the other from horseback. The latter was the most spectacular, for in this kind of match the contestants rode up to each other mounted bareback, grabbed hold and wrestled, and the man who first touched the ground was the loser. The skill was not all with the riders, but involved their horses as well, for the wrestler mounted on a well-trained horse that moved one way or another following the leg-pressure signals of the rider had a distinct advantage. A tall, strong man who locked his toes inside the front legs of his mount, with his legs gripping like a vice, was very difficult to dislodge.

But the sport that was most enjoyed by young and old alike was horse racing. The races were run on a straight-away course of about a quarter-mile between the start and the finish line. The riders, usually youths of light weight, wore only a breech-clout and carried a quirt. Coming up to the start line, they were off at a given signal, whipping their mounts at every stride. Betting could be heavy between families or bands when two famous horses raced, and sometimes caused trouble, as in the famous race described in J.W. Schultz's book *My Life as an Indian*, when a disputed result between Peigan and Kutenai champion horses almost resulted in a war.

Most peaceful were the dances. One of the most popular was called the Assiniboine dance, which involves only unmarried men and women. The two separate groups sit and face each other, while the parents play the drums and everyone sings the dancing song in lively tempo. The dancers come to their feet, rising on tiptoe, then, stepping in time to the drums, advance till they almost meet, then retreat. Back and forth they go, gazing into each other's eyes flirtatiously. Like most Indian dances, it is a long-winded affair, with occasional breaks to chat and smoke. Finally there comes a climax, when one or more of the girls flips her robe over her head and the head of her partner, and thus shielded from view they kiss, to the huge entertainment of the watchers, while the drums beat and the singing grows louder.

The young man thus trapped was expected to give the girl a gift, sometimes as much as one or two horses, depending on how thrilled he was by her looks and the contact. Whatever the feeling, he was expected to give her something, even if it was only a plain bracelet or a cheap string of beads. The Peigans were always a romantic, fun-loving people among themselves, however fierce and unforgiving they and the other Blackfoot were in war.

Sometime during the season of the golden leaves, winter camps were chosen. Their location was influenced by natural shelter from the winter winds for the tipis, the abundance of firewood, the condition of the grass for the horses, the number of buffalo in the area, and the easy availability of water. The river valleys offered these advantages, and while the long, twisting valley of the Oldman was a favourite place for the various bands of the Blackfoot, it was by no means exclusive. They rarely if ever chose the same place each winter, for that would kill out the grass and use up the dry firewood. A camp of a hundred tipis needed a lot of wood and buffalo chips for cooking and heating; while each spring's flood inevitably scattered driftwood along the length of the river, by itself this was not enough. Meanwhile the nearby grazing might have been destroyed by fire.

Prairie fires often burned off enormous stretches of country, leaving the hills and prairies blackened and abandoned by the buffalo until the new grass of spring attracted them back. While the Indians sometimes deliberately set fires to burn off old grass, usually the fires were ignited by lightning or by a spark from a campfire. A grass fire running before a hard wind is a fearsome thing, but the Blackfoot people had their own methods of escaping them, by running off to the side, crossing a river, or back-firing a wide enough strip of grass to protect their tents. Usually the smoke and glare of flames at night gave plenty of warning of an approaching fire and time for moving out from in front of it. A camp getting burned out was a rare occurrence, for such misfortunes are not often mentioned in the legends. Fortunately a tipi, unlike a permanent residence, can be taken down and loaded on a travois in a matter of minutes. In a few hours it can be many miles away in a safe location.

Life in a winter camp set up in a sheltered bend of the river was pleasant. The men conducted patrols, hunted, herded their horses, and generally participated in games of various kinds. Only occasionally did they go in the cold season on raiding expeditions to the camps of their enemies, for snow made it difficult to travel and very hard to stay hidden, while even the most inexperienced child could read tracks in snow. Much time was spent by the men just loafing, storytelling, and gambling, especially on the stick game, which involved moving one marked and one plain object swiftly from hand to hand, then challenging the opponent to guess which was which. Those entrusted with the instruction and education of boys in preparation for their becoming warriors were occupied in teaching the many spiritual rituals and the use of arms. It was a time for making weapons and practising their use. Besides making their own feather head-dresses and clothing, the men also braided their rawhide ropes and carved and decorated their medicine pipes.

The women, by contrast, were always busy in a winter camp, sewing their clothing, tipi covers, and moccasins for all, and embroidering their various garments with dyed porcupine quills or bone beads. This was meticulous, time-consuming work, often conducted by several women coming together around the fireplace of a tipi, where they sat on robes against willow backrests and gossiped as they worked and periodically attended to infants resting in cradle boards.

The women were often out gathering wood and carrying water. Water was transported and stored in stomach bags taken from buffalo, elk, and deer. Buffalo paunches made the most durable containers. The bladders of these animals were also used as containers for various uses, and for toys resembling painted balloons.

Pemmican, which was made of dried meat and berries pounded together with tallow, was stored in rawhide bags around the outer wall of the tipi behind the draft curtain. Other rawhide bags and boxes containing jerky, herbs, dried roots, berries, and articles of clothing were stored in the same way. Fresh meat was hung from a pole rack outside the tipi, high enough to be out of reach of dogs, and the women spent much of their time preparing and cooking food.

The menu for every meal consisted largely of meat, with various other dishes such as meat broth and berry soup added. The early camps of the Blackfoot did their cooking either by broiling over hot coals, or by boiling the meat in crude clay pots or in a hollowed-out section of cottonwood log. Meat and whatever other ingredients were available were mixed with water in the log or the clay pot and then very hot rocks were dropped into the mix as needed to keep it boiling until cooked. Meals were not necessarily prepared at a given time during the day, but something was generally simmering by the fire. If a hunter came home tired and hungry, he was given something to eat and a change of clothing and moccasins by the women of his lodge. The women were proud of their lodge furnishings and kept them neat and comfortable. A well-kept tipi was a happy winter abode for a family.

On good days when the weather allowed, the children would take their sleighs made of buffalo ribs and have a joyous time sliding down a neighbouring steep slope. They would also go to the frozen surface of the nearby river and spin tops carved from wood, which they flung off a string wound around it. Sometimes they competed to see who could make a top spin the longest time and sometimes they threw the top at a mark. A specially carved long stick with a curved end like a sleigh runner was a favourite plaything, called a snow snake. It was flung to glide on the slippery surface and, as in a javelin-throwing contest, it was the distance that counted.

They were, in the old days in the wilds, a very strong and healthy people, powerful children of the outdoors. Their teeth were good because of the kind of food they ate. They did suffer from common colds, but organic problems such as heart disease and other diseases of the main organs were minimal.

Not very much can be written about their remedies or what their medicine men and women used in their treatments because it has always been held sacred, something passed down through the generations by word of mouth. Some of us do know, however, that the depth of their learning is profound, and even though most of us do not have the opportunity to understand it because we do not have the spiritual capacity, this does not mean it is all superstition, with no real power of healing. They were great healers, and many of them still are. Just because medical science does not recognize the worth of their system does not mean it is worthless; it only means that we need broader and deeper vision. Indian medicine has its limitations, just as our medicine has, but that does not detract from its successes or lessen its possibilities.

They were great believers in training to toughen the body as well, as we will see now, as we take a look at a winter camp pitched in a bend of the Oldman, cleverly placed on a flat sheltered to the south and west by a grove of big old cottonwoods, with thickets of willows growing among them here and there. It is dawn on a crystal-clear winter morning with fresh snow on the ground and on the branches of the trees, and the temperature is well below zero. The people are stirring, and smoke columns rise from the tipis in the still air as wood is put on the banked fires, stirring them into flame. The horse herd is bunched up on the bluffs of the valley slopes to the north, a few of them feeding but most of them standing humped up in the cold waiting for the sun. The river skirting the cottonwoods behind the camp is frozen over and silent under its winter blanket of ice and snow.

Out of one of the lodges comes an old man wearing a buffalo-hide robe tied around the waist with a strip of buckskin, his long grey braids framing a weather-wrinkled face that has seen many winters. He is tall, though his shoulders are bowed, but he strides purposefully through the trees towards the river, his moccasins stirring little puffs of the new snow at every step.

When he comes to the river, he walks out on the ice to a place where there is a slight depression in the snow.

Taking a small stone axe from under his belt, he begins chipping at the ice, clearing it from a long, narrow hole that has frozen over during the night. As he breaks it, he pushes the pieces under the ice, where they are carried away by the fast-running current. When he is finished, he has cleared a hole about thirty feet long and three feet wide. The water is about knee-deep and the gravel bottom is clearly visible.

As he straightens up, his austere old face softens and his mouth curls in a slight smile as he nods and gives a soft word of greeting to a young warrior and two boys, one about ten and the other a couple of years younger. They are wearing buckskin leggings and moccasins, and each has a robe slung around their shoulders with the hair side against their bodies. Kicking away the snow, they strip quickly; then, leaving their clothing on the bare ice, the two boys step towards the water. The oldest steps unhesitatingly into it, but the youngest pauses, hugging himself as he looks down and shivers. Before he can move, the warrior steps forward, puts a foot against his buttocks, and gives him a shove that propels him into the water with a splash. With a great gasp he catches his balance and begins to bathe, while his mentor steps in beside him and immerses his entire body before sitting up and beginning to scrub himself vigorously. The bath is short but it is thorough, and when it is through, they dress themselves quickly and head out on a long trot in the direction of the tents. On the way they pass other men and boys on their way to their morning bath – something all the men and boys over five years old do as a daily ritual. It is part of their training, a toughening exercise to make them able to endure exposure to any weather. Only the old men are excused in this kind of weather, for their joints and muscles are stiffening, and when it comes to being tough, they have nothing to prove.

As the morning bathing goes on, the sun comes up, painting the slopes pink, and frost crystals glitter everywhere among the trees. There is laughter as two young boys chase a pup dragging a fragment of hide, their breath showing in puffs of steam as they run. Now people are visible everywhere among the lodges. It is a scene that is alive and utterly beautiful as they move about in the early sun.

They were very clean people, these early Blackfoot, much cleaner, for instance, than their contemporaries in unwashed Europe. Men and women bathed every day, the women in the tipis during cold weather. In summer, they too took to the river, but at a different time from the men. If a youngster became unduly obstreperous, he might be punished by being taken to the river and pushed in, clothing and all, but the Blackfoot never struck their children.

While they were always spiritually close to the rivers, particularly the Oldman, they never used them as a way to travel by either canoe or bull-boat. The latter was a round boat made of buffalo hide stretched over a willow frame, which the Sioux, Mandan, and other Plains tribes used to cross big rivers like the Missouri and the Yellowstone to the south. The Blackfoot people did not try to cross the rivers until they were well past full flood. In the old dog days they waded the shallow crossings, pushing crude rafts that carried their belongings. If they came to a channel too deep to wade, they clung to the rafts and propelled them by kicking their feet. After they got horses, they would take to swimming, either hanging on to the side of the mount or being towed along grasping the swimming horse's tail.

In spite of their close proximity to rivers over countless generations, it is notable that very few of the Blackfoot learned to swim, just as few learned to fish, or to eat the day's catch. One reason for their reticence no doubt lay in their belief that a water monster lived in the Oldman, a legend that may have originated and been sustained when they saw great black sturgeon swimming in it. These big fish sometimes reached a length of fourteen feet and attained a weight of five hundred pounds or more; they were not uncommon in the old days as they ran up the Saskatchewan and its larger tributaries from Lake Winnipeg.

One legend tells of a time when two Sarcee warriors were coming north heading for their camp. They were tired and very hungry when they came to the Oldman and found a "water monster" lying stranded and dead on a sandbar. In spite of dire warnings from his partner, one warrior got off his horse, cut a piece of flesh off the monster, and ate it.

After they had travelled some distance farther towards the Bow, this man complained of feeling very strange, and he told his partner that he was sure he was turning into a water monster. He instructed him that when they got to the Bow, he was to throw him in and leave him. This was done – and from that time on, the Blackfoot people believed that the Bow was also occupied by a water monster.

Despite their concerns about the water monsters or the more prevalent bad spirits who lived in the water, the warriors often broke young horses by leading them into hip-deep muddy backwaters and sloughs. Then, getting on their backs, they would ride them out. Dismounting before the horse could get onto firm footing and buck them off, they would repeat the process until the horse was too tired to buck, and they could ride it anywhere. Less usefully, but for the sheer fun and daring of it, young braves often rode their horses into the Oldman on hot summer days for a swim. Sometimes riding them, sometimes hanging onto the mane or the tail, they would steer them by splashing water at their heads from one side or the other with a free hand.

In those early days, the flats and bluffs by the Oldman were often black with buffalo as far as the eye could see.

Thousands of them were in sight, but that was only a small part of the millions wandering the plains between Lake Winnipeg, the Mississippi, and the Rocky Mountains. It was one of the grandest displays that nature has ever conceived, a magnificent example of an animal completely adapted to its environment, through which the Indian wandered totally in tune with it.

36

THE STONEYS

The Blackfoot tribe went up the Oldman into the valley past the Gap rarely, and then it was only to gather tipi poles from the lodgepole pine of the mountains. They did not go to hunt or to camp for any protracted period of time, for they were hunters of the plains and did not know how to hunt mountain animals on the high, steep slopes. They were also somewhat awed by mountains, and while they travelled through them on raids into the Kutenai country to the west, they never felt at home in them.

DON BRESTLER 98

This was the land of the Stoneys. The mountains from up on the headwaters of the Athabasca River near Jasper south to the American border was the hunting country of the Stoney tribe, and they were a most important part of the Indian culture on the headwaters of the Oldman.

Before the horse came to the northern plains, the Stoneys had split off from the Assiniboine people in Manitoba far to the east. They were part of the great Sioux Nation, who spoke the language of the Nakota branch of these people. When they set out on the trek west across the northern plains and parklands, they were harried by the Ojibway, Crees, and Blackfoot, and their fighting strategy was somewhat limited by the flatter ground, for they were hill people.

Consequently they kept moving, and when they reached some broken country not far west of where Edmonton is now located, a large party of Sarcee warriors of the Black-foot people attacked them. It was a mistake, for here the Stoneys were in rough ground and they out-manoeuvred the Sarcees and gave them a sound beating in a battle that was bloody and ruthless. When the surviving Sarcee warriors limped back and reported on it, they described these enemies as being stony-hearted. And thus, legend has it, they earned their name.

When they came to the mountains west of the scene of this great battle, they looked up at the towering peaks of the Rockies, which made those of their old hunting grounds look like gopher mounds by comparison, and liked what they saw. Soon their hunting country ranged far and wide in the foothills and mountains of southwest Alberta, including the upper valleys of the Oldman River. They hunted the buffalo along the western rim of the plains and foothills east of the Continental Divide. In the mountains they also preyed on the bighorn sheep, mountain goats, deer, elk, moose, and bear as far west as the Kutenal, Shushwap, and Flathead country.

They were great climbers and wore special climbing moccasins soled with the thick neck and rump skin of male mountain goats. These high-climbing animals have short, black curving horns as sharp as daggers and are fierce fighters in the mating season, and somewhat truculent with each other at any time. For protection they have developed skin on their necks and rumps an inch thick, from which the Stoneys made buckskin, tough and spongy, that would cling to the rocks like rubber.

When it came to using steep terrain for fighting and hunting, the Stoneys were great strategists. When hunting, they would deploy hunters in rock blinds located on the saddles and passes at the head of a canyon. When all was ready, the women, old men, dogs, and youngsters would drive quarry out from the valley below with much yelling, yapping, and banging of sticks on the trees. Naturally the animals headed for high ground over familiar trails, and when they passed the hidden hunters they were ambushed and killed. Some of the remnants of these old blinds are still visible.

Unlike the Blackfoot people, they ate fish and were avid fishermen. They were experts with snares and took fish in the clear pools by fashioning a noose made of braided strands of sinew, heavily greased, which they fastened to the end of a long, slim pole. Standing on a ledge over the water or on a logjam, they would slip the end of the pole into the water and with great skill manoeuvre the noose over the head of a trout or a whitefish. Then they would jerk it tight behind the gills and flip the catch out on shore. Such fish were split, sundried, and smoked to preserve them for winter use.

With the help of a dog, the women and children hunted grouse in the same fashion. The dog jumped the birds up into the trees, where they perched, stretching their necks as they watched the animal yapping and jumping about below. While their attention was thus diverted, the hunter lifted the pole and very carefully slipped the noose over the bird's head. A quick jerk decapitated it and another bird was ready for a tasty stew or for grilling over a bed of coals. The youngsters also snared ground squirrels in the same way by placing the noose around the entrance of a den and waiting for the animal to stick its head up for a look around before coming out to feed.

We white-skinned young hunters and gatherers who came later adopted these tricks from our brown-skinned brothers to take fish, birds, and small animals. We substituted brass wire for our nooses and they were very effective. With a little practice, in a few minutes you could take enough fish to make a meal for a whole family out of a pool with a school of whitefish and trout lining its bottom. We never went anywhere in the mountains without a length of brass wire, which not only provided a way of getting food in an emergency but was also handy for mending almost anything that needed it. As a matter of fact, I still carry brass wire as a part of my survival gear, if I am travelling by horse or on foot in the mountains.

Like all the Indians of the west, the Stoneys were a highly spiritual people who hunted only out of need – for food and for the various parts of animals they used every day.

They were migratory people travelling through and living close to the mountains, and, unlike the Plains Indians, they had three kinds of dwellings – seasonal, portable, and permanent. In June, when the sap was up, they peeled the bark off standing spruce trees in large slabs; overlapping one another, these slabs were used to cover lodge poles set up in a cone, the same as the tipi. For their portable tipis, they used the regular skin covers, made from the hides of buffalo, moose, and elk.

Their permanent shelters, to withstand the bitter winters of the mountains, were pole and moss dwellings of two kinds. One was a tipi about ten feet across at the base and from twelve to sixteen feet high. The poles were set in circular tipi style, but with the straight poles wedged very close together, with green moss pushed in tight between the poles. This was overlapped with another layer of poles also chinked with moss to form a double layer. The other type of permanent dwelling was constructed in rectangular shape about twelve feet wide, fourteen feet high, and twenty feet long, with a gable roof. This, too, was of double pole and moss construction. Well insulated, these dwellings were cool in summer and warm in winter. They were located all over their hunting grounds and belonged to nobody, but were used by all members of the tribe who needed them while hunting or on a journey.

In those prehistory times the Stoneys and all other Indians were basically very healthy and active. Scientists tell us that they did not suffer from heart disease to any extent, and cancerous growths were practically unknown, while their diet of meat and wild berries and roots – not to mention the absence of refined sugar – gave them good sound teeth. Their medicine men, who had a profound knowledge of the relationship between the body, the mind, and the spirit, were great healers. The counselling skills of modern-day psychiatrists were well known in their cultures. They did not deal with parts of people but with the whole person. Just as they had no jails or special dwellings for old people not considered useful or any asylums for the insane, they had no fear of death, nor any belief in hell. They believed that a person's spirit went to dwell in a very beautiful and wonderful spirit world when they died. Atheism was unknown among them – they had no word for it in their language, nor any knowledge of it.

Like most mountain people, they had courage and physical strength unsurpassed by any, and their many legends tell of bravery while fighting with their enemies. Many of the stories tell of Stoneys able to change themselves into animals. One particular legend tells of how Wolf-Come-Into-View was approached by a spirit in wolf guise, who gave him a gift, which he could use to get himself out of difficult situations.

On one occasion, he was out among the high hills overlooking the Oldman, scouting for buffalo in the valley below, when he spotted some enemy Blackfoot who were also hunting. They saw him before he could hide, and, whooping in triumph, proceeded to come after him. He ran into some bushes close by and called on his wolf spirit to save him.

The enemy warriors scoured the brush attempting to find him, with no success. Finally one of the Blackfoot warriors pointed and called, "Look over there." The others turned to see a wolf loping away over the skyline on top of a hill. The enemy leader told his men, "Do not bother. That man has turned into a wolf. He must be spiritually gifted, and a great warrior."

So, from that time on, Wolf-Come-Into-View was highly respected by all enemy warriors.

The Stoneys lived close to the mountains and thought of them as sacred. They were the monuments of nature, a constant reminder of the power of the Great Spirit. Warmed by the sun, caressed by the winds, and blanketed in white by the storms of winter, they were a most powerful part of the natural world. To be sure, the mountains could be dangerous and sometimes people were killed by an avalanche or injured in a fall while climbing. At times the lightning of summer thunderstorms set fires that raged down the valleys, burning everything and leaving the trees blackened and dead in their

wake. But always the heat of such fires caused the accumulated seeds of the lodgepole pine to sprout. These trees grew
slim and tall among the deadfall timber of the burn slowly
rotting on the ground, and in time provided an abundance
of poles for constructing lodges.

Old people and the sick made journeys up to the hot
springs on the Bow River, where they bathed and soaked
themselves in the hot water to cleanse themselves and
regained their health and vigour. These medicine baths
were a regular practice of the Stoneys, until after the white
man came and created Banff, Kootenay, and Jasper National
Parks. Then, to our shame, they were barred from the hot
springs, which were developed and used exclusively by
white tourists who knew nothing and cared even less about
the ritualistic healing practices of these Indians.

When the Stoneys got horses and became skilful in
using them for hunting, packing, and pulling travois, they,
like all the western Indians, found life much easier. I
remember as a small boy seeing the tracks and trails used by
their hunting parties on the edge of the mountains some
sixty years ago.

Once, as a young man guiding some guests into the
mountains, I was looking for our horses up on the headwaters of the Oldman River. It was before sun-up on a cold,
frosty October morning when I found a bunch of Indian
horses feeding on a meadow in a twisted little valley. Riding
on to find our bunch, I came upon a very old man walking.
He did not speak much English and I knew no words of
Stoney, but by use of sign language and by drawing a map
and some pictures in the dust of the trail, it was not long
before we understood each other. I had found his horses
and he had found mine.

I went on and soon came to a Stoney camp, a hunting
party led by a big strong Indian known as King Bear's Paw,

son of the Stoney chief Bear's Paw. They had meat hung up and a fresh bear hide laced into a pole frame. A woman was busy scraping the fat off the bear hide, another was working with a deer hide, and there were several black-eyed youngsters standing around looking at me very solemnly. King Bear's Paw, who spoke good English, told me with much gesturing and enthusiasm how his dogs had fought with the bear and then chased it up a tree, where he had shot it.

When I had gathered my horses and was driving them back towards our camp, I met the old man riding a pony bareback and herding his horses up the trail. He was puffing away happily on a huge cigar one of our guests had given him at our camp, and carrying a roll of toilet paper – a somewhat droll gift from the same source. He also had a bag of tea in one of his pockets that Bert Riggall, the head guide, had given him.

Pointing to the roll of toilet paper, I asked with a smile, "What's that for?" The old Indian grinned from ear to ear and said, "Give'm squaw. Buck use'm stick!"

One time I was sitting visiting with Chief John Snow of the Stoney tribe telling stories when the question of how Indians came to be called Indians came up. I commented that when Columbus came to North America, he thought he had found India; consequently he called the natives he encountered Indians in his logbook, and the name stuck. John quietly digested this bit of historic information for a while, then his eyes gave away his humour as he said, "Good thing he wasn't looking for Turkey!"

John Snow is a highly educated man, an ordained minister of the United Church, who presided over a church at Morley, Alberta, for a number of years before being elected as chief of the tribe. Disillusioned by Christianity, he has gone back to his native religion. He is the author of the book *These Mountains Are Our Sacred Places*, one of the finest books ever written on the history of native people and a very thorough account of the Stoney tribe, past and present.

The Oldman River knew his people and their ways well. Some of the old trails they made along the steep slopes and over the passes of the Rockies drained by it are still visible, though in places there are big trees growing on them at least seventy-five years old.

37

COWBOY DAYS

They were an impressively tough, enterprising lot, these cattlemen who took over the great grasslands from the Indians. In the country up along the Oldman above the three forks just east of the mountains, some of the ranchers were British army officers retired from service in India, members of wealthy families in England and steeped in the traditions of aristocracy. They built big, well-furnished homes of logs and stone, solid and comfortable.

— DON BRESTLER

Later, it was in this area that the Prince of Wales established his ranch near the Highwood River.

There were others of British extraction, some of whom owned land temporarily, who generally were not known for their practicality. These were "remittance men," black sheep of wealthy families, who had been sent to the colonies with a quarterly stipend to sustain them – and to keep them as far away as possible. Some steadied down to become respected citizens, and others squandered their money in colourful ways, finally fading into obscurity. But they all made an important contribution to a part of the country where money was scarce, for they generally spent theirs like water.

All these ranchers had something in common with the Indians, for their lives were totally dependent on horses, which they rode or drove in harness. Most of them would not walk from the house to the barn if there was a horse to ride, and usually there was one handy. Youngsters born on the ranches generally rode before they could walk. Because it was not considered genteel for them to ride astride, the ladies of some of the families in the higher strata of society rode side-saddle. The more practical ones adopted regular stock saddles, wore heavy, long divided skirts, and rode astride like men. For the most part, they were excellent riders, and some of them could handle cattle and use a rope or a gun.

One lady who came north with her husband and a herd of cattle to take up a ranch had spent her younger years riding with him in a touring wild-west show. She was a very independent, no-nonsense type who could handle herself in just about every circumstance. Once, when her husband was away on business, she caught a neighbour helping himself to firewood out of a dead stand of trees in the valley below the ranch buildings. She waited till he got his wagon all loaded, then rode up and accosted him. He was very cheeky about it, grinning as he started his team towards home. But the grin rapidly faded when she reached into a saddle-bag, drew a six-shooter, cocked it with an ominous click, and pointed it unwaveringly at his belt buckle. Then she ordered him to drive to the ranch buildings, where she made him unload the wood and stack it neatly. It was a chastened, very respectful man who finally slunk off in the direction of his home.

The heartland of the old ranching frontier from the earliest days down to the present was the foothill country around the Oldman. Life for the early pioneer cattlemen was hard, but it had its frivolous moments.

On one occasion, Sam Howe, a colourful, hard-riding rancher, brought his crew into town after a long, hot, and dusty round-up to give them a chance to unwind. This they did with great enthusiasm at the local hotel, until in the course of the festivities one cowboy passed out so completely that everyone present became concerned. He was duly examined, pronounced dead, and then laid out in state in a makeshift coffin. A wake was held that went on till sunrise.

A funeral for their deceased comrade was organized, a flatbed rack on a wagon was brought to serve as a hearse, and a grave was dug in the cemetery. Then the funeral procession, complete with a long column of pall-bearers and mourners, headed for the graveyard. When they reached the graveside, it was very hot, and everyone was thirsty, so all and sundry left to go back to the hotel for refreshments, leaving the hearse standing unattended by the open grave. After a while, "the body" stirred in the casket and then sat up, rubbed its eyes, and looked around. Even in the throes of a horrendous hangover, it was easy for the cowboy to take in the details of his surroundings – the freshly dug grave and the headstones of preceding unfortunates and the general aspects of a funeral, which, from the way he felt, was obviously supposed to be his. He shuddered, climbed shakily out of the coffin and down to the ground, and went for his horse. He left riding west for British Columbia on the other side of the mountains. It was said that he was a total abstainer for the rest of his life.

The Indians have always been noted for their inability to handle liquor, but some later white-skinned arrivals were no more immune to alcohol. Some of them made a habit of stealing other people's horses and cattle, too, with no compunction about the rules of the game. All of which kept the Mounted Police busy and resulted in the building of some very escape-proof jails wherein to keep those unlucky enough to get caught.

When Louis Riel's band of Métis revolted and, with the help of some Crees, killed some people at Frog Lake, and a number of Mounted Police in another skirmish, the whole plains country of western Canada was in an uproar. Various groups of volunteer rangers were organized in the ranching country to patrol and guard the scattered communities of settlers, for it was feared that the Blackfoot warriors would join the Métis and Crees in a general uprising. But, thanks to the influence of the chiefs and the general respect for the Mounted Police – along with the valuable help of two missionaries, the Reverend McDougall and Father Lacombe – the Indians around the Oldman remained at peace. It was, nevertheless, a very anxious time, for the scattered population of white settlers was extremely vulnerable if the Indians had chosen to go on the warpath.

However, there was justified bitterness among the Indians. A few years earlier they had been free-roaming hunter-gatherers living off the buffalo, and now they were confined to reserves as wards of the government, dependent on inadequate hand-outs of beef from government agents who were sometimes downright dishonest. When a hungry Peigan killed a rancher's cow and was arrested, he gave testimony at his trial that the white man had killed the Indians' buffalo without permission, and asked why he was not allowed to kill a cow. Presenting the hide with its brand, the police explained he could not kill the cow because it was branded with the mark of the owner. The prisoner reflected on this and said, "We should have branded the buffalo."

The Indian did not always understand the law, though it is amazing how much he respected it. He did not comprehend, for instance, that a man arrested by the police was innocent until proved guilty by trial in court. In the old days under the laws of the tribes, he had revered and lived by the decrees of the chiefs and band councils. Now he saw governing white men breaking their own laws, and there were too many times when they got away with it, in a totally confusing hodgepodge of manipulation. To him the white man's law was something of an enigma, though it could be fatally efficient.

There was Charcoal, a Peigan warrior, who caught his wife making love with a fellow tribesman. In a fit of understandable rage, he blew his wife's lover off her body with a shot through the head. Had he gone and given himself up to the police, he likely would have gone free, after the discomfort of staying in jail waiting for trial. At that time there were no Indian lawyers to represent him or to give him advice, and he did not speak or understand English. He was sick with tuberculosis, and he believed that the only honourable thing left for him to do was to go on the war trail towards inevitable death and take as many high-ranking white men with him as possible to the spirit world.

First, he ambushed the reservation agent at his home, but the bullet meant to kill him only broke his arm. Accompanied by his wife and her sister, Charcoal ran away up onto the heavily timbered heights of the Porcupine Hills overlooking the Oldman River valley. His camp there was eventually located by a group of police officers and their Indian scouts in the late evening of a cold, snowy fall day.

But before they could close in, he got the women away to the horses and escaped in a blaze of rifle fire.

Under cover of the storm, he made his way south. The continuing pursuit under bad conditions was not very well organized. Though the Peigans were not altogether sympathetic to him, they did not totally cooperate with the police, either. Back and forth between the Oldman and the border the chase continued, following rumour as much as fact. There was another shoot-out in a camp on the upper reaches of the Belly River in thick timber, from which Charcoal got clean away with his two women. Half-starved, cold, sick, and totally desperate, he continued to elude his pursuers for weeks.

At one point in the hunt, he rode right into the police headquarters at Fort Macleod looking for a chance to kill the commanding officer. But he settled for stealing a highly prized, very fast horse and made a run back up the Oldman, eluding the astonished police officers who were trying to cut him off. Meanwhile, his women had abandoned him, and he was all alone.

At a spot south of the Oldman near the Waterton River, Sergeant Wilde of the N.W.M.P. saw him and rode hard to intercept him. Bravely, but very foolishly, the officer rode right up to him, whereupon Charcoal shot him out of his saddle and escaped again. Finally, exhausted and starving, he rode back to his home cabin on the reserve, where he was overwhelmed by his own people, tied up, and turned over to the police. He was subsequently tried for murder, pronounced guilty, and hanged. But he hasn't been forgotten, for his defiant feat of endurance was magnificent in spite of its utter tragic futility. When he was captured, the ranching country up along the Oldman generally breathed a sigh of relief and everyone in the outlying areas slept much better at night.

38

PEOPLE ALONG THE RIVER

DON BRESTLER '98

From the home ranch near Waterton Park to our base camp on Racehorse Creek inside the Gap was about ninety miles. We made an average of two round trips a season trailing forty-odd head of loose horses. It was a two-day ride each way, which took us across a number of tributaries of the Oldman, just a few miles east of the mountains. At first there were two of us making the trip, but later I persuaded Bert that I could trail the bunch alone, for I liked the work and knew the country well enough to make it easy. When a bunch of horses become accustomed to one man, they handle even better than with two riders. A lone rider doesn't get his concentration sidetracked and can better anticipate problems before they happen.

Well into the shank of an afternoon one long, hot day, I was heading south up out of the Crowsnest River valley past a bench inside a rancher's field. There was an open gate leading to the field, and perhaps hoping I would stop and camp for the night, the leaders of the bunch trotted through it and fanned out to feed. I was riding around to haze them back out onto the road when I suddenly noticed an old hidden tipi ring of stones, which the Indians had used to hold their tents down in this windy country. I soon found that it was only one of about a hundred such rings on the bench, and they had been there a long time, for many of the rocks, six to eight inches through, were barely showing in the sod, and it takes a lot of years for sod to build up around surface rocks of this size. Sitting there on my horse, it was easy to visualize the big camp that was once pitched here with probably three to four hundred people. Old buffalo hunters, these ones, people who had ranged up and down this valley before there were any white people.

It was not the first time that I had found tipi rings along these rivers, nor would it be the last. But it was always a thrill, like riding into a historic review of the past, when this was all unfenced, open country with buffalo dotting the hills on an ocean of grass running far beyond the horizon, and halfway across the continent. It was something to think about as the horses jogged on south towards the Castle a few miles farther on.

It was evening when I came down to the river, the horses spreading out at the near edge of the shallow crossing to drink. For some reason known only to herself, old Cee-Cee, the lead mare, turned upstream instead of heading into the river and led the bunch under a steep bank. I rode up along the top of it to head her off and stepped my horse out near its edge to yell at her and turn her back. Immediately I smelled smoke and to my amazement saw a stovepipe sticking out of the ground almost under my left stirrup. At the same time a voice down below yelled, "Get the hell off the roof, before you come through!" My horse jumped sideways just as a man appeared on a little shelf a few feet down the bank against a clump of willows.

My surprise was complete as I sat there on my horse looking at him. He was of medium height and indeterminate age, with a face as brown and wrinkled as a sun-cured prune and a pair of eyes that were clear blue and sharp.

"Seeing as how you rode out on my roof, you might as well get down and come in, Russell," he said with a grin. "I've seen you cross down below with that string of broomtails often enough to know who you are."

I stepped down and picked up a rock to shy ahead of old Cee-Cee with a yell to go with it. She plunged into the river and headed across. The idea of a cool swim must have seemed like a good one, for the whole bunch followed her across, including the packhorse. My sleeping bag was on top of the pack and out of the water, which was a comfort.

Climbing down to where my unexpected host was standing, I grinned at him and shook his hand. Although I had not seen him since I was half-grown, I knew who he was. For Bill was something of a legend: hunter, trapper, cowboy when he felt like it, and on occasion there were rumours that he was a moonshiner. He was a crack rifle-shot and spent a large part of every winter ranging far and wide across the hills hunting coyotes for their skins.

"Got a nice bull trout this afternoon," he told me. "It's about suppertime. When you get your camp set up, better come and have a bait."

I accepted his invitation and went back to my horse and rode back down to the crossing. By the time I had caught and saddled a fresh horse and spread my bed under a tree, the sun had dipped behind the hills. Riding back across the river, I hobbled my horse on a little meadow among some aspens and climbed down to Bill's dugout. The door stood open and Bill was busy at the stove. The inside of the place was neat and the walls and roof were lined with old weathered rough planks that looked as if they had once been the flooring of a bridge. They were supported by a log centre beam and two side beams, each of which were held up by three stout posts. The stock of a rifle peeped out of a buckskin case hung on two pegs set into one of the beams, and a miscellany of equipment was tucked under the bunk at the back of the dugout. The table was a couple of wide boards on two oak barrels, and on the well-swept board floor a row of stone crocks stood along the base of one wall with a coil of copper tubing over them.

When I had washed off the dust in a washbasin on a shelf outside the door, Bill poured a measure of clear liquid out of a jug into a cup and handed it to me.

"Sample some of my white mule to celebrate," he said, "seeing as how you're the first to ride on my roof."

He poured some for himself in another cup, and by way of a toast he laughed and said, "Here's to your ornery old packhorses and mud in your eye!" whereupon he downed it in one gulp.

I took a sip and almost choked, for that so-called white mule had a kick like one – pure liquid fire.

"Don't be scared of it," Bill said with a grin, "it's pure stuff filtered in charcoal to take out the gook. Make the hair grow on your chest!"

I took another cautious sip and thought it would more likely burn the hair off.

We had a good supper of fresh fried trout, Dutch-oven biscuits, and boiled new potatoes, topped off with canned peaches, which we ate off our knees as we squatted outside where it was cool. Then we lit up smokes and sat back to trade some stories.

That was a fascinating evening, for Bill was in an unusually loquacious mood. He told me about riding north to Canada from the States many years before through this country along the Oldman – a fugitive from a gunfight with a rancher who had some vengeful relatives.

"I kept right on going to hell and gone beyond, away north into British Columbia. Figured on staying there, but it wasn't in the cards. I remembered this country and came back. Been here ever since."

He had a real love for this mountain and foothill country and knew the river from its headwaters to away down on the prairie. Like me he had come to know it and to love the spirit of its movement through feeling the push of it against his legs. We had both fished it and trapped beaver up along the creeks in spring. We could talk about it, though there was no need. Like the Indians, we had looked and learned something about how to really see and feel its power. Like the smell of campfires burning under a starry sky, or the whispering and roaring of the wind in the trees and among the high rocks, it was something we shared in our blood.

Bill told me that, more out of the challenge of it than anything else, he had been making the odd batch of "white mule" on and off for several years. He had been careful where he sold it, going far enough away so his still wouldn't be easy to find. When he had dug out this place, he had planted the willows outside to hide the front of it. In winter the snow drifted down deep over it; he had a log cabin farther up the Castle, where he lived most of the time.

"But lately," he told me, "I been having bad dreams about windows with bars on them, and wake up in a cold sweat. Reckon a couple of close shaves with the Mounties started it. Got a feeling that landing in jail would kill me. I been free as the mountains for too long. If you had come a couple of days later, this would be only a hole in the ground. I'm quittin' while the quittin' is good!"

When I rode down the trail towards the home ranch the next morning, I knew I had met a real character. Bill lived for more years after that visit, enjoying the mountain trails, and with no more bad dreams about bars on windows.

There are few straight lines in the designs of nature: almost everything about it is a combination of interwoven curves, subtle sweeping outlines of form and motion. Some are obvious and some are hidden, and the understanding takes time. A river is the ultimate proof of it, for the water lifts and eddies, swirls and curls back on itself, jumps and falls in a myriad of interwoven patterns so simple and yet complex. This complexity will always be a real challenge to a fisherman presenting a tiny lure of fur, feathers, silk, or tinsel, so that it will drift naturally without dragging and giving itself away for the fraud that it is. The skill involved with fly fishing makes it an art, and sometimes an exasperation. It is not enough to tie the fly so that it closely resembles the insect on which the trout is feeding; the good fisherman must present it with sufficient skill and delicacy to make it irresistibly attractive to the fish. The eyes of a trout are sharp and discerning, and really big ones do not get that way by being careless.

It is not necessary to be a fly fisherman to truly love a river, but it helps. This love of rivers and the pursuit of trout have shaped and moulded some very special characters I met along the river.

There is Bob, who first came to know the Oldman while courting a rancher's daughter, with his mind on things other than fish. It took some time and concentration to persuade the girl that life with him would be utter bliss, during which he somehow did not elaborate unduly on the fact that at times she would be a fisherman's and hunter's widow. She, being a smart girl, no doubt knew this already and loved him anyway.

For a while Bob gallantly ignored the river, but one fine summer day they went on a picnic at a spot overlooking a pool, where they sat in the warm sun and wove dreams for a while, blind to everything but each other. Suddenly the quiet of the afternoon brought the unmistakable slurping sound of the rise of a big trout to his ears. He was suddenly totally alert, like a pointer dog with a noseful of the scent of grouse. A minute or two went by before that slurping sound came again, and this time he turned to see the rise beside a half-sunken driftwood log sticking out from the bank sixty feet or so up on the far side of the pool. Mumbling something, he rushed to the car parked nearby and extracted from its trunk a cased rod and a fishing vest with numerous pockets well stuffed with various things. With deft fingers he put the rod together, fitted his reel to its handle, strung the line through the guides, and then carefully tied a fly – a Letort Hopper – to the tippet of the leader. Without the slightest thought for his polished shoes or the sport slacks he was wearing, he went to the edge of the pool and waded out into the shallows at its tail until he was thigh-deep and directly below the end of the log. With consummate skill, he worked out the line with two or three false casts, at the same time stripping a bit more from the reel, which he held in a loop with his left hand. Without breaking the rhythm of the rod, he gracefully shot the fly upstream, dropping it with delicacy and precision on top of the log. The gentle drag of the river on the line nudged the fly off the log into the water, where it floated with saucy daring on the surface directly over the trout's lair.

There was a quick swirl and Bob lifted the rod tip with a firm hand. A heavy rainbow trout exploded out of the water, fell back, and then came out again to tail-walk in a shower of spray before falling back to bore down towards the log. Bob did not yell – he is not the yelling kind – but he turned the fish out into the pool, where the dancing rod and the screaming reel told the story of its wild efforts to throw the tiny hook in its jaw. After a dramatic few minutes, Bob slowly backed out to the edge of the gravel bar, finally leading the tired fish to his feet. Stooping, he caught it by the gills and lifted it triumphantly out of the water.

Remembering that he had company, and with due regard for the girl's sensitivity, he turned his back to give the trout the *coup de grâce* on the head with a rock. He then carried it to her in triumph, and she, with shining eyes expressing admiration for his skill and daring, threw her arms around his neck and gave him a kiss of some duration. It was later that he became aware that he had forgotten to put on his waders.

Bob is a lawyer, and a bit of an eccentric, though inclined to dress in conservatively traditional pinstripe suits in his office. On the stream, he generally resembles a dignified bum, wearing clothes that are well marked by service, topped by a disreputable fly-strewn hat that looks as if it had been trampled by a herd of stampeding buffalo. He takes his fly fishing and hunting just as seriously as his law, but tempers it by writing delightful stories and articles about it. He purely loves the Oldman and regularly abandons his office to go fishing there at every opportunity. One can imagine his secretary answering a call at such times.

"Sorry, sir, but he is not in the office today. Where can he be reached? By four-wheel drive and waders somewhere in the Oldman River, I believe. It's trout season, you know."

After a lot of years, he is still married to the same woman, which says something.

One summer a few years back, Bob was fishing the Oldman near the forks when he came upon a boy about twelve years old sitting by the sawed-off stump of a big driftwood red-fir log. He was carefully counting the annual rings of the tree on the bevelled butt of the stump, which had been smoothed with a razor-sharp axe to reveal them. Filled with curiosity, Bob introduced himself and the boy gave his name as Rob.

"That's short for Robert, the same as mine," Bob told him and then asked about the log.

"Grandpa and I found it. It was washed down here on last spring's flood, I guess. He cut two gateposts off it. He thought it would be good if I counted the rings and found out how old it is. He says this big stump is about the best history book there is. I guess he's right. I've been having trouble with history at school."

"How's it going?" Bob asked.

"Pretty slow," Rob told him. "The rings are awful close together in some places. Grandpa says those are the dry years. See these ones here," and he pointed to some very fine rings not far under the bark. "Those are the dry years in the 'hungry thirties'." Then he pointed to a dark ring farther down. "This was when a fire went through, burning the grass and brush."

He went on to explain how fir trees have thick bark resistant to fire and how it doesn't kill the tree unless it gets up into the green needles among the branches. "Grandpa says little fires on the ground are good for fir trees. They keep the brush down so flames don't get high enough to burn the top of the trees."

He had marked certain rings with a sharp pencil and noted dates. "This one I marked is 1905. That's when Alberta became a province. This one here is 1874 when the Mounted Police came and built Fort Macleod down the river. Here's 1877. That's when they signed the treaty with the Indians." Then he pointed positively to another ring: "This one is 1753. That's the year Anthony Henday came, two hundred and seventeen years ago. He was the first white man to see the mountains. That's the last date in my book about this country. I guess I'll have to go back in Canada's history before 1753 now."

Bob could remember the dismally boring history books of his early school years. This boy had a smart grandfather who had seen a way to bring history alive for him, and at the same time open up an inquiring mind. As much as Bob had been around, up and down the rivers from the Red Deer River south to here, this was the first time he had really seen a tree right down to its heart. He asked how old this one was. The boy pondered for a while. "I guess I won't know for sure till I count all the rings. But it will be easier towards the middle. You see, the rings are farther apart there. Trees like this grow faster when they are younger. But it must be close to eight hundred years."

"That will take you back into European history," Bob said. "Look, Rob, I've got a chainsaw in my Scout back about half a mile, and I think we can cut off this bevelled piece. It's too heavy to carry very far, but we can put it in the river and float it down to the car. Then we'll take it down to your place, for you to show at school. And I'd like to meet your grandfather and your parents."

It was mid-afternoon by the time Bob got back with the saw and cut off the required section of the stump. In the meantime, the boy had stripped down to his shorts and sneakers. They launched the awkward piece of wood into the river and Rob went with it, swimming with the smoothness of an otter in the deep places and pushing it along in the shallows. When it got stuck, Bob waded in to help him wrestle it free.

"This is the way Grandpa got the posts down," Rob said, "only he used his horse and rope. They were awful heavy. Kept getting hung up. Made ol' Baldy snort." He chuckled, then, "Grandpa cussed when he broke his rope."

When they loaded the piece of log into Bob's vehicle and drove down to the ranch buildings along a twisted trail, the two thick posts were standing upright on each side of the driveway entrance in freshly dug holes. Rob's father and grandfather were there and the boy introduced them.

"I started out fishing today, but I got sidetracked in history," Bob told them. "This boy has been teaching me something I've never thought about before."

Bob had supper with the family, and when he drove to his father-in-law's ranch later, he knew that sometimes there is a lot more to fishing than just catching fish.

ACKNOWLEDGEMENTS

Grateful acknowledgement is made for permission to reprint the following:

"The Land of the Sky," "Dangerous Game," "Chalk One Up for Us," "Being Your Own Packhorse," and "Camera Hunting," from *Horns in the High Country* (New York: Knopf, 1973).

"First Steps" (excerpt from the story "By the River"), "A Joke on Cap," "Green Englishman" (excerpt from the story "The Remittance Men"), "Meeting the Judge" (excerpt from the story "The Wilderness Fishermen"), and "There My Stick Floats," from *Trails of a Wilderness Wanderer* (New York: Knopf, 1971).

"Wapiti Land," "Mountain Streams," "Wings Over the Mountains," "Relative to Riches," and "The Speedster and the Slowpoke," from *The High West* (New York: Viking Press, 1974).